PIENZA

PIENZA

The Creation of a Renaissance City

CHARLES R. MACK

Photographs by

MARY S. HAMMOND

With a Section of Texts Translated from
the Latin by Catherine Castner
and an Appendix of Papal Documents

CORNELL UNIVERSITY PRESS

ITHACA AND LONDON

First published 1987 by Cornell University Press.

International Standard Book Number 0-8014-1699-X
Library of Congress Catalog Card Number 86-24269
Printed in the United States of America
*Librarians: Library of Congress cataloging information
appears on the last page of the book.*

*The paper in this book is acid-free and meets the guidelines for
permanence and durability of the Committee on Production Guidelines
for Book Longevity of the Council on Library Resources.*

The chapter headpiece is a wrought iron horse-tie ring, attached to the
wall of the Palazzo Lolli.

*For Ilona and Katrina
and in memory of my mother,
Mary Dirnberger Sundbeck*

CONTENTS

PREFACE

IN 1460, the Italian sculptor, builder, and architectural theoretician Antonio Averlino, called Filarete, wrote this forceful admonishment to his contemporaries:

I advise everyone to abandon the modern [i.e., Gothic] style [of architecture] and not be advised by those masters who use this crude system. May he who invented it be cursed! I believe that none other than barbarians brought it into Italy. I shall give this illustration to show the relation of ancient to modern architecture. It is the same as in literature: that is, as the relation of the speech of Cicero or Virgil to that used thirty or forty years ago. Today writing in imitation of the classical past is the best usage, contrary to the practice in the past. . . . The same occurred in architecture. The man who follows the ancient practice in architecture does exactly the same thing as a man of letters who strives to reproduce the classical style of Cicero or Virgil.[1]

The masters of the Italian Renaissance saw literature and the arts as complementary parts of the great humanistic revival of the classical spirit. Accordingly, the statuary and ruined buildings of Roman antiquity received much the same devoted study as did the manuscripts of the ancient authors. The artists and architects of the period strove to recreate the visual mood of the glorious age of Rome in much the same way that such humanists as Leone Battista Alberti, Niccolò Niccoli, Giannozzo Manetti, Leonardo Bruni, Francesco Filelfo, Flavio Biondo, and Aeneas Silvius Piccolomini emulated the ancient poets, playwrights, and rhetoricians. It was this last mentioned scholar, Aeneas Silvius Piccolomini, who, as Pope Pius II, was responsible for the creation of the fifteenth century's most complete architectural embodiment of the total humanist concept.

Pope Pius II died on 15 August 1464 in Ancona, Italy, as he prepared to embark upon a new crusade against the Turks. Thus the primary objective of his eight-year papacy—the liberation of Constantinople—was not achieved. Also left unfinished at his death was the manuscript of his memoirs, the *Commentarii*, certainly one of the freshest and finest literary creations of the age.[2] On the final page of this work, Pope Pius had written: "The foundations of a very great war have been laid. . . . We shall imitate the architect who, having begun a great building, goes on with it according to how his patron supplies the funds. If he furnishes what he needs in abundance he promises him a splendid house. If he withholds what is needed he either discontinues his work or produces something inappropriate or ridiculous. We shall be dependent upon the outcome."[3] The pope's use of an architectural analogy in the *Commentarii* was quite natural for, during the previous five years, he had had much to do with buildings and architects. His architectural association resulted in what must be regarded as the most complete and enduring memorial to the Piccolomini papacy—the creation of the city of Pienza, a very model of Renaissance urban thought and a testimonial to architectural taste in the Age of Humanism.[4]

Pope Pius had hoped that Pienza might serve as a refuge from the frequent ravages of the plague in Rome and might even become a summer retreat for the members of his Curia. His death ended his dream for Pienza, however, and the little community quickly reverted to its former provinciality. Only one or two of the dead pope's cardinals, who, like Pius, found particular delight in the town's pastoral setting, continued to frequent the city. Yet Pienza, even if abandoned by the clerical nobility, was no longer the scruffy little hill town it had been before the papal intervention. It had been ennobled not only by great dreams but also by beautiful buildings that gave it a unique architectural character.

Pius had devoted considerable space to his urban creation in the *Commentarii,* and it was also described in the writings of his humanist courtiers, Flavio Biondo, Lodrisio Crivelli, Giannantonio Campano, and Porcellio Pandoni. Its place in the history of Renaissance architecture was recognized as early as the 1820s by the distinguished historian C. F. von Rumohr and later in the century by such scholars as Jacob Burckhardt and Carl von Stegmann. Increasing appreciation of the town's great patron, demonstrated by the publication of several biographies (Voigt, 1856–1863; Cugnoni, 1883; Boulting, 1908; Ady, 1913) also helped direct attention to Pienza. Soon a growing number of archivists and local historians were busily discovering, documenting, and describing Pienza's place in the story of Renaissance architecture.[5] Chief among Pienza's devotees was the cleric G. B. Mannucci, who spent a lifetime publishing a host of articles and notes about Pienza, its buildings, and its patrons, eventually gathering much of his work into the invaluable *Pienza: Arte e storia,* which first appeared in 1927. All subsequent scholarship on Pienza is greatly indebted to his systematic research. The monograph by Armando Schiavo that appeared in 1942 also contributed to our knowledge of the Renaissance reconstruction of Pienza. Of greatest importance, at least to an architectural appreciation of Pienza, was the critical article "Pius II als Bauherr von Pienza," published in 1937 by Ludwig Heydenreich. The guidebooks of Piero Torriti (1956, 1965, 1980), the handsome volume by Enzo Carli (published in 1967 and devoted to a general consideration of the town's history, its rebuilding, and its artistic treasures), and the superbly written little book of essays by Don Ivo Petri (1972) summed up many of the earlier investigations. Currently, Pienza is receiving a new spate of enthusiastic attention from a variety of scholars, most clearly evidenced in a recent issue of *Studi e documenti di architettura* devoted to the city.

That Pienza represents one of the major architectural masterpieces of the Italian Renaissance is acknowledged in most of the basic surveys of Renaissance art and architecture. Frederick Hartt (*History of Italian Renaissance Art,* p. 194) has described it as "the first of the new Renaissance town designs that was actually built"; Ludwig Heydenreich (*Architecture in Italy, 1400–1600,* p. 43) has called it "the first ideal city of the Renaissance to take on visible form"; and Peter Murray (*The Architecture of the Italian Renaissance,* p. 77) has noted that "it contains one of the first pieces of regular town planning since Roman days." The impact of Pienza's sheer beauty, both physical and conceptual, as well as the uniqueness of many of its individual elements assures it a most prominent place—beyond local or specialized interest—in any consideration of Renaissance style and urbanistic concepts, especially since the physical state of Pienza has, for the most part, altered but little since the days of Pope Pius. The town is, in effect, a Renaissance Williamsburg without the artificiality of restoration.

My own familiarity with Pienza began while I was a graduate student at the University of North Carolina at Chapel Hill and wrote a paper on the Renaissance building campaign for a course on Renaissance architecture taught by Harold Dickson. My interest in the town was deepened in Italy in 1968–1970 when it formed an important part of my dissertation research on the architectural career

of Bernardo Rossellino, carried out under the direction of John W. Dixon, Jr. My work at this time was supported by a doctoral fellowship from the Samuel H. Kress Foundation. In the course of my investigations, I studied Rossellino's contributions at Pienza and thoroughly examined the relevant papal account books preserved in the State Archives in Rome. Much of that documentary material had been published almost a hundred years earlier by Eugene Müntz, but I was delighted to discover a quantity of documentation that had not appeared before. A long chapter in my dissertation was devoted to Pienza, and an appendix presented all the pertinent entries from the Roman records.

Although Pienza maintained its fascination for me, it was not until 1982 that I had an occasion to revisit the town and evaluate its architecture anew. In that year, I received an invitation to take part in a symposium dealing with new towns and the urban transformation of fifteenth-century Italy, which was held in Pienza under the sponsorship of the International Center for the Study of Regional and Urban Evolution (CISPUT), headquartered in the town. There I met a number of scholars who had developed an interest in Pienza and learned of a variety of new archival and topographical discoveries relating to the town. The presence, for instance, of the twelve documented row houses on the so obviously named Via delle Case Nuove had escaped my attention earlier; for some reason, I had thought that the street name referred to a postwar rebuilding. My own experience in the intervening years with Brunelleschi, Alberti, and Rossellino also allowed me to see what had happened in Pienza from a different perspective. I realized that it was time to reevaluate the previous research on Pienza and make new critical assessments.

My visit to the CISPUT symposium in Pienza in 1982 had been made possible through travel grants from the American Council of Learned Societies, from the Samuel H. Kress Foundation, and from my own institution, the University of South Carolina. I returned to Pienza once again in the summer of 1984 for further research and to arrange for a series of fresh photographs. In this work I was again assisted by the Kress Foundation, by a Summer Research Grant from the National Endowment for the Humanities, and by a grant from the University of South Carolina Research and Productive Scholarship Committee.

As I have suggested, much new work has been done on Pienza since my first visit in 1968. Some of it has been published, but much is still in the investigative stage. The work of Italian architectural historians and architects, including Giancarlo Cataldi of the University of Florence, Luciana Finelli, Sara Rossi, Fausto Formichi, and Lero Di Cristina (the last two fortunate residents of Pienza), has done much to define individual building problems and general urban patterns. To their efforts have been added those of Henry Millon, dean of the Center for Advanced Study in the Visual Arts at the National Gallery of Art in Washington, D.C., Nicholas Adams of Lehigh University, and many others. Through their efforts, the picture of what took place in Pope Pius' Pienza is becoming clear—but also far too complex for one book to treat comprehensively. Certainly a great deal will be added in the future to our knowledge of Pienza, about its separate elements and about its total civic character. My present intent is to offer the first "complete" history of Pienza's Renaissance renewal in English, to summarize the research to date, to raise a variety of questions, and to make some personal observations and proposals. I also hope to clarify Pienza's significant position within the general context of late medieval and Renaissance urbanism and to suggest its continuing importance as a model of humane city design. I hope, too, to enable the reader to visualize some of the gracious majesty of Pienza's communal environment, where, as Leonardo Benevolo has so neatly put it, "love of form and human participation come together in a mood of literary serenity."[6]

The focus of this book is both specific (on the architecture of the Renaissance renewal and not the town's earlier or later life) and general (the entire Pientine architectural project and not just the famous monumental area around the main piazza). I have, for instance, deliberately omitted any discussion of the furnishings of the cathedral—its altarpieces, choir stalls, books, and the like—believing that material to be tangential to my architectural objectives. I have also avoided many interesting socioeconomic aspects of Pius' intervention. Such topics will likely be presented by my colleagues in future publications, as will the more archaeological examinations of specific buildings in Pienza. I have chosen simply to outline some of the problems these buildings present and to direct attention toward how the individual units fit into the general scheme for the town as devised by Pope Pius and his architect.

My debts in the writing of this book are many. As indicated, I have enjoyed generous financial support from the National Endowment for the Humanities, the Samuel H. Kress Foundation, the American Council of Learned Societies, and from my own university. At the Kress Foundation, I am particularly indebted to the former executive vice-president, the late Mary Davis, and to her successor, Marilyn Perry. Much of my work has been based upon documentary evidence found in the archives of Rome and Siena, and I greatly appreciate the kind assistance of the directors and staffs of the Archivio di Stato di Roma and the Archivio di Stato di Siena. I also found much needed but hard to obtain secondary materials in the library of the Kunsthistorisches Institut in Florence, and the director and staff of that splendid institution have my appreciation for their help and consideration. Additional library work was done at the University of North Carolina's Joseph Curtis Sloane Art Library, whose librarian, Philip A. Rees, has my especial thanks, as does the staff, particularly that of the Interlibrary Loan Division, of my own university's Thomas Cooper Library.

For complete access to the Palazzo Piccolomini in Pienza, I am indebted to Avvocato Lao Cottini, the Società di Esecutori di Pie Disposizioni di Siena, and the building's custodian and guide, Vincenzo Stacchiotti, whose courtesy and assistance were exceptional. I also am deeply appreciative of the complete cooperation of Pienza's mayor, the Honorable Vera Petreni. Invaluable also has been the kind help and inspiring conversation of Pope Pius' spiritual successors in Pienza, Monsignore Aldo Franci and Monsignore Ivo Petri, both expert in the history of their community. It was through Don Aldo's good offices that I was able to enter many of Pienza's private residences. I thank the present-day owners of homes once occupied by Pius' associates: Osvaldo Colombini and his family, Ingegnere and Signora Simonelli, Signora Pincelli, Signora Leonella Pellegrini, and others. The enthusiasm shown for my project by all the *pientini* I met is a tribute to the town's lasting pride in what Pope Pius did for his birthplace. I would be remiss if I did not also acknowledge the hospitality of Signor and Signora Brogi and the staff of Pienza's comfortable Albergo Corsignano.

I owe much to conversations with other scholars: Sharon Cather, Christoph Frommel, Elisabeth MacDougall, Werner Oechslin, Brenda Preyer, Howard Saalman, Andreas Tönnesman, Carroll William Westfall. The generous assistance of Nicholas Adams, Giancarlo Cataldi, Lero Di Cristina, Fausto Formichi, David Friedman, and Henry Millon has been of particular and constant value.

Whatever worth this book has would have been diminished greatly were it not for the skills of Catherine Castner and Mary Sayer Hammond. My colleague from the University of South Carolina's Department of Foreign Languages, Professor Castner has translated Latin texts about Pienza written by Pope Pius' contemporaries. In rendering her translations she received valuable assistance from Professor Aldo Scaglione of the Department of Romance Languages of the University of North Carolina at Chapel Hill. Professor Hammond of George Mason University has executed, with impressive sensitivity, the series of new plates which complements my text. That her "assignment" became a labor of love is obvious.

The staff at Cornell University Press has been a pleasure to work with from start to finish. Eric Halpern gave me great encouragement from the moment I submitted my proposal, and Carol Betsch, Kay Scheuer, and Judith Bailey have been both patient and efficient in helping me shape my manuscript and in guiding it toward publication. Throughout the period of research and writing, I have been fortunate to enjoy the constant support of the chairman of my department, John O'Neil.

Finally, I wish to express my appreciation for their sympathetic understanding to the members of my family into whose lives my work has been projected, especially to my wife, Ilona, who has shared my affection for Pienza from the beginning and who knows its streets and stones as well as I.

CHARLES R. MACK

Columbia, S.C.

PIENZA

Chapter 1

From Corsignano to Pienza

The Project Begins

IT WAS getting on toward midday when, on Wednesday, 21 February 1459, the papal party wound its way up the hillside above the Orcia River valley to arrive before the Tuscan village of Corsignano.[1] The travelers must have been on the road since before daybreak to have covered the fifty kilometers from their overnight lodgings at Sarteano. They had set out from Rome a month earlier on what was to be a five-month progress northward to Mantua and the pan-European conference convened there by the pope in preparation for a new crusade against the Turks. What an occasion this visit must have been for Corsignano, a modest community of some 320 houses and no more than fifteen hundred inhabitants.[2] The papal entourage consisted of a troop of cavalry and six cardinals with all their retinue; it must have made a splendid appearance—certainly the finest this little hill town had ever seen.[3] And at the head of this distinguished party was the newly elected Pope himself, Pius II, born Aeneas Silvius Piccolomini here in Corsignano in 1405. This was Piccolomini's first recorded return to his birthplace since he had left the town in 1423 to pursue his notably successful career as scholar, author, secretary-adviser, diplomat, and, most recently, cleric. In all probability, he had revisited his hometown before this, on his frequent travels between Germany and Rome in the 1440s or later, during the nine years he had served as bishop and then cardinal of nearby Siena. This, however, was his first entry into Corsignano as pope.

The citizenry did all they could to make the return of their native son memorable. As Pius himself recorded in his celebrated *Commentarii:* "The town was wonderfully decorated. The people were excited and in holiday mood over the presence of the Pope, who they boasted had been born among them, and they could not look at or cheer him enough." Despite the festivities and the genuine outpouring of affection shown him by the townsfolk, the fifty-four-year-old pontiff was less than thrilled by his visit. "He was disappointed," says the *Commentarii,* "for most of his own generation had died and those who were left kept their houses, bowed down with old age and illness, or, if they showed themselves, were so changed as to be hardly recognizable, for they were feeble and crippled and like harbingers of death." The gout-afflicted and neuralgic pope added, that "at every step the Pope met with proofs of his own age and could not fail to realize that he was an old man who would soon drop."[4] No doubt the town itself, like its citizens, seemed "bowed down with old age." Physically, the medieval hamlet would have seemed unworthy of its sudden historical importance as the birthplace of the Vicar of Christ.

On the day of the pope's arrival, there was little but his own presence to distinguish Corsignano from any of the other little farming villages of the region. Pius gave the following description of his birthplace:

A high mountain rises from the valley of the Orcia River, crowned by a plateau a mile long and much less broad. In the corner which in winter looks toward the rising sun there is a town of little repute but possessed of a healthful climate, excellent wine, and everything else that goes to sustain life. Travelers to Rome from Siena, after leaving the Castle of San Quirico and going straight ahead to Radicofani, pass Corsignano on a gently sloping hill to their left three miles from the main road.[5]

The Corsignano visited by Pope Pius II in February 1459 would have been little changed, but the transformations that followed his visit, which would remake the town into Renaissance Pienza, have made it difficult today to reconstruct the physical history of the pre-Pientine community. Some believe that the basic configuration of Corsignano/Pienza originated in a Roman foundation, which would have established an enduring axial street pattern common to many Roman colonial communities.[6] The east-west orientation of the present Corso il Rossellino would, in this view, correspond to the ancient *decumanus* while the Via Marconi would follow the original line of the *cardo*. If so, the forum of this hypothetical Roman town would probably have stood at the intersection of these two principal streets, occupying what would later be the site of the modern Piazze Pio II and del Mercato. One, in this case, could speak of a continuity of location and function which would have placed, almost through tradition, the religious and civic buildings of the Renaissance on ground once occupied by their Roman counterparts—an antique city plan reborn some fifteen hundred years later through the intervention of a humanist pope.

Alas, such pleasant speculations on ancient origins and orthagonal layouts appear to have no true substantiation. At least there have been no archaeological excavations to support such an attractive thesis and the urbanistic evidence points in other directions. It seems far more likely that whatever community there might have been in ancient days (and there is no hard evidence that there was such a town) grew up along the east-west road connecting the Via Cassia (the Medieval Via Francigena) with Montepulciano at a point of intersection with the track leading down to the hamlet of Monticchiello and the valley of the Orcia. The first houses of such a roadside village would have been built along the sides of the thoroughfare with other streets starting to lead away from it at

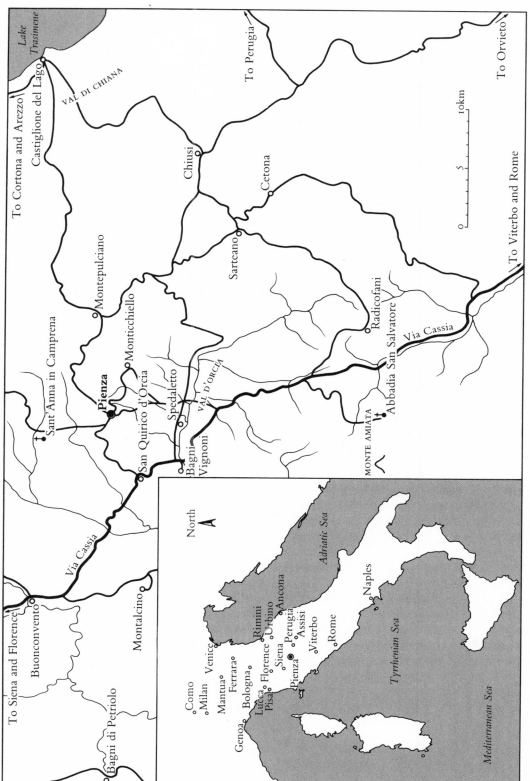

Italy and the Pientine Region

To Cortona and Arezzo

Lake Trasimene

Castiglione del Lago

VAL DI CHIANA

To Perugia

To Orvieto

Chiusi

Cetona

10 km

5

0

To Viterbo and Rome

Montepulciano

Sarteano

Monticchiello

Radicofani

Sant'Anna in Camprena

Pienza

San Quirico d'Orcia

Spedaletto

VAL D'ORCIA

Abbadia San Salvatore

Via Cassia

Bagni Vignoni

MONTE AMIATA

Via Cassia

Buonconvento

To Siena and Florence

Montalcino

Bagni di Petriolo

North

Adriatic Sea

Naples

Como

Milan

Venice

Mantua

Rimini

Ferrara

Urbino

Ancona

Genoa

Bologna

Lucca

Florence

Perugia

Pisa

Siena

Assisi

Pienza

Viterbo

Rome

Tyrrhenian Sea

Mediterranean Sea

PLAN OF PIENZA

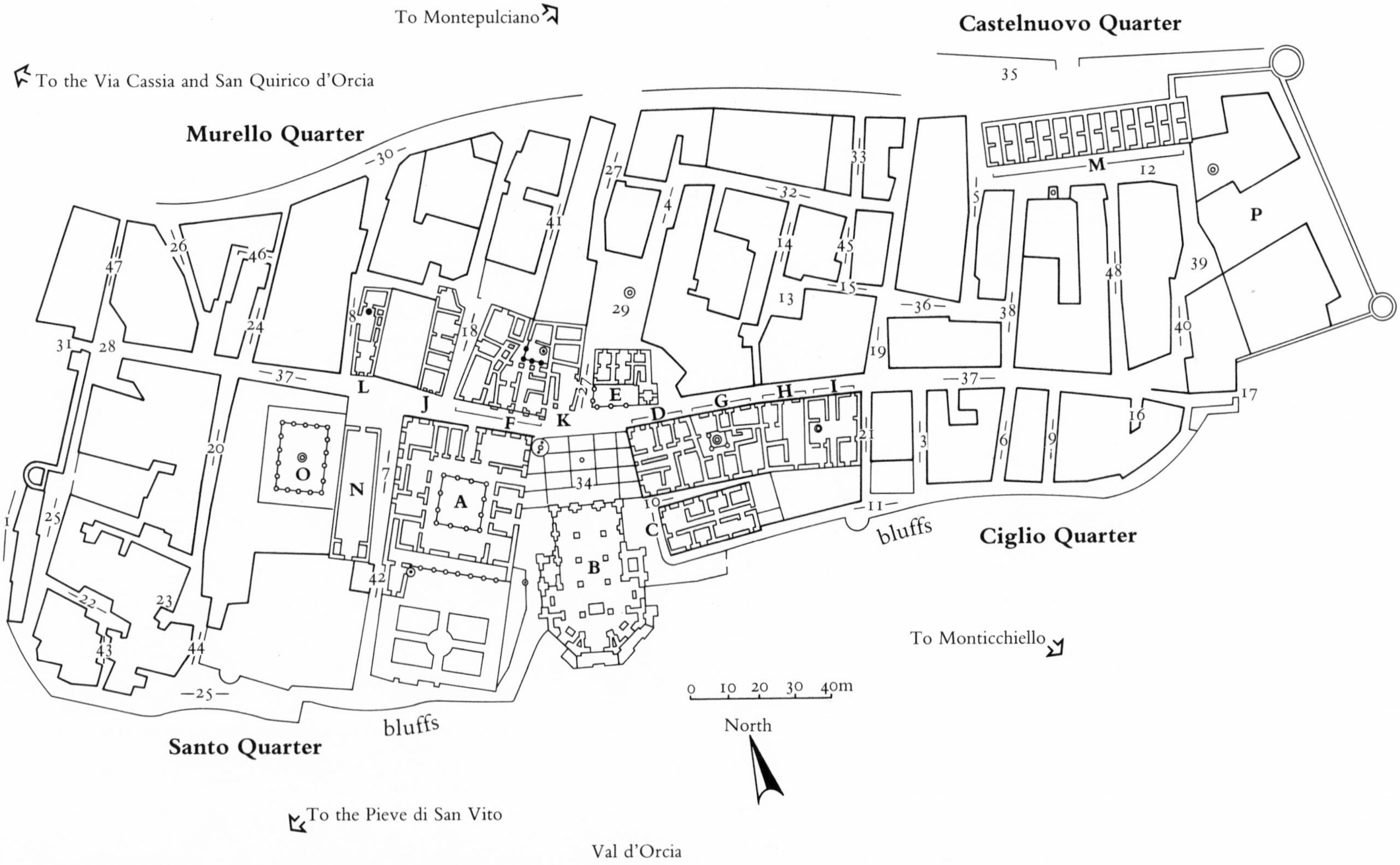

Castelnuovo Quarter

Murello Quarter

Ciglio Quarter

Santo Quarter

To Montepulciano

To the Via Cassia and San Quirico d'Orcia

To Monticchiello

To the Pieve di San Vito

Val d'Orcia

North

0   10   20   30   40m

bluffs

bluffs

Building Index

A. Palazzo Piccolomini
B. Cathedral
C. Palazzo Canonica
D. Palazzo Vescovile (Borgia)
E. Palazzo Comunale
F. Palazzo Ammannati
G. Palazzo Jouffroy (Atrebatense)
H. Treasurer's Palace (Palazzo Buonconti?)
I. Palazzo Lolli
J. Palace of Salomone Piccolomini (?)
K. Palace of Tommaso Piccolomini (?)
L. Possible Site of the Inn or Hospice
M. The Twelve *Case Nuove*
N. San Francesco
O. Cloister of San Francesco
P. The Castelnuovo

Street Index

1. Addobbo, Via dell'
2. Alighieri, Piazza Dante
3. Amore, Via dell'
4. Angelo, Via dell'
5. Apparita, Via dell'
6. Bacio, Via del
7. Balzello, Via del
8. Buca, Via della
9. Buia, Via
10. Canonica, Vicolo della
11. Casello, Via del
12. Case Nuove, Via delle
13. Chiocarella, Largo della
14. Chiocarella, Via
15. Chiochina, Via della
16. Cieco, Vicolo
17. Ciglio, Porta al
18. Condotti, Via
19. Dogali, Via
20. Elisa, Via
21. Fortuna, Via della
22. Fosso, Via del
23. Galletti, Piazza (post–World War II)
24. Giglio, Via del
25. Gozzante, Via
26. Lione, Via dei
27. Marconi, Via Guglielmo
28. Martiri della Libertà, Piazza
29. Mercato, Piazza del (di Spagna)
30. Mura, Via della
31. Murello, Porta (al Prato)
32. Pia, Via
33. Piano, Vicolo
34. Pio II, Piazza
35. Roma, Largo
36. Rosa, Via della
37. Rossellino, Corso il
38. San Andrea, Via
39. San Carlo, Piazza
40. San Carlo, Via
41. San Pasquale, Vicolo
42. Santo, Porta al (?)
43. Serve Smarrite, Vicolo
44. Solleciti, Vicolo dei
45. Stretti, Via
46. Torta, Via
47. XV Giugno, Via
48. Volpe, Via della

right angles as the community expanded. In any case, we actually hear nothing of a town on the site until the medieval era.

The provocative mists of history which envelop the early days of Corsignano begin to lift with the dawn of the Middle Ages. Apparently the hypothetical ancient town vanished for a time with the decline of Roman rule in the wake of the barbarian onslaughts. It was not until sometime before the seventh century that a Christian church, the Pieve di San Vito, was erected. It was built not on the hill where the present town is located, however, but at a spring below the escarpment some three hundred meters away. This church, modified, expanded, and finally rebuilt in its present form in the eleventh and twelfth centuries served an informal community that developed around it and, later, upon the more defensible hilltop. Despite its inconvenient location, San Vito remained the only church in Corsignano during much of the Middle Ages. Even after new churches were built in the precincts of Corsignano, San Vito continued preeminent until the construction of Pope Pius' cathedral. It was to San Vito that the children of Corsignano were carried for baptism, the infant Aeneas Silvius Piccolomini among them.

In the ninth century, the area came under the rule of Cistercian monks from the Abbey of San Salvatore at Monte Amiata and remained in their hands for the next three centuries. They established a small monastery at the top of the hill above the Santo Gate. Their *corte,* as the monastic property was termed, was later to be occupied by the houses of the Piccolomini and, in turn, by the great papal palace. The monastic feudalism that governed the little peasant village broke up in the twelfth century and by the middle of the next century the Sienese were established as the new overlords. It was during this period that the physical character of Corsignano was established. As the town matured and grew, a second church was erected, this time in the heart of the commune. The Church of Santa Maria was later supplanted by the Renaissance cathedral, but traces of its medieval foundations were uncovered in 1932 during repairs to the cathedral.[7] Fragments of sculpture found in the excavations make a date in the twelfth century likely for this medieval Santa Maria.[8] The excavators concluded from the traces of foundation walls and piers they discovered that the Romanesque church ran at an approximate right angle from the western wall of the present cathedral across its nave to terminate somewhere in the vicinity of the old Priors' Palace (replaced in the Renaissance by the Palazzo Vescovile). That reconstruction seems to me to be less than certain. The only trace of a doorway was found not in the supposed western facade but along the southern flank, and the foundations of walls and piers are of such size that the apse would necessarily have trespassed on the area of the Priors' Palace. It seems more likely that the facade of the medieval church faced south, toward the brow of the hill and Mount Amiata, with its apse reaching into the present Piazza Pio II, perhaps as far as its northern edge.

In the following century, yet another religious institution was founded in Corsignano, the Franciscan Church and Monastery of San Francesco. This Gothic church is one of the long "preaching barns" favored by the followers of Saint Francis, with an interior uninterrupted by aisles or architectural adornment. The adjacent monastic complex dates from the late fifteenth century and the patronage of Cardinal Francesco Todeschini-Piccolomini (the future Pope Pius III) but may replace an earlier cloister and monastery.[9] The Church of San Francesco and its dependent properties took up a substantial portion of the medieval community, pointing to the growing impact of such clerical foundations upon the internal fabric of the Italian communes during the late Middle Ages. Other thirteenth-century religious institutions included the Church of San Giovanni in the northwestern quarter and the small Benedictine nunnery of San Gregorio located a hundred meters north of town on the Montepulciano road. At the eastern edge of town, just inside the Porta al Ciglio, the lay Fraternità del Corpus Domini built its oratory and headquarters in the fourteenth century. These were the religious institutions that gave to Corsignano a new architectural personality and substance in the final years of its medieval life.

The most important secular building built during this period was that which housed the new communal government of Corsignano. The Palazzo dei Priori was constructed immediately to the east of the Church of Santa Maria on the south side of the present Corso il Rossellino; its ogive arched windows and doorways can still be discerned beneath the veneer of the Renaissance Palazzo Vescovile. Sienese soldiers were stationed in the town to ensure that the city fathers and the citizenry of Corsignano would remain loyal to the government of Siena. This practice was begun in 1251 when a captain and twenty-five men were sent. Eight years later the force was increased by a troop of fifty horsemen, and undoubtedly, the military presence was reinforced in 1388, when the town of Montepulciano, a scant fifteen kilometers distant, passed into the hands of the Florentines. Corsignano thus became a strategic border outpost for the Sienese and it was perhaps at this time that the fortress, or castelnuovo, at the northeastern corner of town facing in the direction of Montepulciano, was begun. In archival documents, thereafter, the town is often referred to as Castro Corsignano.[10]

These were the major buildings of Corsignano before it became Pienza. But what of the rest of the medieval town? What was it like? There is little outwardly medieval in the streets of modern-day or, better, Renaissance Pienza, so extensive was the work undertaken in the 1450s and 1460s. Behind the reconditioned facades undoubtedly stand structures of medieval origin, but they are not easy to detect in passing. In only a few parts of town—notably in the southwestern corner along the Via Gozzante, the Via del Fosso (Plate 1), or the Via Elisa (Plate 2)—can some relatively untouched medieval housing be observed. Yet even here little remains, for this area was heavily damaged during the last war.[11] In recent years the dedicated efforts of a handful of scholars have brought a clearer picture of the medieval community into focus. Their work has included site and structural analyses and some archaeological investigations, which, while concentrating largely upon the Renaissance features of Pienza, have also provided information on medieval Corsignano. Some of the most revealing material in this regard has been reported by Nicholas Adams, whose work has

1. Medieval house on the southern side of the Via del Fosso in the Santo Quarter.

2. View north along the Via Elisa (Santo Quarter) to the Corso il Rossellino. The remnants of a medieval house can be seen on the right. The house with the sgraffito coats of arms is at the middle left. Across from it is the palazzo with figural sgraffiti.

been undertaken not only in the streets of Pienza but also at the reading tables of the State Archives of Siena. There he has discovered a number of documents that make possible a reconstruction of the social and physical fabric of the pre-Pientine commune.[12]

Among the extensive archival materials in Siena, Adams discovered a property evaluation survey made at Corsignano in 1320 (*Estimo 41*). His insightful use of this record gives us a substantially improved picture of Corsignano in the century prior to its metamorphosis. At the beginning of the fourteenth century, Corsignano consisted of some 350 houses in which approximately 1,750 people lived. Although we must allow for some shrinkage in population and a consequent abandonment of dwellings or amalgamation of adjacent housing units due to the black death of 1348 and the reoccurrence of the plague throughout the rest of the century and on into the next, the basic pattern of life probably had altered but little by the time of the Pope's visit in 1459. *Estimo 41* shows the vast majority of the inhabitants, not unexpectedly, engaged in agricultural pursuits. What is, perhaps, a bit more surprising is just how one-sided the economic base of Corsignano was. Few listed their occupations as anything but farming; there were hardly any craftsmen (Adams could find only one person who could be so identified) and virtually no middle class. This was a bedroom community of farmers and field hands who spent their days working in the wheat fields, olive groves, orchards, and vineyards beyond the town walls. Wealth in the hill town appears to have been unevenly distributed, with an unusually high percentage of citizens at the bottom of the economic ladder. Curiously, however, their housing did not reflect the poverty of the inhabitants. While only a few of the houses listed in the *Estimo* were of good size and substantial value, there were just as few upon which very low property valuations were placed. This apparent anomaly might be explained if we suppose that a general economic decline had already set in by the early fourteenth century, producing a situation in which many whose earnings were now drastically reduced continued to live in housing built in better days. Economic depression appears to have persisted into the next century when it was alluded to in Pope Pius' rather gloomy description of what he found on his return to his birthplace. The state into which his hometown evidently was sliding may well have influenced his decision to rebuild the town and reverse the trend.

From the *Estimo* of 1320, we also learn something of the physical character of medieval Corsignano. For one thing, there seems to have been little empty space in the village. Only one *piazza comunis* is mentioned, and its location was, unfortunately, not recorded. Perhaps it was at the Monte Piccone where the Piazza Pio II is today, but more likely, especially if this space was occupied by the Church of Santa Maria, as I have suggested, it is to be identified with the present Piazza del Mercato, also known as the Piazza di Spagna.[13] Only a few properties described as open spaces or garden plots were listed, almost all of them associated with larger houses. Empty lots were rare in 1320, but by the middle of the next century they formed a substantial part of the urban environment, evidence, perhaps, of continued economic erosion and population slippage resulting in the decay and collapse of abandoned houses. In any case, since little free space was recorded in the *Estimo* of 1320, we can picture the dusty streets of fourteenth-century Corsignano lined with contiguous row houses or units of *isola* surrounded by streets. Corsignano looked, in short, as undistinguished as any other hill town in the area on that special afternoon in February 1459. What did set it apart was that it had produced a pope.

While one might question Pius' spiritual suitability to assume the Fisherman's place, there can be no doubt of his intellectual and scholarly qualifications. Aeneas Silvius Piccolomini was a brilliant child of the quattrocento and one of the most delightful sons of the Age of Humanism, but when he was born in Corsignano on 18 October 1405, his success could not really have been foretold.[14]

The Piccolomini certainly had seen better days. In the thirteenth century they were among the most powerful of Siena's merchant families, with banking houses in Genoa, Venice, Trieste, Aquileia, France, and Austria.[15] The family also possessed considerable property in the Sienese countryside and from an early date were established in Corsignano. In 1351, for example, Enea di Corrado Piccolomini is recorded as having purchased a *palazzetto con piazza* in the town. Thus, when the Piccolomini clan was banished from Siena in 1385, along with other members of the aristocratic establishment, it was only natural that they should wait out their period of exile in Corsignano.

The future pope's father, Silvio, was born in 1370, the posthumous son of Silvio d'Enea Piccolomini. It was he who was forced to retreat to Corsignano and who tried to redeem the fortunes of his family through a military career in the service of the Visconti of Milan. His hopes were not realized and he returned to Corsignano to live the life of a rural landholder, an important man in a very unimportant community. Silvio married Vittoria Forteguerri, who, like himself, possessed a noble Sienese name but little else. Of their eighteen children only three reached adulthood, their firstborn, Aeneas Silvius, and his two sisters Caterina and Laudomia. Aeneas Silvius grew up as a country lad but with his mind undoubtedly filled with the aspirations of his formerly powerful family. Success as a soldier had eluded Silvio, so he determined that his son should try another route to escape the rustic captivity of Corsignano. Aeneas had shown himself an apt pupil of his first teacher, the parish priest Fra Pietro, and in 1423 his father sent him to Siena to lodge with his paternal aunt Bartolommea Lolli and pursue a course of study at the university.[16]

In Siena, Aeneas studied grammar, rhetoric, theology, and law, and there, from 1425, he listened to the inspirational preaching of Bernardino da Siena.[17] In 1429 Aeneas Silvius traveled to Florence to begin a study of Greek literature under the celebrated Francesco Filelfo.[18] He remained with Filelfo for two years and then, armed with letters of introduction to the greatest scholars of the day, set off on a tour of Italian cities, visiting Pavia, Milan, Padua, Ferrara, and Bologna. He returned to Siena in the winter of 1432, just in time to encounter the entourage of Cardinal Domenico Capranica.[19] The young Aeneas evidently impressed the cardinal with his scholarly skills and personality, for he was offered a secretarial position on Capranica's staff and journeyed with him, via Genoa and Milan, to the Council of Basel. His attendance at this reforming and later schismatic assemblage of churchmen introduced the young scholar to a large circle of theologians and intellectuals. He thrived in their company.

After two years in Cardinal Capranica's service, Aeneas Silvius found new employment, first with Bishop Nicodemus of Freising and then with Bartolommeo Visconti, bishop of Novara, with whom he traveled to Florence in 1435. There he joined the brilliant staff of humanists surrounding Cardinal Niccolò Albergatti. Albergatti's remarkable following included the humanist Pietro di Noceto and the future Pope Nicholas V, Tommaso Parentucelli. Aeneas returned to Basel with Albergatti, accompanied him on several trips through northern Europe, and was sent by him on a special ambassadorial mission to Scotland and England. Upon his return, he served the Council of Basel in a variety of secretarial capacities and became a polemicist for the candidacy of Amadeus VIII of Savoy as Antipope Felix V against Pope Eugenius IV. His official duties allowed him sufficient time to follow the pursuits of a humanist writer, treating a variety of diverse matters from love to theology in beautifully phrased Latin prose and verse. His literary and oratorical talents soon earned him a position of respect and prominence. In 1442 Aeneas accepted a post in the chancery of Emperor Frederick III and followed the imperial party to Austria. That year, the emperor bestowed on Aeneas the laurel wreath of court poet. He served Frederick in a

number of capacities and in 1445 was sent to Rome as the imperial envoy to Eugenius IV. He eloquently made his peace with the pope he had denounced only a few years earlier and who now encouraged Aeneas to think of a career in the papal service. Aeneas used his considerable skills of persuasion on Eugenius' behalf and helped to secure the submission of the German princes. Soon his patronage became papal rather than imperial, and in 1446 he was made a pontifical secretary; eight months later he was appointed an apostolic subdeacon. In 1447, the direction of his career clearly charted, Aeneas foreswore the worldly life he had led (as attested not only in many of his writings but also by the two illegitimate children he had fathered in the north) and accepted ordination into the priesthood.

With the accession of his former colleague Parentucelli to the papal throne in 1447 as Pope Nicholas V, Aeneas prospered and soon was nominated bishop of Trieste. In 1450 he was given the bishopric of Siena, a prize that must have seemed something of a triumph for the son of an exile. His imperial contacts were also maintained during this period, for he traveled to Milan on the emperor's business on two occasions and went to Naples in 1450 to arrange the engagement of Frederick to Eleanor of Portugal. Two years later, Bishop Aeneas Piccolomini finalized those arrangements when he brought the couple together at Siena and journeyed with them to Rome for their marriage by Pope Nicholas and Frederick's official coronation as Holy Roman Emperor.

Although Aeneas spent much of Pope Nicholas' reign at his bishoprics or in Germany, he was in Rome long enough to be inspired by the architectural impact Nicholas was having upon the city.[20] The projects undertaken during the papacy of Nicholas V are well known from a number of sources, including the report of Giannozzo Manetti, one of the pontiff's own secretaries.[21] Shortly after Nicholas' death in 1455, Manetti composed a biography of his patron in which he devoted considerable space to recording the pope's deathbed oration and the long description of the architectural program it contained. It would seem that Pope Nicholas, an astute politician, recognized the importance of visual display and symbolic gesture. As part of his program of consolidation, restoration, and expansion, Nicholas determined to give to his possessions an appearance worthy of his vision of the temporal majesty of the Roman church. Aeneas Silvius himself was sufficiently impressed with those efforts to remark that Nicholas "erected magnificent buildings in this city, though he began more than he finished."[22] In his history of the Council of Basel, too, Aeneas listed among Nicholas' catalogue of virtues, "curam rei familiaris maxime delexit, architectus mirificus."[23]

Manetti in his report wrote that Nicholas had concentrated first upon the necessary repairs to Rome's fortifications, the renovation of her important churches, and the restoration of her bridges, aqueducts, and fountains. This work seems to have been related directly to preparations for the jubilee year of 1450 and for the subsequent visit of Emperor Frederick III in 1452. Nicholas' biographer also claimed that a number of building projects of a similar nature were undertaken in various towns in the papal states.

What is remarkable about Nicholas' program is its projected second stage—those celebrated projects Manetti said were planned but never effected. If death had not intervened, according to Manetti, his pope would have set about three visionary projects. We are told that he wished to convert the Vatican Palace, already being enlarged, into an enormous complex resplendent with gardens, loggias, aqueducts, fountains, chapels, libraries, a theater, and a new conclave hall. He also intended to reorganize the Borgo district, lying between the Tiber and Saint Peter's, creating order out of its confusion of tiny streets by laying out three loggia-lined avenues leading into the piazza in front of Saint Peter's. And finally, the pope's most ambitious dream of all entailed the total rebuilding of the old basilica. In short, according to Manetti's biography, if Pope Nicholas had had his way and if time and health had been more accommodating, the seat of the papacy would have been given a splendor and grandeur not seen in the cityscapes of Western Europe since the days of imperial Rome.

The papal proposals are described in such detail by Manetti that they seem tangible; yet nothing, or very little, ever came of them, and it is not at all certain that anyone ever really imagined such a gigantic undertaking could be accomplished. Perhaps they were seen as more of a descriptive gesture, a propagandistic symbol of the revivified papacy of Nicholas V, meant to be spoken of and never seen. On his deathbed, Nicholas is reported to have said that to solidify his rule and the authority of the Church, he had found it necessary to "conceive such buildings in mind and spirit." Manetti may well have been describing a utopian dream, a parallel or sequel to the *De re aedificatoria* presented to Pope Nicholas in 1451 by his secretary and architectural advisor Leone Battista Alberti. Yet traces of the concepts embraced in this grand design did materialize half a decade later in much more realistic scale. It was really in the Pienza of Pius II that the Rome of Nicholas V came alive.

The humanistic environment nurtured by Pope Nicholas withered for a time during the short reign of his successor Calixtus III Borgia (1455–1458), whose primary preoccupation, aside from bestowing favors on family members, was championing a new crusade against the Turks. Though many of the humanists were discouraged by the Spanish pope's indifference to the Renaissance of learning and art, Aeneas Silvius continued to advance his career. In December 1457, he was given a cardinal's hat, a not unremarkable achievement for a secular scholar who had first made his priestly vows a scant ten years before. When Calixtus died in 1458, Cardinal Aeneas was in a good position to make his bid for the chair of Saint Peter.

The name taken by the Piccolomini pope upon his election on 19 August 1458 reflected his humanist background and his new religious dedication as well as, one must believe, his keen wit. The name Pius recalled not the name of his obscure second-century papal predecessor but Virgil's great epic and the words of its protagonist, the founder of the Roman race: "Sum pius Aeneas."[24] Like the Virgilian hero, Aeneas Silvius Piccolomini had found a new calling and a divinely directed destiny.

Pope Pius' intense enthusiasm for the artistic as well as the literary Renaissance would undoubtedly have been even more demonstrable had he lived longer and not been so involved in time- and finance-consuming political affairs. Then, too, he was sincerely committed to Calixtus' promise of a crusade, and most of his attention was devoted to that cause. Pius did resume much of the construction Nicholas had begun in Rome and its environs.[25] Though the enormous building dreams of that pope were curtailed, the records of papal expenditures during the years of Pius II's reign are filled with payments for a wide variety of restorations and repairs to churches and buildings throughout Rome, and most of these projects appear to have been simply sequential to those begun by Nicholas V.[26] Pius also continued one major phase of the work at Saint Peter's. Under Pius' sponsorship a number of realizable projects intended to ennoble the approach to the great basilica were continued or initiated. Most significant were the construction of a new flight of stairs leading from the piazza to the level of the forecourt of the basilica, the reorganization of the piazza itself, and the erection of the splendid Benediction Loggia. The new pope was a realist, and as Christoph Frommel has pointed out, "The piazza project of Pius II proceeded, in contrast to that of Nicholas V, less from the Utopia of an ideal piazza as from the traditional function and the topographic situation of the old piazza."[27] The major architectural contribution of this program was the Benediction Loggia. Its design was based upon the example of the Colosseum or the Tabularium and so emphatically "antique" was its appearance that the name of Alberti comes immediately to mind although those of

Bernardo Rossellino and, most recently, Francesco del Borgo have been advanced.[28]

Pius' respect for antiquity was made clear not only in his own writings, his visual preferences as demonstrated by the Benediction Loggia, and his patronage in other matters but by the landmark papal bull that he published in April 1462 protecting the ancient monuments of Rome.[29] Pius had a sincere interest in the archaeology of Italy. Seven years before, he took time on a trip to Naples to survey the "skeletons of ancient cities" along the Bay of Naples.[30] Yet Pius was no Albertian antiquarian thoroughly committed to classical revival. He could also admire the Gothic churches of England, the paintings of Giotto, and the medieval sculptures of Lorenzo Maitani.[31] It is thus not surprising that the plans he approved for the rebuilding of his birthplace included a cathedral whose interior and apse were obviously Gothic in style set next to a classically motivated palace.

Pius' aesthetic was also shaped by a true love of nature; he was, in the words of William Boulting, "a wooer of nature."[32] His joy in the outdoors comes across clearly in the *Commentarii* in glowing descriptions of trips into the countryside, in the verbal *vedute* of sights seen, and in refreshing rememberances of "picnic" consistories.[33] This sympathy for nature, certainly in keeping with the humanist tradition of Petrarch, was to be firmly imprinted on the new town he would create out of his birthplace.

Pius spent but two nights in Corsignano in February 1459, perhaps sleeping in a chilly tent or lodged in uncomfortably cramped quarters in one of the Piccolomini family's old dwellings. He doesn't tell us. On Thursday, 22 February, he celebrated the Mass of Saint Peter's Chair in the Church of San Francesco and on the next morning departed Corsignano to push on with his party along the road to Siena. It had been a brief homecoming for Pius but a stay long enough for him to determine to make a glorious example of Corsignano. As he later wrote in the *Commentarii*: "He decided to build there a new church and a palace and he hired architects and workmen at no small expense, that he might leave as lasting as possible a memorial of his birth."[34] In his intentions to transform his birthplace, Pius must have wished to emulate the noble actions of earlier rulers, both imperial and papal, among them Emperor Septimius Severus, who sponsored lavish architectural projects in his native Lepcis Magna, and Popes Innocent III and Boniface VIII, who in the thirteenth century had attempted the same at their common birthplace of Agnani south of Rome.[35] Pius also saw the opportunity of finally actualizing, in more realistic fashion, some of the visionary urban symbolism of which Pope Nicholas had dreamt.

The *Commentarii* suggests that the pope was prompt in hiring "architects and workmen," but he could not have done this on the spot, for such artisans were not available locally. One has but to remember the paucity of any sort of craftsmen in 1320. It is possible that Pius hired his work crew in Siena during his two-month stay there, but his chief architect was not to be a Sienese compatriot but a man identified in the *Commentarii* as a certain "Florentine named Bernardo."[36] A variety of documents prove that this Bernardo from Florence was the well-known sculptor and architect Bernardo di Matteo di Domenico di Luca Gamberelli, better and more briefly known as Bernardo Rossellino (1409–1464). The Vatican accounts of the work at Corsignano/Pienza identify the architect in charge as Master Bernardo da Fiorenza and he is further linked in those entries with a Master Puccio di Paolo da Fiorenza, "his nephew and colleague."[37] This same Puccio di Paolo is to be identified with Puccio di Paolo di Giovanni di Luca Gamberelli, a grand nephew of Bernardo Rossellino.[38] Absolute confirmation that Pius' Bernardo is Bernardo Rossellino is to be found in a document preserved among the accounts of the Cathedral of Florence and dated 14 December 1461, which records that "advice about certain stones" was sought from "Bernardo Mattei, stone worker, who at present is the director of the cupola and lantern [of the Florence Cathedral] . . . who was in Corsignano."[39]

Born in the village of Settignano in the hills north of Florence as the second son of a farmer and quarry master, Bernardo Rossellino received his first training as a stonemason in the family workshop.[40] His brothers were all active in the trade, and the youngest, Antonio, won especial fame as a sculptor. Prominent as a sculptor himself, Bernardo Rossellino began his architectural career in 1433 by directing the completion of the facade of the chapter house of the Fraternità di Santa Maria della Misericordia in Arezzo.[41] Despite the underlying awkwardness of this youthful endeavor, the direction he would follow was already discernible. The facade reveals Rossellino's interest in the sculptural handling of surfaces. Even

later, when purely architectural considerations came to dominate his thinking, he continued to retain this love for the decorative. Such a tendency might be construed as a survival of a taste for the Gothic; yet from the beginning he appears to have consciously rejected the conservative and latently medieval solutions of many of his competitors. The architectural phraseology of the facade of the Misericordia Palace illustrates Rossellino's enthusiastic acceptance of the progressive and classicizing tastes of the most avant-garde artists of his day. This constant commitment to *il modo antico* would set Rossellino apart from most other Florentine stonemasons, even Michelozzo, and place him in the forefront of the humanist movement in architecture only a few steps behind Filippo Brunelleschi and Leone Battista Alberti.

In his desire to implant an antique—and consequently a "modern"—spirit in his architecture, Rossellino employed many of the innovations of more senior masters. Although he was not a learned man in the accepted sense, Rossellino had a quick mind. He easily borrowed, absorbed, and synthesized the motifs of those more familiar with antiquity than himself. While never an imitator and seldom, if ever, an out-and-out plagiarist, he was a selective eclectic. His genius for innovative eclecticism, quite obvious at the Misericordia Palace, much less so in his later projects, became a fundamental ingredient of his style. Rossellino constantly appropriated the vocabulary of others, but he so reworked the borrowed phrasings that the result was a highly personal language of his own.

Bernardo Rossellino returned to Florence in 1436 to work under a certain Antonio di Domenico who was rebuilding the cloister at the Badia Fiorentina.[42] For this project, Rossellino furnished a distinctively elegant doorframe and a curious window that combines elements of the traditional twin-lighted *bifora* and the cross window. He may also have been responsible for the cloister's most novel feature, the use of superimposed pilaster strips above the columns of the two stories of loggias. In any case, Rossellino would later use pilasters in this way, to articulate the wall surface and to provide a balance between vertical and horizontal, in the Palazzo Piccolomini at Pienza. During the same period, Rossellino directed the construction of, and perhaps designed, the Cloister of Santa Maria alle Campora, which, with Michelozzo's cloisters at San Marco in Florence, was among the first to display a pure Renaissance style in a monastic context.

Bernardo Rossellino's allegiance to the classical mainstream of Renaissance art is apparent in his two great pieces of architectural sculpture of the 1440s, the portal of the Sala del Consistoro in the Palazzo Pubblico of Siena and the funeral monument to Leonardo Bruni in the Florentine Church of Santa Croce. By any estimation, these two works stand out as highpoints in the development of the Renaissance style. The richly decorated and gracefully classical doorframe in Siena is arguably the finest example of the type to have been done in the first half of the fifteenth century, and it is certainly one of the most sumptuously elegant of the entire Renaissance. The Bruni tomb in Santa Croce was a tour de force in classical devices and the Florentine Renaissance interpretation of ancient architectural decoration. Significantly, it

displayed Rossellino's interest, as yet only at second hand, in the *maniera all'antica* and showed his uncompromising efforts to master the classical style of architecture. Even before his trip to Rome in 1451–1455 and his subsequent close contact with Alberti, Bernardo Rossellino had demonstrated a thorough appreciation for the nature of the classical revival. This sympathy for the meaning of classicism extended beyond details of decoration to an understanding of the harmonious relationships, balance, order, stability, and grandeur found in the best products of antiquity, qualities evident in the finest architectural accomplishment of Rossellino's early years, the Spinelli Cloister at Santa Croce (1448–1451).[43]

The rhythmic beauty of the Spinelli Cloister is due to a well-conceived design based upon a series of mathematical ratios and Euclidean relationships that echo those employed by Brunelleschi at the Hospital of the Innocents. Although not really a Brunelleschian, Rossellino seems to have understood better than most of his contemporaries the fundamental principles of the master. Throughout the Spinelli Cloister, architectural details were handled with inventiveness and sculptural precision. The unusual design of the capitals and corbels with their fluted bells and turned-down acanthus leaf volutes (possibly a Rossellino innovation), the finely delineated archivolts, the magnificent doorways—all these elements clearly represent the products of artisans working under the expert supervision of an accomplished master.

During the same years he was at work for Tommaso Spinelli at Santa Croce, Rossellino was also in the employ of another wealthy Florentine banker,

Giovanni Rucellai. Around 1448, he began to remodel several houses owned by Rucellai into the core of a unified residence. The only significant feature of this phase of his work at the Palazzo Rucellai was its courtyard, with its stately Corinthian columns reminiscent of Michelozzo's work at the Medici Palace. The famous facade was not to be executed until Rucellai had acquired sufficient property, and in his plan for it Rossellino was to follow and refine his own design for the Piccolomini Palace in Pienza.

The watershed of Bernardo Rossellino's architectural career was his tenure on the building staff of Pope Nicholas V.[44] The available documentary evidence indicates that Pope Nicholas' biographer, Giannozzo Manetti (and Giorgio Vasari who repeated his story a hundred years later in his *Lives of the Artists*), greatly exaggerated not only the amount of what was undertaken but also the extent of Rossellino's actual involvement. According to Manetti, Rossellino was entrusted with the design and execution of all the projects visualized by the pope, but the available documentary evidence strongly disagrees. The records of papal expenditures indicate that Rossellino participated in only two building projects, the construction of the Torre Magna at the Vatican and the restoration of the Roman Church of San Stefano Rotondo.[45] Yet Rossellino was the highest-paid member of the pope's extensive architectural staff, and he must have done more to justify the size of his retainer.

His main employment may have been not at the construction site but at the planning table, working out the second, far more ambitious phase of Pope Nicholas' program. If so, then it was there that Rossellino would have acquired those ideas about urban design which were to be of such importance in the major architectural accomplishment of his career. As his instructor in these matters, he would have had one of the greatest humanist scholars and aestheticians of the age, Leone Battista Alberti.

From the early 1440s on, Alberti was writing his monumental *De re aedificatoria,* in which can be found glimpses of some of the ideas Manetti said the pope wished to accomplish. It was through the plentiful treasury of the Vatican that Alberti may have seen the possibility of putting his antiquarian researches, architectural theories, and ideas about living into practice. His dedication of the treatise on architecture to the pope probably was meant to whet Nicholas' appetite for the elaborate proposals of its author—it was a sort of fifteenth-century architect's prospectus. If this suggestion is correct, then it would have been at this point that Bernardo Rossellino, who arrived in Rome at precisely the right moment, would have become involved—after Alberti had presented the general concepts for the new palace, Borgo district, and basilica to the pope. Alberti was a theoretician and brilliant dilettante of the arts but not a professional architect or engineer. The experienced Florentine stonemason, therefore, was brought into the inner planning circle and given his substantial monthly retainer and a few odd jobs with which to busy himself when not otherwise on call. Certainly a protracted contact with Alberti and a close familiarity with the theories contained in his treatise is indicated by Rossellino's later designs for the buildings and spaces at Pienza.

Little, if any, of this phase of the papal program in Rome was put into execution, yet Rossellino benefited greatly from the experience. He enjoyed the tutelage of Alberti who introduced him to a deeper understanding of the nature of classical architecture and encouraged him to think beyond the level of individual architectural units, to appreciate the essence of spatial volume and the essentials of urban planning. Rossellino may have built little in Rome, but his high-ranking position on the papal building staff and even, perhaps, as an architectural adviser to the pope seems to have raised the estimation of his worth both in his own eyes and in those of others. Certainly, after his return to Florence, Bernardo Rossellino was no longer regarded as a simple stonemason or building contractor. His status had risen above the level of the craftsman, and as Michelozzo slipped into some measure of disfavor, Rossellino became the most respected and sought-after architect in Florence. Upon his return, although he worked on certain sculptural commissions (e.g., the Tomb of Orlando de'Medici in Santissima Annunziata), most sculpture commissions were left to members of his thriving workshop led by his brother Antonio. His attention was now on architectural affairs.

During the last decade of his life, Rossellino's architectural work in Florence included participation in the completion of the Hospital of the Innocents and on the Oratory Chapel of the Annunciation in Santissima Annunziata, as well as on architectural repairs in the Church of San Miniato ai Monte.[46] Through his workshop, he was also involved with the construction of the mortuary chapel of the Cardinal Jaime of Portugal in San Miniato.[47] Rossellino's two most important projects in Florence during this period involved palaces. Around 1459, for his old patron Tommaso Spinelli, he remodeled some existing structures on the Borgo di Santa Croce into a palace remarkable for its architectural sculptures, extensive use of sgraffito decorations, and the perspectival illusionism introduced in the entrance passage.[48] He also returned to Giovanni Rucellai's employ and completed the distinctive facade for the Palazzo Rucellai. Other unsubstantiated but likely architectural programs with which his name has been connected include work at the Badia Fiesolana and construction of the apse of the Church of San Martino in Gangalandi, from which Alberti enjoyed a benefice.[49] In 1461 Bernardo Rossellino was made architectural superintendent of the Florence Cathedral, an appointment of the highest prestige which recognized his position as the leader of the most important architectural and sculptural workshop in Florence.

Despite Bernardo Rossellino's recognized place of importance in the architectural establishment of the day, we may still ask why Pope Pius selected him to direct the work that would transform Corsignano into Pienza. There are several possibilities. If we accept the statement in the *Commentarii* at face value, then we must believe that Rossellino was given the assignment during the pope's brief stay in Corsignano, 21–23 February 1459. Such a supposition presupposes, of course, that Rossellino was a member of the papal party and, consequently, was in Rome prior to the pope's departure on 22 January. There is no proof that he was there, however, and considering the number of projects with which Bernardo Rossellino was involved in Florence during the late 1450s, such an eventuality, although not impossible, does appear unlikely.[50] What is more plausible is that the pope did not appoint his architect until he arrived in Florence on 26 April.[51] If this was the case, the choice of architect was based upon Rossellino's recognized preeminence among the available Florentine builders; his previous position of trust on the architectural staff of Nicholas V, and Pope Pius' possible acquaintance with him at that time; and upon the suitability of the Rossellino shop (then the biggest in Florence) for such a large-scale undertaking. Related to this theory is the possibility that Leone Battista Alberti was involved in the decision.

Alberti was surely a member of the papal entourage that accompanied the pope northward, for his presence in Mantua is well established. Alberti had left the papal service with the election of Calixtus III in 1455. He probably spent the next three years in Florence, during which time he enjoyed the patronage of Giovanni Rucellai, for whom he designed the facade of Santa Maria Novella, built the Chapel of the Holy Sepulcher in San Pancrazio, and perhaps, gave Cosimo de'Medici advice on the remodeling of the Badia Fiesolana.[52] He resumed his Vatican career once again with the accession of Pius II, either immediately returning to Rome in the summer of 1458 at news of the papal election or joining the pope's party as it passed through Florence in April of 1459. It would have been only natural for Pius to have sought Alberti's advice in planning the reconstruction of Corsignano and to have consulted with him on the selection of a suitable architect to direct the project. Although the pope's only mention of Alberti in the *Commentarii* was to describe him as his guide through the ruins of the Castelli Romani, south of Rome, and to praise him as "a scholar and a clever archaeologist," it may well have been upon Alberti's advice that preference was given to a Florentine rather than to a Sienese architect.[53] Who would Alberti have considered better suited to the task than Bernardo Rossellino? Alberti knew Rossellino from the days of Nicholas V; both had enjoyed the patronage of Giovanni Rucellai; and Alberti may even have used the Rossellino shop in rebuilding the apse of his church at Gangalandi. Among the stonemasons then practicing in Florence, Bernardo Rossellino was most capable of appreciating the artistic aims of Alberti and building according to those principles of *il modo antico* desired by the pope. By this argument, it was upon the advice of Alberti that Rossellino became the chief architect for Pienza.

According to the *Commentarii,* the pope's first intention as he left Corsignano that Friday morning in February 1459 was to give his birthplace two new buildings—a church and a palace. One can easily understand the perceived need for the palace (presumably, he meant it from the beginning to serve his family as well as himself). His two-night sojourn in Corsignano had probably convinced him that the papal Piccolomini deserved better than the house into which he had been born. But why would he have thought that the community needed a new church? The remains of the Romanesque Church of Santa Maria, found beneath the paving of the Renaissance cathedral, indicate that it was almost as large as the building that replaced it. Despite the apparent size and prominence of Santa Maria, however, Pius had chosen to celebrate the Mass of Saint Peter's Chair in the smaller Church of San Francesco. He did so perhaps because his father had been buried there, but why, indeed, had Silvio Piccolomini been interred in San Francesco instead of in the larger Santa Maria? Perhaps the Piccolomini had a preference for the Brothers Minor, but was that the only reason? From the very beginning, there seems to have been no question but that the new Pientine structure would stand upon the site of the medieval Santa Maria. Of course, that was the logical location; it was in the center of town, along the main street of Corsignano in the area known in the fifteenth century as the Monte Piccone; it was also convenient to the Piccolomini properties upon which the new palace was to be erected. Even so, one would expect the destruction of the principal church of Corsignano to have stirred some recorded murmur of protest among the citizenry. Yet not only is there an absence of opposition in the records, but there is no mention of the demolition of the church. Certainly, it would have been easier and far cheaper for the pope simply to have had the medieval building modernized but not even a fragment of it was reused in the new fabric, nor is there any correspondence in alignment. It would seem, therefore, that the medieval Santa Maria no longer existed in the 1450s, having been destroyed at some earlier time perhaps in a fire or some other calamity. In such a case, Pius would have felt compelled to order a new church for Corsignano, and this site would of course have been chosen. No matter what its orienta-

tion had been—west to east as proposed in the excavation report of 1932 or south to north as suggested here—the old church was not a physical factor. At most, Rossellino's work crew had but to remove some rubble and level off the area.

The history of the renovation of Corsignano may be traced in a series of ninety-two entries from the Vatican account books in which papal expenditures for the project were recorded (see Appendix 2). These records are amplified by additional documents, including letters, Sienese government deliberations, papal bulls, literary descriptions, and passages in the *Commentarii*. Most recently, the written documentation has been fleshed out considerably by some fifty property transaction statements found by Nicholas Adams in the tax summaries (*gabella dei contratti*) preserved in the archives of Siena.[54] Taken together, this material allows for a rather complete reconstruction of just how Pius and his builders went about reshaping the medieval village into a Renaissance city.

Actually, even before Pius' departure from Rome, some preliminary papal expenditures had been made at the town. On 19 January 1459, three days before he left the papal city on his trip to Mantua, the account books of the Vatican treasury noted that two hundred florins had been dispatched to Corsignano for the installation of a chapel in the Church of San Francesco, perhaps to honor his father who had died eight years before and was buried in that church. The next allocation in favor of Corsignano was made on 27 March, a month after the pope's visit and while he was on his long Sienese layover. The 325 ducats sent to Corsignano on this occasion were for "restorations of the walls of the fortress of Corsignano."[55] The *castelnuovo* of Corsignano suffered grave damage during World War II, but Pius' additions to its fabric are still to be seen in the two round towers standing at the northeastern and southeastern angles of the curtain walls (Plate 3).[56] These towers, with their battered bases in the new quattrocento style, are similar to those erected during the reign of Pope Nicholas V at the Vatican and in Fabriano and elsewhere in the papal states.[57] Their type also resembles the Pientine towers ordered for the *Rocca* of Assisi in January 1459 and at the *Arx Pia* of Tivoli in 1461.[58] The two towers at Tivoli, by the way, were described by the pope as having heights of 100 and 130 feet, and today, with their projecting battlements, give a good idea of the original appearance of the towers of Corsignano, now sadly truncated.

Pius had probably presented the first of his requests concerning Corsignano to the government of Siena before his departure from that city in April of 1459. Nicholas Adams has shown that a variety of provisions favorable to the well-being of the town were submitted at that time, including proposals for a suspension of taxes levied on the market fair held in Corsignano each May, a reduction or suspension of the tax on the sale or transfer of property in the town, the cancellation of a debt owed by Corsignano to the neighboring town of Castel San Quirico d'Orcia, and a drastic reduction of the debts of anyone agreeing to relocate in Corsignano.[59] Pius, it seems, aimed not only at the architectural enhancement of his birthplace but also at the revitalization of its social and economic fabric.

Clearly it could be an advantage for a town to have produced a pope. Nevertheless, some of what Pius was about to initiate was not favorably received by the citizens—at least in the short run— for over the next several years, with the support of the town's Sienese overseers, the pope, his family, and his associates rather ruthlessly set out to acquire desired property at Corsignano for private palaces as well as public buildings.[60] Many of the citizens must have been happy to sell, especially at the inflated prices offered, but many undoubtedly were forced to sell against their wishes and others simply dispossessed. Then, too, many in the town who did not own their homes but rented them were rudely evicted.

The pope's next official step concerning Corsignano was made in Florence just before he left to continue his journey to Mantua. By this time he had a more definite idea about what he wanted for his town and probably had selected his architect and formulated the initial plans for the architectural program. On 8 May 1459, the records of the Sienese council note that a petition had been received from the "most distinguished Pontiff," informing the Sienese of his intentions "for the construction of a temple and house at the town of Corsignano" and asking the government to "give license to the architect and supervisor sent by his Holiness for procuring stone, making furnaces, cutting fir trees and wood and other things necessary to the said edifices."[61] The stone was obtained nearby. The sandstone, locally called *tufa,* of which most of the buildings are constructed, came from a quarry cut into the hillside above the Pieve di San Vito only a few hundred meters away, and the

3. The northeastern tower of the *castelnuovo* built in 1459.

travertine from a quarry at nearby Radi-cofani. The timber was cut from the slopes of Mount Amiata, twenty-five kilometers distant. The pope noted in the *Commentarii:* "In a secluded fold of the mountain there grow also lofty firs, which furnish splendid timber for the buildings of Rome as well as of Siena. Here Pius bought the beams for his palace at Pienza."[62]

Over the next year and a half, while the pope was in Mantua attempting to induce the heads of Europe to support his crusade, his agents in Corsignano were busy. The *gabelle* of Siena list nine sales of property in Corsignano to the pope or his relatives between May 1459 and Pius' next visit to the town in September 1460.[63] The property purchased ranged in price from eight to two hundred ducats. Apparently private funds were used for these transactions since there is no mention of them in the account books of the Vatican. All but two of the purchases seem to have involved houses and land on the site of the future Piccolomini Palace and were made between May and December 1459 when, presumably, enough property had been put together for the work of demolition and then construction to have begun. That things went with a speed unconventional for the fifteenth century is attested in the *Commentarii* and other reports of the time. Pius passed through Corsignano on his return from the Congress of Mantua and spent twelve days there from 11 to 23 September 1460 recuperating from an illness. "When he was recovered to health," he wrote, "he was highly delighted to see rising in his native place buildings which seemed likely to equal any in Italy."[64] Progress on

the project also was reported in an official document of the town council of Siena, dated 5 October 1460. The council voted to allow "any member of the court of our Lord Pope Pius II of Siena who wishes to construct any house and piazza by the side of the principal street to do so. . . . those who own said houses and piazzas must and shall sell them to his courtiers for an agreed price for the house arranged by two arbiters chosen by the respective parties and if they do not agree on the price then at that time the *podesta* of Corsignano will fix the price."[65] Apparently, although the pope had hired his architect and the workmen with just a new church and family palace in mind, his plans were becoming more ambitious. During the months spent in Mantua, he either persuaded himself or was persuaded (by Alberti?) to sponsor a much grander concept. That Pius had found the time to think of Corsignano is suggested in a letter dated 13 December 1459 and written by Marquis Lodovico Gonzaga of Mantua to Leone Battista Alberti, who apparently was billeted a short distance from Mantua. Ludovico requested that Alberti lend him a copy of the architectural treatise of Vitruvius to be used by his papal guest.[66] Pius, it would seem, wanted to brush up on matters architectural with his new Corsignano/Pienza project in mind. One might also assume that he consulted a manuscript of Alberti's *De re aedificatoria* as well. The plan for the pope's birthplace was growing. The new design called, at the very least, for the reconditioning of the main thoroughfare running past the two great new buildings and, more likely, for a more extensive urban renewal of Corsignano and its transformation into a virtual secondary seat for the papacy. Not only had he decided to invest personal and official monies in the project, but he was actively encouraging others to do so as well. Nothing was to stand in the way, least of all the possible protests of local homeowners. It was perhaps to discuss the expanded project that Bernardo Rossellino came to Rome in July 1461.[67] Although our only documentation for this visit concerns his supplying of stone cannonballs, this task could hardly have been of sufficient import to have called him away from Corsignano and certainly must have been incidental to the real reason for the trip.[68]

Pius' sister Laudomia Todeschini-Piccolomini had already purchased a house in the northeastern quarter of town near the Porta al Ciglio and the *castelnuovo* in August 1460; Another relative, Salomone Piccolomini, acquired a house in June; in September the loyal Cardinal Giacomo Ammannati of Pavia bought four houses and a garden out of which he was to fashion his palace; and in the next month the papal vice-treasurer, Giliforte dei Buonconti da Pisa bought three houses and an adjoining lot along the southeastern escarpment east of the cathedral.[69] Some of these purchases may have been for Buonconti's own use, but since some of the property had been obtained from the commune and may have been situated next to the old Priors' Palace, it is likely that some of the property had been bought for the future Canons' House. In this matter, Buonconti probably acted as the pope's purchasing agent. For a time the Sienese records are silent. The acquisition of properties seems to have stopped until

the summer of 1462, when, in July, Jean Jouffroy, cardinal of Arras, began to negotiate for property on which to build a residence.[70]

An entry in the papal ledgers for 28 December 1460 was the first in a series of twenty-one recorded expenditures from the Vatican treasury for work undertaken at Corsignano ending on 1 September 1462.[71] Clearly the pope was not bashful about using church funds to satisfy his personal whim. The money was paid out for what the documents describe quite simply as *la frabica di corsignano* or, later on, for *la frabica di pientia*. These official appropriations (or misappropriations) totaling 24,500 ducats, were handled through one of two bankers, either the Sienese Ambrogio Spannocchi or the pope's private treasurer Alessandro de Mirabelli-Piccolomini. Although the description in each entry is frustratingly generalized, it would seem that the work referred to involved the construction of the cathedral and the palace. In fact, the first entry in which the name of Bernardo Rossellino was mentioned, dated 21 August 1462, described the architect as "Master Bernardo of Florence who builds the church and palace of Pienza."[72]

When the pope visited the town in the summer of 1462, the two great buildings were all but completed, and the town in which they had been built had been renamed in the pope's honor. On the first day of June 1462 an entry in the Vatican account books speaks of Corsignano; another, eighteen days later, refers to Pientia (Pienza).[73] The *Commentarii* records the event: "At this time, Pius brought up in the senate the question of raising his native place to the rank of city-state. This was unanimously voted and the name of the place was changed from Corsignano to Pienza."[74] It is rather curious that the change in name and status could have been accomplished in Rome and did not require action in Siena. Seemingly the Sienese govern-ment chose not to object to the papal seizure of effective control over the com-mune. Siena was perhaps content to wait, while all the investments and im-provements were made, until the pope was dead to reclaim authority in the town.

Chapter 2

The First Phase

The Monumental Area

Pius II arrived in Pienza for the third visit of his papacy sometime in July 1462 and remained in the town until the end of September.[1] He viewed the new buildings with enthusiasm. "This morning," the Sienese commissioner at Pienza, Niccolò Severini, wrote to his superiors, "His Holiness was taken throughout the palace, above and below, and also through the church, and with great pleasure he has seen it. It seems to him that he has done worthy things, worth the money spent and well made, not just for the buildings in themselves but because they are appropriate and well composed."[2] His delight is also expressed in the loving detail with which Pius described in his memoirs every facet of what he saw. The description he has left in the *Comentarii* remains the most thorough and enjoyable guide to the major monuments of his new city.[3] It leaves little doubt that the pope was able to reside in his newly completed palace, and it was of the Palazzo Piccolomini that he wrote first.

The Palazzo Piccolomini

The great palace Pius described in the *Commentarii* stood upon ground long associated with the Piccolomini clan. In fact, a year later, in a papal bull conferring the palace upon his nephews, Pius described the building as "in fondo paterno destructa domo."[4] It was a convenient act of fate that had placed the house of his birth in the center of town and next to the ruins of the medieval Church of Santa Maria soon to be replaced by his great cathedral. The close physical association of palace and church, of secular and spiritual life, was fortuitous.

Presumably the house of his father had passed into the pope's hands with the death of his parents. According to records of sale (the *gabella dei contratti*) preserved in the State Archives of Siena, more than seven other houses and structures, plus gardens and open areas, may once have stood upon the spacious site of the future palace.[5] Although the records state only that the buildings were "in the quarter of Monte Piccone," since they were all bought by either the pope or one of his family, it can be assumed that they were obtained for the project. All of the buildings, with the possible exception of a single nostalgic remnant, were demolished to make way for the great family palace.

Orders for the first purchase were given only a week after Pius had left Florence and his discussions with Rossellino and Alberti. On 10 May 1459 "a cellar under the proposed palace of His Holiness our Lord Pius" was acquired from a Giovanni di Mino Battista Piccolomini. This curious transaction might refer to the purchase of a ruined house of which only the foundations remained. The next acquisition did not take place until 12 September when purchases were made from three owners, one of whom was Salomone Piccolomini, who would later remodel a house for himself in Pienza. Two other properties were obtained in November and another house was purchased just before Christmas.

The palace that rose in place of the several properties acquired by Pope Pius was one of the most remarkable domestic buildings to have been erected thus far in the Renaissance.[6] In its proportions and decorative qualities, the Palazzo Piccolomini made a decided break with medieval traditions in secular construction. Its spacious, open character is in marked contrast to the towerlike verticality of many earlier family palaces, such as the Palazzo Davanzati (Davizzi) in Florence or the Palazzo Tolomei in Siena; its inviting exterior is opposed to the forbidding fronts of many earlier palaces, including even Michelozzo's Palazzo Medici. The Palazzo Piccolomini represents, in fact, the creation of a new standard in domestic design and clearly indicates the increasing sophistication of the Renaissance life-style, which placed a new emphasis upon comfort, elegance, grace, and not least, tasteful ostentation.

For two generations, the Piccolomini had been relatively impoverished, exiled from their native Siena and their "rightful" position among the aristocracy. The ascension of Aeneas Silvius Piccolomini to the papal throne in 1458 raised the name of his family once more to a position of regional prominence and gave it a new international luster. It befitted the family of the pope to possess a palace that would adequately reflect its newly achieved power and prestige as well as the humanistic attainments of its *pater familias*.[7] Pius must have stressed these considerations in his conversations with his architectural advisers. No doubt he also directed his architect in the arrangement of certain rooms and conveniences (e.g., as few stairs and steps and, when they were necessary, as gradual in ascent as possible to ease the strain on his gouty legs) and, in particular reference to his love of the outdoors, the disposition of loggias and gardens.[8] The actual details of design and execution were left, however, to the imagination and skill of the papal architect.

The Palazzo Piccolomini, unlike most previous Italian palaces, is a massive, freestanding block unhampered by adjoining structures. No shop entrances penetrate its ground story, as was often the case with earlier Italian palaces.[9] It occupies an area 150 meters in circumference. The principal (northern) facade, which fronts on the present Corso il Rossellino, is 36 meters in length. The eastern and western sides of the building are 39 meters long "on account of the porticoes which projected to the south from the main square of the palace."[10]

The three (northern, eastern, and western) facades of this sizable structure are identical in form, except for the number and placement of the portals. They display the first trabeated articulation of a wall surface on a secular building in the Renaissance (Plate 4).[11] Three tiers of superimposed pilasters vertically divide the facades into a series of regular bays. The effect is quite consciously "classical." The pilasters of the first story rest upon a continuous podium, interrupted only by the entrances to the palace. Each row of pilasters supports an entablature, that of the third story being the projecting cornice of the roof.

A different architectural order is used for each tier of pilasters. The Doric order appears in the lower story; in the next a simplified Composite capital is used; and finally, in the upper story a variation of the Corinthian. In keeping with this scheme, the proportions of the pilasters are also altered. The three stories diminish in height from the first through the third. The effect is to increase the impression of height and stateliness made by the entire building.

A vertical balance to the horizontal spread of the palace was originally more apparent, for the upward line of the pilasters was continued beyond the physical height of the building. "On the very top of the roof, where the smoke from the chimneys emerged, were built twenty-three towerlike structures ornamented with pinnacles and buttresses and various paintings, which could be seen from a distance and added much to the splendor and charm of the building."[12] This decorative transition between structure and

sky has unfortunately vanished but its existence must be appreciated in calculating the proportional distribution of the palace and in understanding the relationship of the building to its environment. In a sense the Palazzo Piccolomini had a fourth story, but one that was more ephemeral than tangible. One thinks ahead to the Conservator's Palace of Michelangelo on the Capitoline Hill in Rome, to Sansovino's Library in Venice, or to the Palaces of Andrea Palladio.

A uniform channeled rustication enlivens the surface of the wall against which the pilasters stand. "The blocks were cut round the edge a finger's breadth and the jointings made at the cuttings, so that the surfaces of the blocks stood out like tiles."[13] The pope's architect was, no doubt, mindful of Michelozzo's earlier use of rustication on the Palazzo Medici as well as of other even earlier examples, but his more elegant and "antiquizing" design rejected the use of cyclopean masonry and the vertical graduation of surfaces through the stories.[14] Instead, the handling of the exterior of the Piccolomini Palace illustrates the calm order and static stability that were seen as virtues of ancient design.[15]

Anyone having even the barest acqaintance with the architecture of the Italian Renaissance will be quick to note the similarity between the facade of the Piccolomini Palace and that of the better known Rucellai Palace in Florence, though the former is more in harmony with its surroundings.[16] At first glance, the two palaces seem almost identical, and because of the usual dating of the Rucellai Palace (1446–1450) and its customary attribution to Alberti, the Palazzo Piccolomini has been called a copy,

4. View from the tower of the Palazzo Comunale of the Piazza Pio II with the well and the Palazzo Piccolomini.

plagiarized by Rossellino. Based upon an analysis of Giovanni Rucellai's tax records, however, and the use of emblems on his palace which are not likely to have been used before 1460, I prefer to reverse the chronology of the two buildings. Indeed, it is hard to believe that a knowledgeable Sienese pope would accept for his own palace a design already used for the home of a Florentine banker. It is my contention that the palace in Pienza predates the facade of the Rucellai Palace (at least in concept) and that if Alberti has to be associated with either building, it is with the one built for Pope Pius.

If the facade of the Piccolomini Palace is accepted as predating (or, at least, as being contemporary with) that of the Rucellai Palace, many of the questions that have centered around the latter building must be directed to a consideration of the palace in Pienza. The foremost among these questions concerns the role Alberti might have played in drawing up the design.

Several details of the facade of the Piccolomini Palace recall points contained in Alberti's *De re aedificatoria*. Alberti's general advice for the location of a palace nicely describes the situation in Pienza. "The palace of a king should stand in the heart of a city, it should be easy of access, beautifully adorned and rather delicate and polite than proud and stately. . . . It looks noble to have the palace of a king be near . . . to the theater, the temple and some noblemen's handsome houses." The trabeated articulation of the exterior of the palace, divided into three levels of bays, also seems to have been indicated in Alberti's discussion of the "porticoes of the houses of the principal citizens." Alberti wrote:

"The whole entablature must be in height one fourth part of the shaft. If there is to be a second order of columns over the first, let that second order be one fourth part shorter than the lower one; and if there is to be a third order over this, let it be one fifth part shorter than that below it. In each of these the pedestal or plinth under each order of columns must be in height one fourth part of the column which it supports.[17] If the height of Alberti's pedestals is combined with that of his columns, the Albertian proportions are almost identical with the system Rossellino used for the pilasters of the facade of the Palazzo Piccolomini.

Seemingly, therefore, Alberti had a direct influence on the design of the palace, perhaps even the controlling influence.[18] Yet the humanist's possible participation in preparing the plans should not be overemphasized. After all, the remainder of Alberti's description of the ideal palace was quite unlike the Piccolomini Palace. Alberti said that "the front of the vestibule may be smaller [than a temple's] pediment. The rest of the front on each side of this pediment may be adorned with a small plinth which may rise somewhat higher at the principal angles."[19] The superimposed orders of pilasters which delineate the Palazzo Piccolomini and the arrangement of loggias on the palace described by Alberti are really antique in origin. Rossellino would have needed no specific instruction by Alberti to have come up with the plan but could have arrived at the scheme on his own. While in Rome during the early 1450s, he would have noted a similar articulation on such monuments as the Theater of Marcellus, the Colosseum, the exedrae of the Forum of

Trajan, or the Anfiteatro Castrense. The latter structure has a lower order of arcades springing from piers decorated with engaged Corinthian columns supporting an entablature. A similar arrangement enlivens the upper story of the Anfiteatro with pilasters taking the place of the columns.[20] More direct palatial sources were to be seen in the Septizonium of Septimius Severus below the Palatine Hill (now destroyed) and the mid-second-century *villa rustica* of Le Mura di Santo Stefano near Lake Bracciano just north of Rome, which could have been specifically pointed out to Rossellino by Alberti, whom Pope Pius described in his memoirs as "an eminent archaeologist."[21] The rectangular building of three stories articulated by regularly spaced pilasters, each bay pierced by a round-arched window, is strikingly similar to the Palazzo Piccolomini.[22] The Porta Palatina in Turin could have been yet another source through either drawing or description.[23]

Such obvious allusions to classical architecture tell us immediately and emphatically that we stand before the dwelling place of no merchant or banker or petty tyrant but a scholar-prince, well versed in the learning of the ancients and receptive to progressive ideas. The adaptation of the antique scheme of articulation to the facade of a palace is also quite in keeping with the productive plagiarisms that characterize Rossellino's entire style. The articulation of wall surfaces through the use of pilasters, too, had been part of Rossellino's method from the very beginning. His development of the theme had begun at the Misericordia Palace in Arezzo, was continued at the Aranci Cloister, and found its most recent expression in such sculp-

tural monuments as the Tomb of Orlando de' Medici (1456–1458) and the Tomb of the Beato Marcolino da Forli (workshop, ca. 1458). It should also be noted that Rossellino had recently been working at the Hospital of the Innocents in Florence and probably had access to Brunelleschi's plans for the story above its portico, which, according to Antonio di Tuccio Manetti, showed "small pilasters that were to rise from the lower cornice that functions as the sill for the windows up to the upper cornice."[24] It would have been typical for Rossellino to have formulated his scheme upon this sort of unexecuted design. Still, the similarity between the facade of the Piccolomini Palace and such antique monuments as either the Colosseum or the villa of Le Mura must have been consciously stressed. The classicizing design represented not simply an architectural statement *al modo antico* but a visual allegory to the supposed ancient origins of the Piccolomini as well as to the humanistic scholarship of its *pater familias* and to Pius' present position as the Roman pontiff.[25] The facade of the Palazzo Piccolomini was an allegory of lineage, status, and achievement.

Although the Palazzo Piccolomini with its orderly division into bays offers the first actual architectural use of this form of articulation, there had been a few fictive prototypes earlier in the century, including the sgraffito facade of the Palazzo Gerini in Florence (ca. 1450) and the palace shown in Fra Angelico's scene of Saint Stephen preaching in the little Chapel of Nicholas V in the Vatican.[26] This sort of palatial ordering was already in the air, then, but the Palazzo Piccolomini is to these earlier examples of represented articulation as the true perspective of Brunelleschi and Alberti is to the pragmatic attempts at spatial construction of the trecento. It is in its deliberateness, consistency, and definite associations with the antique that this palace achieves its novelty.

Despite the fact that the three stories of the Palazzo Piccolomini are to be read collectively and not separately as is the case with the Palazzo Medici, there is a subtle distinction between the bottom story and the two upper stories. Each of the two upper stories is penetrated by "rows of windows remarkable for size and design, twenty-three windows in each row equidistant from one another."[27] This airy and open effect contrasts with the more massive and closed impression given by the first story. There, aside from the portals, the surface of the wall is broken only by unframed mezzanine windows. In addition, the pilasters of the first story are rusticated while those of the other two tiers have smooth faces that visually detach them from the surface of the wall. The lower pilasters seem to blend with the wall behind them or rather to emerge out of it to assert their independence in the two upper levels. These differences, although far subtler than the surface treatment employed by Michelozzo for the Medici Palace, produce the effect of a massive pedestal upon which the two upper stories rest. This is one of the more distinctive differences between the designs of the Piccolomini and Rucellai Palaces.[28]

The large windows of the second and third stories are aligned not only with themselves but with the mezzanine windows and portals of the first story, thereby displaying a greater unity in design than that shown, for instance, at the Palazzo Medici. The large windows in the two upper stories have round heads set off by smooth voussoirs. Each window is vertically divided by a mullion in the form of a colonnette, with a capital of the type previously used in Bernardo Rossellino's Spinelli Cloister. The elegant bipartite design is borrowed from the windows of the Palazzo Medici. Yet these windows show features typical only for Bernardo Rossellino. The bold relief of the tracery in the area of the lunette is reminiscent of the frames Rossellino had installed in the *bifore* of San Stefano Rotondo in Rome in 1453, as well as of his earlier window at the Badia Fiorentina of 1436. The similarity between this latter window and the windows of the facade of the Palazzo Piccolomini is especially close. They, too, are "*bifore*-cross" rather than simple bipartite windows, for they are horizontally divided by transoms (Plate 5). This horizontal division is repeated by the stone bar separating the upper lights from the area of the lunette. The combination of Tuscan *bifore* with the Lombard-Roman cross windows was unique to Rossellino and was one of his many contributions to the vocabulary of architectural design in the fifteenth century. The crossing of mullions and transoms echoes the horizontal and vertical statement of pilasters and entablatures which establishes a gridlike pattern across the exterior surface of the palace.[29]

The organization of the facade of the Palazzo Piccolomini is so reminiscent of a sheet of graph paper that one is tempted to project upon and through it definite mathematical or geometrical relationships. Recently, George Hersey has done just that in a book devoted to the utilization of Pythagorean geometry by Renaissance architects. His examinations

5. East front of the Palazzo Piccolomini as seen from the doorway of the Palazzo Vescovile.

of the Medici and Rucellai palaces in Florence led him to certain definite conclusions concerning the underlying principles upon which they had been designed. According to Hersey, the ground plan of the Palazzo Medici was based upon a Pythagorean modular system in which "practically all the columns [real and imagined] strike walls, ceilings, or axes." Hersey concluded that "despite its rough exterior the Medici Palace harbors a decent hypostyle skeleton." None of this was possible at the heterogeneously composed Palazzo Rucellai; instead the application of Pythagorean geometry may be seen on that building's exterior elevation. "Unlike the Medici . . . the Rucellai is a visible and explicit, as opposed to an implicit, three-story hypostyle." Hersey regarded the Palazzo Piccolomini as "the child procreated by the Medici-Rucellai liaison," which united the interior grid of the one with the facade grid of the other. He pointed out that on the main (Corso il Rossellino) facade of the Palazzo Piccolomini the central bay is the widest while the three superimposed stories decrease in height upwards. "In the Piccolomini facade," wrote Hersey, "there are two types of movement—the vertical ascent and descent within the bay stacks, and also a duity movement from the sides, culminating in the central bay [which is a square]." Hersey saw this system in operation not only upon all the faces of the palace but internally as well, in plan and elevation.[30]

Yet a careful measuring of the exterior of the palace does not indicate quite so rigorous an application of the rules. In fact, measurement of the bays of the Corso il Rossellino facade reveals that the central bay is not the widest, that bay widths vary by as much as 1.7 meters, and that there seems to be no logical mathematical or optical explanation for the inconsistencies. The same sort of irregularity appears on the other facades of the palace and in the internal organization. Perhaps the architect aimed at a Pythagorean harmony but did not achieve it in the structure as executed. At this point, one is reminded of a curious passage in the description of Pienza left by Pius' secretary, Flavio Biondo.[31] Flavio apparently toured the new buildings in the company of Rossellino and found some fault in the design of the palace. Rossellino, he said, blamed the papal staff for the problems, "saying that they had not allowed him from the beginning to construct small sections but had persuaded him to add them to the already finished work." The meaning of this admittedly obscure passage may help to explain the inconsistencies in the measurements. The same accidental (?) variations in the measurements also becloud other attempts to provide some deeper theoretical structure for the design of the palace, including that proposed by Paul von Naredi-Rainer, who has attempted to fit the proportions of the building into the framework of musically determined harmonies.[32]

"The magnificent great main door," wrote the pope, "was on the north side. In the east side, where an entrance could not be made in the middle there were two smaller doors symmetrically placed, one of which was walled so as to appear closed and the other left open for everyday use. The west side was treated in the same way."[33] The curious arrangement of the portals on the eastern side of the palace was, as Pius indicated, dictated by necessity. The addition of a bay to flank the loggia at the southern ends of the eastern and western facades meant the creation of eight rather than seven bays (the southern tiers of windows actually look out from the rear loggias and not from the interior of the palace in a manner that calls to mind the little villa of Cardinal Bessarion on the Via Appia in Rome of ca. 1450).[34] Thus, a centered single entrance was ruled out. If, furthermore, a doorway had been set in the fourth bay of the eastern side, it would have been too close to the northwest corner of the nearby cathedral. Rossellino accordingly decided to use two doorways located three bays in from each corner. Since only one actual entrance was suitable (the one opening onto the piazza before the cathedral), he made the other a false door.[35] The same arrangement is repeated on the western facade with the actual doorway (a service entrance) opening onto the little square in front of the Church of San Francesco.

The portals of the Palazzo Piccolomini have rectangular frames with jambs and fillets that turn in at the base. Topping the lintel of each of the doorways is a cornice consisting of a cyma recta. Rossellino first used this device for his doorframes inside the remodeled Church of San Stefano Rotondo in Rome and, most recently, on the *lavacro* in the courtyard of the Palazzo Spinelli in Florence.[36] The principal entrance is, as the pope said, on the northern side of the palace fronting the narrow Corso il Rossellino (Plate 6). There are seven bays in this facade and the portal is centered in the fourth bay. It is distinguished from the other portals by its more ornate treatment. Rossellino used the standard doorframe that characterizes all the entrances to the palace but added a torus

strip and set it off against a surround, the face of which is recessed. The cornice is detached from the frame below and rests upon two classical consoles.

As innovative as the design of the northern, eastern, and western facades of the palace is, it is almost surpassed by the revolutionary character of the southern, or garden, front of the palace (Plate 7). There, in contrast to the public facades, three stories of loggias rise the entire height of the building. Pius described their effect and purpose: "On the fourth side, which has a most delightful view of Mt. Amiata to the south, were three porticoes raised above one another on stone columns. The first with its high and splendid vaulting provided a delightful promenade near the garden. The second, which had an elaborately painted wooden ceiling, made a very pleasant place to sit in the winter [Plate 8]. It had a balustrade which, with its cornice, was as high as a man's waist. The third was similar to the second but less elaborate in its coffering."[37] The Piccolomini Palace was the first building of the Italian Renaissance to wed the light and airy loggias of the country villa of Tuscany to the traditionally severe block of the urban palace.

The use of the loggia screen reflects both the rural atmosphere of Pienza and the personal taste of Pius, who reveled in nature and landscape. While the three classically articulated facades of the palace which faced upon the activity of Pienza expressed the humanistic concerns of the Piccolomini and their historical connections with the patrician families of antiquity, this more private face of the building offered both an opportunity for reflective meditation and a position from which to survey the country holdings of

6. The main (north) entrance to the Palazzo Piccolomini with axial view through the *cortile* to the garden.

7. The garden loggias of the Palazzo Piccolomini.

8. The piano nobile loggia of the Palazzo Piccolomini with the cathedral beyond.

the family. The mood here is elegantly bucolic, and appropriately so, for since the days of Pius' grandfather, the Piccolomini had been rural rather than urban in outlook. As Eugenio Battista points out, "In Pienza contemplation of landscape is also associated with pride in feudal possessions. Pius II looks at his dominion like Christ viewing the cities of the world, but he does this with a sense of quiet and permanent gratification."[38]

Despite the novel way in which the tiers of porticoes were integrated into the design of the palace there were some precedents. As far back as ca. 1320, Giotto had represented a loggia-topped palace in the background of his fresco *Saint Francis Renouncing His Inheritance* in the Bardi Chapel of Santa Croce in Florence. Similar "attic" loggias (*altana*) are to be found in several actual buildings of the fourteenth and early fifteenth centuries, including the Florentine palaces of the Davanzatti (Davizzi) and the Lotteringhi-della Stufa, the suburban palace of the Strozzi at Bellosguardo above Florence, and the Villa Medicea at Careggi. Even more similar in mood and appearance is the palace of Cardinal Giovanni Vitelleschi built in Tarquinia between 1436 and 1439.[39] Here, three stories of loggias look out upon an enclosed garden and a vast panorama of the Latian coastline. Vitelleschi's palace may actually have been built in partial imitation of a feature of the Vatican Palace. A fresco by Benozzo Gozzoli, executed in 1465 in the church of San Agostino in San Gimignano, shows a two-story loggia on the eastern side of the Vatican apartments. This fresco was evidently based upon studies Gozzoli had made in Rome in the mid-1450s. The Vatican

loggias may have formed part of the building constructed during the reign of Pope Nicholas III (1277–1281), or they may have belonged to the program of Nicholas V (1448–1455). In any case, the double loggia at the Vatican overlooked the private gardens of the pope just as the loggias of Pius' palace in Pienza were intended to do.[40] In both palaces, these sheltered and breezy walkways provided a pleasant position from which to view the secret "paradise" gardens below and a wide vista beyond (Plate 9).[41] One cannot help but be reminded of the *Madonna and Chancellor Rolin* by Jan van Eyck (ca. 1433) or of Rogier van der Weyden's imitative *Saint Luke Drawing the Virgin* (ca. 1435–1437). The palace painted by Benozzo Gozzoli at the Camposanto in Pisa (ca. 1468), too, with its three stories of loggias may somehow be inspired by the palace in Pienza.

The disposition of the three levels of loggias at the Palazzo Piccolomini corresponds to the treatment given the other facades of the palace; it is as if the walls of the building were punched out and the pilasters transformed into columns, which, once again, assert their supportive function. The first and second tiers are arcuated; the upper level is open beamed. There are curious "hoods" dropped below the arches of the second story loggia which would certainly have been among the imperfections criticized by Flavio. This visually clumsy device was necessitated by the vaulting of the second tier. Without hoods, there would be no space for vaulting, but there remains the question of why Rossellino decided to vault the second level of loggias. Rossellino also elected, rather strangely, to reverse the progression of the orders—Corinthian capitals were

9. View from the piano nobile loggia of the Palazzo Piccolomini across the hanging garden and the Val d'Orcia toward Mount Amiata.

used in the first level, those of the Spinelli Cloister type in the second, and Doric capitals in the third story. A purist might complain that Rossellino had deviated from good classical (and certainly Albertian) theory, but in actuality, there was antique precendent. The very same reversal of orders occurs on the Roman villa of Le Mura di Santo Stefano, and this similarity makes it more likely that Le Mura was a source for the Palazzo Piccolomini.[42]

Behind the palace and below the porticoes was laid out a *giardino pensile* almost equal in size to the area of the palace "extending up to the town walls."[43] It is possible that the idea of the "hanging garden" was an addition to the first plans for the palace and was suggested to his architect by the pope following his visit to Florence on his way to and from the Congress at Mantua. On one or both of these state visits, he certainly would have visited the newly completed Palazzo Medici, one of the attractive features of which is the walled garden at its rear. It was an idea the pope could have brought with him when he revisited Pienza in September of 1460.

The *Commentarii* described the appearance of the pope's garden in 1462: "Around the garden were stone seats and a balustrade breast high ornamented with painted pinnacles, which from a distance presented a very gay appearance. If you entered the palace by the great north door you could see straight through the peristyle and court, then through a back door to the lower portico and as far as the very end of the garden and could walk the whole length smoothly without stepping up anywhere."[44] Just how this spacious enclosed garden was organized we do not know. Other than the pope's

rather vague mention in the *Commentarii* of plans "to make a hanging garden with vines and trees," there is little to go on.[45] Apparently, the gardeners had not yet had time to do their work before the pope's visit in the summer of 1462. Some general idea of what Pius might have anticipated can be found in Giovanni d'Iuzzo's description of Cardinal Niccolò Forteguerri's palace in Viterbo, which was laid out in 1470 with "garden, fountain, fish pond, aviary and places for animals with a pleasant garden area and so beautiful that one might almost say it was an earthly paradise."[46]

The nature of such a Renaissance "paradise garden" is given even more graphic description by the anonymous author of a poem celebrating the visit of the young Galeazzo Maria Sforza to the Palazzo Medici on the occasion of Pope Pius' passage through Florence in April 1459:

And this palace has a handsome garden
   with court, loggias, vault, and water and
     green,
   and it was done and flowered in a single
     morn.
And it is embellished with such genteel
     arrangements
   of laurel, myrtle, orange and box,
   that one look shows what is planted there.
A dance is there, as gentle as one can say,
   of jasmine, violets, roses and lilies,
   and flowers blue, yellow, white and red.
Nor is there anyone who finds it strange
   that there should be animals and little birds
   which do not take fright if one picks them
     up.[47]

To the delightfully paradisiacal description of the Medici garden, perhaps more poetic artifice than truth, we might add the more detailed and accurate remarks of Sforza's counselor, Niccolò de' Carissimi da Parma, about the topiary artistry practiced in that garden. In a letter to the duke of Milan, Francesco Sforza, full of lavish praise for Cosimo de' Medici's palace, Niccolò described a garden done "in the finest of polished marbles with diverse plants, which seems a thing not natural but painted. And among other things there is an adder in the form of the device of Your Excellency, and beside it there is the shield and arms of the aforementioned Cosimo. This adder and arms are of new-planted grass in a piece of ground so that, the more the grass grows, the more the device will grow." Carissimi also described the palace and garden as an "earthly paradise," something the Milanese ruler might well emulate.[48] Surely Pope Pius would have wished to surpass it. The crescent-shaped moons of the Piccolomini and the crossed keys of the papacy are sculpted throughout Pienza, from the great *tondo* of the cathedral's facade to the capitals of columns; how nice to imagine them as naturally embellishing the papal garden.[49]

The plein-air atmosphere established on the southern side of the Palazzo Piccolomini might have been intensified by decorating the walls of the palace behind the loggias. Perhaps fictive gardens were to be frescoed on those walls as they had been in Rome at the Casa dei Cavalieri di Rhodi and at the urban *villino* of Cardinal Bessarion on the Via Appia Antica.[50] Both of those Roman examples are datable to the 1460s or 1470s.

From the main entrance passage of the palace, the visitor's eye immediately travels across the internal court and through the door opposite to the expansive vista of the Tuscan hills beyond.[51]

Once the garden is entered, however, the effect changes. The emphasis shifts from a boundless view to the quiet and meditative atmosphere of the enclosed *giardino segreto*. Not only were such "secret gardens" popular in the chivalric literature and representations of the period, but they also figured in theology. The Virgin Mary was often portrayed within the enclosure of such a purely idyllic environment intended to remind the viewer of the lost Garden of Eden. It also recalled the monastic cloister as espoused by Saint Bernard, with its isolated sense of perfection and its allusions to the awaited paradise.[52] What an appropriate setting for the strolls of a humanist pope! Such private gardens with their heavenly suggestions were to be found at the medieval Vatican Palace and were given a renewed emphasis in the plans of Pope Nicholas V for the new papal residence.

Today, from the level of the garden, the valley and hills beyond can be appreciated only from three archways (not described by the pope and likely a later modification) that pierce the high surrounding wall. It is probable that Pius intended to lay out a more public garden stretching down the hillside below the palace, for seven orchards were purchased on the Pope's behalf on 4 and 5 September 1462 (Appendix 2, Docs. 34–40). Some of the properties were described as *in loco dicto la porta la Sancto,* evidently referring to the quarter of town near the Church of San Francesco. Since it is doubtful that these gardens were within the walls of the town, it is not illogical to imagine them spreading across the slope of the hill below the palace. Indeed, one cannot help wondering if the multi-terraced approach to the Temple of Fortuna Primigenia at Palestrina might not have inspired the arrangement at Pienza. Certainly the Roman temple complex and the Piccolomini Palace share a love of a bird's-eye view of nature.[53]

In a sense the whole design of the Palazzo Piccolomini centered around the concept of uniting enclosed spaces with limitless nature. A passage in the *Commentarii* devoted to what the pope could see from his new palace indicates the importance Pius placed upon this feature of the building's design:

The view from the upper floor of the palace extends to the west beyond Montalcino and Siena to the Pistoian Alps. As you look to the north diverse hills and the lovely green of forests are spread before you for a distance of five miles. If you strain your eyes you can see as far as the Apennines and make out the town of Cortona on a high hill not far from Lake Trasimeno, but the valley of the Chiana, which lies between, cannot be seen because of its great depth. The view to the east is less extended reaching only as far as Poliziano . . . and the mountains which separate the valley of the Chiana from that of the Orcia. The view from the three porticoes to the south is bounded . . . by towering and wooded Mt. Amiata. You look down on the valley of the Orcia and green meadows and hills covered with grass in season and fruited fields and vineyards, towns and citadels and precipitous cliffs and Bagni di Vignoni and Montepescali, which is higher than Radicofani, and is the portal of the winter sun.[54]

This conscious incorporation of the outdoors into the design of the Palazzo Piccolomini was one of the revolutionary features of the palace. Not only did it reflect the pope's own love of nature, but it recalled many of the ideas found in the never-executed plans of Nicholas V for the Vatican Palace.[55] Those plans, which featured a "theater" loggia and a symbolic emphasis upon a paradise garden and were probably based on Alberti's concepts, would have been familiar to Rossellino as well. The Palazzo Piccolomini, although there were some precedents, was the first major building of the Renaissance to utilize these ideas with such deliberateness and to take into account the natural setting and the existence of a landscape vista. In this respect it looked back to such ancient examples as the Villa of Hadrian at Tivoli (which the pope knew well) and anticipated the Belvedere Palace of Giacomo da Pietrasanta at the Vatican, the Ducal Palace at Urbino, the Villa Madama of Raphael, and even the Palazzo Farnese of Sangallo and Michelangelo.

The enclosed *giardino pensile* behind the Palazzo Piccolomini was demonstrably of the utmost importance to the pope, for it was necessary to erect it upon great masonry vaults projecting beyond the edge of the hillside (Plate 10).

Here Pius intended to plant a garden, but the ground was uneven and sloped sharply. Very thick walls were built on a stone base and between columns of brick or stone it had arched openings which could provide stabling for a hundred horses and workshops for blacksmiths. Above them was left some twelve feet of solid wall and above that was a second row of arches. On these was heaped earth deep enough to make a hanging garden with vines and trees, care being taken that the rain should not penetrate to the vaults or wet the stables.[56]

This stable beneath the garden is one of the most innovative aspects of the vast

10. View eastward along the Via Gozzante showing the stables beneath the hanging garden.

palace project. The stately courtyard of the noble palace of the Piccolomini was not to be filled with the clatter of carts or the noise and smell of horses. Provisions could be brought directly to the "service entrance" beneath the garden, unloaded there, and carried along passageways connecting the stables with storage rooms in the cellar of the palace. The horses themselves could be quartered comfortably in the spacious stables and fed conveniently from the haylofts above them through which circulated air from the second row of arches. All this resembles the arrangement of the stables beneath the Ducal Palace of Federico da Montefeltro at Urbino constructed more than a decade later by Francesco di Giorgio Martini. As a youth, Francesco di Giorgio (1439–1502) may well have worked under Rossellino at Pienza, so his stables at Urbino may be directly inspired by the functional arrangement at Pienza.

Because, as the pope noted, "the Palace had no kitchen" a seperate wing exclusively designed for this purpose was added. It projects out into the garden from the western side of the rear porticoes (Plate 11). Pius' statement seems to imply the impossible—that his architect had forgotten to provide for a place to cook. What is more likely is that the kitchen wing was added later to replace facilities originally planned for the palatial block. Evidence for this view can be found in the clear break in fabric between kitchen wing and palace proper which is apparent along the Via del Balzello and the fact that columns at the western end of each story of loggias have been walled up where the facility is attached to the core of the palace. Certainly the revision

in plan was a happy choice. Pius writes of the kitchen wing: "A square building as high as the palace itself was built near the cistern . . . and in it were three kitchens with their various offices built one above the other and connected with the palace by porticoes, thus making it possible to serve the three floors with the greatest convenience. They were not troubled by smoke or wind and drew water with a rope from the nearby cistern."[57] The practicality of this arrangement does credit to Bernardo Rossellino's ingenuity. Meals could be sped to whatever level of the palace had been chosen for dining straight from a kitchen on the same floor, and separate meals could be prepared and served at the same hour to different members of the household. The separation of kitchen and residence also reduced the danger that fire might spread to the palace from the kitchens.

Another interesting feature of the garden area is the *lavacro* set into the eastern wall of the lower portico (Plate 12). The frame resembles that of the *lavacro* in the courtyard of Rossellino's Palazzo Spinelli, but here the fluted and triangular base has strong connections with ecclesiastical ciboria.[58] The design was appropriate for the palace of a pope. Incorporated into the garden wall next to the *lavacro* are the remnants of what appears to be a medieval doorway and the fragments of the wall of a house. It is pleasant to think that these might be the remains of the house in which Pius was born, the *paterno destructa domo* mentioned in the papal bull of 19 July 1463.[59] The pope evidently wished to preserve a portion of his humble birthplace as a reminder of his origins and a contrast to

11. The western flank of the Palazzo Piccolomini with attached three-story kitchen wing.

12. East garden wall of the Palazzo Piccolomini with columns of the loggia, the *lavacro,* and the possible remains of the house in which Pius II was born. Antique fragments are recent inserts into the wall.

the sumptuous palace he had erected in its stead. It was a nonstalgic statement of both humility and pride.

"From the main door to the peristyle there extends a gleaming arched portico as long as the width of the dining rooms on each side."[60] A similar passageway leads from the eastern door to the *cortile*. These two barrel-vaulted passageways mark one of the first such uses of that type of vault in the Renaissance and have their source in the entrance passage of the Palazzo Medici. The columns that flank the courtyard ends of these passages are quite special (Plate 13). They have Doric capitals and, together with the Tuscan Doric columns of the upper level of the garden loggia and those of the little *cortile* of the Palazzo Jouffroy on the Corso il Rossellino represent the first certain architectural use of that order in the Renaissance. It is curious that they have remained unmentioned in literature dealing with Renaissance architecture. The use of the Doric illustrated a shift in Rossellino's architectural style, perhaps under the influence of Alberti, who discussed the order in the *De re aedificatoria*, though he never used it on any of his projects. It was a move away from Rossellino's earlier decorative manner toward a new and disciplined severity. Rossellino died before he could give full expression to his change in taste but his was the first use of the form favored by Bramante and the High Renaissance.

The open courtyard of the Palazzo Piccolomini follows the pattern of that of the Palazzo Medici (Plate 14). It is almost square in plan with three arcades on every side, which spring from "monoliths sixteen feet high and proportionately thick with bases and capitals skillfully set."[61] The capitals of these columns are a simplified variety of the Composite order. The cross vaults of the peristyle are carried by these columns and by corbels in the same order, in which the usual conical calathos is often replaced by the shield of the Piccolomini.

A simple frieze defined by string courses runs along the top of the arcades. It resembles the same feature in Rossellino's courtyard of the Palazzo Rucellai. The windows of the piano nobile rest upon the "cornice" of this abbreviated "entablature." These "square windows divided by a stone cross"[62] were the first pure cross windows to be used by Rossellino. Without question they were inspired by similar windows (of Lombard design?) used at midcentury in Rome with which he had become familiar during his service with Nicholas V.[63] They also mark the first certain appearance of the true cross window in Tuscany.[64] In the third story, cross windows were used on the northern and southern sides of the *cortile,* but open galleries—the traditional *altana*—face the courtyard in the other wings (Plate 15). Slender columns with either Ionic or Spinelli Cloister–type capitals support the wooden roofs of these upper loggias.

The walls surrounding the courtyard were originally resplendent with gaily colored painted decorations. The remaining traces of red, blue, and gold colors seen today actually date from a renewal undertaken in 1911.[65] If that restoration followed the original design, there were three areas of entablatures with painted festoons suspended from *tondi* containing either rosettes or the shield of the Piccolomini. The cross windows were set off by fictive colonnettes and crowned by painted "shell lunettes," providing a far less austere appearance than the

13. Detail of the columns and corbels in the northeastern corner of the *cortile* of the Palazzo Piccolomini.

14. Southwestern corner of the *cortile* of the Palazzo Piccolomini.

15. The *cortile* of the Palazzo Piccolomini.

courtyard presents today. The whole effect would have been splendidly festive, but it is unclear if the pope saw any of this, for he did not describe these embellishments, and they may have been added later.

Most of the rooms opening off the courtyard were given over, as was customary, to utilitarian purposes, but Pius did record that on either side of the main entrance "there are dining rooms for winter and summer and the seasons in between, chambers fit for kings."[66] A curious feature of the palace is the corridor that parallels the western wall. It was along this passageway that food could be sped from the kitchen wing to the papal table in the winter dining room. The corridor is interrupted by a room in the center of the western wing where, we may assume, the meals could be transferred from kitchen dishes to dinner service. It made for a practical and efficient arrangement typical of the many niceties of this palace. One of the rooms adjoining what probably was the winter dining room (northwest corner) contains a *lavacro* framed by slender columns carrying an entablature. A more simply framed *lavacro* is in the summer dining room, together with a handsome fireplace (Plate 16).[67]

Beneath the palace were extensive storage facilities, "for when they excavated for the foundations of the palace they quarried out the very hard rock to a depth of about sixteen feet and constructed vaulted cellars for wine and oil and other provisions. Certainly," the pope added, "a noble larder and one it would be hard to fill."[68] Filling it was made easier for the palace staff by the passageways from the stables, which lay under the east and west wings of the

palace. A "window" cut through the northeastern foundation wall opens directly into the shaft of the communal well on the Piazza Pio II so that fresh water might be easily obtained from within the palace.

A flight of stairs next to the main entrance leads to the piano nobile. The description of this level of the Palazzo Piccolomini which Pius left is remarkably thorough and can scarcely be improved upon. Its precision and accuracy should leave no doubt as to just how complete the palace was on the occasion of the pope's visit in 1462.

At the top is a gallery which on three sides looks down into the court through square windows divided by a stone cross. Its ceiling is skillfully constructed and decorated in various colors. As you follow it to the right you come to a square hall out of which open two splendid chambers one of which gets the western sun and the other the north light as well, and this also has a strong room where valuables can be kept. At the end of the gallery is a hall seventy-two feet wide and a third again as long with six doors [Plate 17]. Two look into the gallery, two give access to the middle portico that looks toward Mt. Amiata, and the others to two large and elaborate chambers, one of which receives the light of the rising, the other of the setting sun. The hall itself is lighted not only by the doors but by large windows toward the court and smaller ones toward the portico. It has a fireplace cunningly wrought of white marble and the coffered ceiling is remarkable for the precision of the woodwork and the variety of the paintings. There is never a time when the place is not comfortable since it does not feel the extremes of heat or cold.

If you turn left in the gallery you will come on another staircase exactly like the first

16. The interior of the "summer dining room" with doorway now covered.

17. The hall with six doors with the doorway to the bedchamber of Pope Pius II beyond.

leading to the third floor. Passing by this you come to a door which divides the gallery into two parts. If you choose to turn right you enter the hall which we have said adjoins the second portico, but if you go to the left you will find yourself in a summer dining room or hall larger than any of the others with four windows on the north giving on the street and two on the east giving on the square. From this hall you pass into an oratory and the eastern apartments, that is three chambers, the last of which is connected, as we have said with the hall of six doors and the adjoining portico. In this room the Pope lodged and he had given orders that it should be paneled in fir so that the dampness of the new walls should not trouble him. Every chamber had its fireplace and everything else that was necessary. Everywhere were paneling and fir beams worth one's notice and suitable in size and beauty to the building itself. The beams and timbers contributed magnificence not only of themselves but by the painting and gold leaf upon them. The floors were of polished brick and without any unevenness whatever—everywhere the same level surface; in going from room to room and place to place you never had to step up or down.[69]

A comparison of this contemporary description with the present arrangement of the piano nobile shows that several major changes have taken place, most probably dating from the early sixteenth century. The second of Pius' "splendid chambers" has been decreased in size, for instance, and one window, in consequence, has been walled up. The first of these chambers, referred to as the hall "of the setting sun," has been partitioned into two sections. Perforce, the ceilings of these rooms have also been replaced or modified.

Indeed, the interior of the palace reflects the continuous remodelings of generations of occupants. The palace remained in the Piccolomini family until the death of Count Silvio Piccolomini della Triana in 1962, when it passed to the administration of the Società di Esecutori di Pie Disposizioni di Siena. The "hall of six doors," for instance, was turned into a *sala delle armi* by Count Silvio; the "summer dining room" had been converted into a theater before count Silvio restored the room and turned it into a library and family archives.[70]

The eastern wing of the palace has also been extensively altered. The religious nature of the chapel described in the *Commentarii* has vanished, along with its original orientation. The introduction of a staircase has meant the relocation of the northern wall of the pope's bedchamber. This room, originally paneled to halt the damp, was thoroughly refurnished and decorated in late quattrocento or early cinquencento style, perhaps for Cardinal Francesco Piccolomini, who would briefly reign as Pope Pius III. Although Pius II stated that "every chamber had its fireplace"—some twenty-three of them—many of the fireplaces presently in the palace may not be contemporary with the original construction but installed or reworked with appropriate coats of arms by successive generations of Piccolomini occupants. The same is true for many of the doorframes, although several original portals remain throughout the palace. Each of these bears in its lintel the arms of the Piccolomini set against vine tendrils (Plate 18). These sculptural decorations, executed in a manner closely related to that of the heraldic wreath in the *cortile* of the

18. The doorway to the "summer dining room."

Rucellai Palace, should be considered as the products of the Rossellino workshop.

The arrangement of the piano nobile illustrates a new concern for order and decorum. The very fact that the pope thought it important to point out the evenness of the floors and that it was not necessary to step up or down between rooms illustrates how different this palace—built from the ground up in a single building campaign—was from many palaces of the day. Most Italian palaces (e.g., the Rucellai and Spinelli palaces) were amalgamated from several different structures. They were often hodgepodge in their internal arrangements, and steps between rooms were common.[71] In the Piccolomini Palace, however, one is reminded of Alberti's advice about making the passage from room to room in a palace "without the least ascent or descent, but all . . . upon one even floor or at least the ascents . . . as easy as may be." In plan, the distribution of rooms is generally in keeping with Alberti's emphasis on "conveniences for living with health, dignity, and politeness."[72] These considerations helped to determine the location of the rooms and their functions. The pope, for instance, was troubled by neuralgia and attacks of gout; accordingly, his bedchamber was located in the warmest and sunniest corner of the palace. In contrast, the summer dining room was situated in the coolest area.

Alberti expressed his interest in such arrangements on more than one occasion. In *De re aedificatoria,* for instance, he discussed the placement of houses within a town so that "there will be no house but what in some part of the day, will enjoy some sun; nor will they ever be without gentle breezes." He advised that "the bedchambers for the winter should look towards the point at which the sun rises in winter and the parlor, towards the equinoctial sun-setting; whereas the bedchambers for summer should look to the south, the parlors to the winter sun-rising and the portico for walking in to the south." Alberti also directed that "all summer apartments stand open to the northern winds, all winter ones to the south, and all those for spring and autumn to the east. Baths and supper parlors for the spring season should be towards the west. And if you cannot possibly have all these exactly according to your wish, at least choose out the most convenient places for your summer apartments: for indeed, in my opinion, a wise man should build rather for summer than for winter."[73] These basic precepts are followed in Pienza, except that the pope's bedroom was placed in the southeastern corner where it received the breezes blowing across the Orcia Valley and enjoyed the grand view of Monte Amiata. That Alberti meant to practice what he advised is demonstrated by his autograph notations to one of his few surviving drawings.[74] Alberti, on a recently discovered proposal for a bathing establishment, explained that "this whole bath building will be warmed by the rays of the sun . . . [and] the loggia which is in front of the vestibule will have sunshine not winds in winter; in the summer it will have winds not sunshine."[75] How fortunate it was that Rossellino could position his porticoes to take advantage not only of the view toward Mount Amiata but of the southern exposure recommended by Alberti.

Alberti's ideas themselves seem to have been derived from ancient advice such as that offered by Pliny the Younger when describing his so-called Laurentian Villa and from Vitruvius as well.[76] In *De re aedificatoria,* Alberti had pointed out that "the ancients favored making the portico facing south, so that in summer when the sun traces a higher orbit, its rays should not enter, whereas in winter they should enter."[77] Such reawakened standards of comfort were part of the spirit of the new age of Alberti, Rossellino, and Pope Pius.

The staircase to the piano nobile continues to the third floor, the plan of which "is like or very nearly like the second. The ceilings are a little lower; they have no painting or color and are conspicuous only for the dignity of the beams."[78] Actually, Pius here seems to have been less accurate in his description (perhaps he had little occasion to climb the steps to this upper level of his palace), for there are no ceilings but rather an exposed system of rafters and tie beams. It is, of course, possible that the original ceilings have been removed thus revealing the great wooden trusses. Clearly these must be examples of the "splendid timber," which the pope said had been cut for his palace from the slopes of his beloved Mount Amiata.[79]

On the roof of the palace a cistern made of large stone blocks and "set five feet back from the wall [which] received the rain water that collected in gutters and distributed it to a distance through iron pipes. . . . The reservoir on the roof carried off some of the rain outside . . . and carried some down into the court, so that, after being filtered through gravel, it might fill the cisterns, of which there were three: two in the palace and a third very large one in the garden, which was ample to provide for a numerous household."[80] Forethought for utility as well as beauty was a key element in the design of this palace.

Each wing of the palace had its definite purpose in a systematic ordering in contrast to the heterogeneous character of most medieval and Renaissance palaces and in keeping with Alberti's advice that "the principal parts may be allocated to the principal occasions; and the most honorable, to the most honorable."[81] The similarities between the organization of the Palazzo Piccolomini and the recommendations of Alberti do not warrant, however, an assumption that Bernardo Rossellino specifically followed either Alberti's written treatise or his oral advice. Rather, both book and palace point up the growing emphasis being placed in the fifteenth century upon rational and gracious living.

The relationship of the interior of the palace to the natural setting, expressed in the tiers of porticoes and the enclosed garden, has already been demonstrated. Even within the building itself, the pope's desire to remain outside while inside was manifest. An arcadian mood was firmly implanted in the Palazzo Piccolomini particularly in the overriding concern for illumination. "If as some think, the first charm of a house is light, surely no house could be preferred to this one, which is open to all points of the compass and lets in abundant light not only through outside windows but through inside ones looking on the inner court and distributes it even down to the storerooms and the cellar."[82] The pope abhorred the sort of dark, dank rooms endured by the conclave that elected Antipope Felix V at Basel, of which, he wrote, "almost all were without light. . . . In the middle cells there was permanent darkness and no one could either read or eat without a candle. In these there was one night lasting seven days. The lower rooms . . . were even more inconvenient since, built on the cold ground, they afforded places better suited to fishes than to human bodies."[83] In the land of darkened rooms, it is the manipulation of light that unifies the Palazzo Piccolumini both in its internal distribution and in the relation of the entire complex to its surroundings. A similar concern is displayed in the great Cathedral of Pienza and is one of the most visible leitmotifs of the entire program in Pienza.

The spirit of antiquity also exerted its influence upon Rossellino's overall design for the palace. The palace is emphatically symmetrical, as the pope pointed out with his description of the palace as seen from the entry through to the garden, and was one of the first palaces of the Renaissance to enforce such a rigidly classical discipline. Alberti had said, "We should be sure to have a good courtyard, portico, places for exercise, and some garden."[84] These features, found, of course, in the villas of ancient Rome, were the ones that determined the plan of the Palazzo Piccolomini. The aesthetics of the ideal villa of antiquity with its balanced and orderly distribution of the living units, its peristyle court, and viridarium were revived by Rossellino in his design for the pope's palace. These features, coupled with the classicizing elements of the trabeated ornamentation of the facade, make the Palazzo Piccolomini the first truly "modern" palace of the postmedieval period.[85] Bernardo

Rossellino had constructed a home worthy of a humanist pope.

Pius enjoyed his palace but briefly, on three separate occasions—his first long visit in Pienza in the summer of 1462, later in the same year between 11 and 19 November, and finally, on his way to Ancona between 13 and 19 February 1464.[86] Yet he intended the palace for more than his infrequent personal enjoyment. On 20 February, the day after he had left Pienza on his last visit, Pius ordered ten ducats paid to Benedetto da Bologna "for rooms made [or decorated or furnished] at the command of His Holiness" in the palace (Appendix 2, Doc. 87). He had already given the palace to his nephews Antonio, Giacomo, and Andrea Todeschini-Piccolomini and their male descendents in a papal bull dated 19 July 1463.[87]

It is difficult to say no to a pope, even if he is your uncle, and so the three brothers found themselves in possession of an enormous and unwanted palace with a most expensive upkeep. They expressed their dissatisfaction with the pope's bequest in the tax declaration they made in February 1465, only two months after the pope's death. The brothers listed the palace in Pienza among their assets, but they noted that it was a property "which as everyone knows was done at very great cost without any usefulness." Accordingly, they asked the Sienese government to "lighten the taxes in consideration of the great expenses which we have there."[88]

The Cathedral

"Such was the palace," wrote the pope, "and next it stood the church built in honor of the Blessed Mary Ever a Virgin'' (Plate 19).[89] The construction of a cathedral in Pienza signaled the elevation of the town to episcopal status.[90] A papal bull published on 13 August 1462 decreed the formation of the new bishopric of Pienza and Montalcino (some fifteen kilometers to the east) and the election of Giovanni Cinughi, former bishop of Chiusi, to preside over the new diocese. "On the Feast of the Beheading of St. John the Baptist [29 August 1462] the Pope dedicated the church and the altars, the Cardinal of Ostia [Guillaume d'Estouteville] officiating. He himself anointed the front of the high altar and when the relics of the saint had been deposited in it he affixed the seal."[91] A few days later, on 7 September, another papal bull officially dedicated the new cathedral to the Virgin Mary, thus preserving the name of the medieval church the Renaissance cathedral replaced. On 16 September, a further bull prohibited any changes from being made in the newly completed and furnished building.

In beginning his project for the cathedral, Bernardo Rossellino first cleared the area between the site of the Palazzo Piccolomini and the old Palace of the Priors (the area called Monte Piccone). It was here that he would lay out the distinctive parvis square, and at its southern end, he started the construction of the cathedral. Several circumstances handicapped his work. The physical situation necessitated the abandonment of the conventional east-west orientation (the Duomo of Pienza has a north-south axis), and the lack of adequate space meant that part of the cathedral had to project out over the precipice beyond the old perimeter of the town walls.

Rossellino was forced, therefore, to support the apse of the church upon an artificial foundation, much as he did the garden of the Piccolomini Palace and as Francesco di Giorgio was to do at Urbino when building the Cathedral of San Bernardino. Unfortunately, on this occasion the situation was less favorable and the structural solution less satisfying:

When they started to dig for a foundation, they went down fully a hundred and eight feet before they found any and even then it was none too good, since when they cracked the crumbling stones in their effort to strike a solid base, they kept coming on fissures and sulphurous exhalations. While they were trying to shut out the fumes, the sides of the pit, which were not sufficiently protected, gave way and some of the workmen were killed. Therefore they constructed very broad arches from rock to rock and laid the wall on them without having sufficiently investigated the solidity of the rocks. Though they were very large it was uncertain how firmly they were set in the earth and a crack in the building running from bottom to top gave rise to a suspicion as to the security of the foundation. The architect thought the crack was caused by the settling of the mortar while it was hardening and that they need not fear for the safety of the structure. Time will tell. The walls are very thick and adequate to carry their own weight and that of the two rows of arches above them.[92]

The unusual situation and resulting "split-level" design did permit the creation of a "crypt church" (baptistery) under the apse similar to that of the Siena cathedral. This lower church was dedicated to Saint John the Baptist, and it was there that the saint's relic

19. Facade of the cathedral.

would later be housed. "The lower church," wrote Pius, "was reached by a door and thirty-six broad steps [at the east side of the church beneath the bell tower.] Two columns [really squat piers] in the middle supported the entire structure. Three large windows let in ample light for the whole church and the four altars and beautiful white marble font in one of the chapels [Plate 20]. The very aspect of the church causes emotion and a devout reverence in all who enter."[93] The great piers, thick walls, and massive cross vaults of the lower church recall other examples of Renaissance "foundation rooms," such as the one under Michelozzo's Novitiate Corridor at Santa Croce in Florence (1440s) and those under the Greek and Latin libraries of the Vatican Palace of Nicholas V (built by Antonio di Francesco da Firenze, ca. 1447–1450).[94]

The upper church is one of the most unusual creations of the early Renaissance (Plate 21). I have already noted the pope's concern that buildings let in a lot of light. As far as the Cathedral of Pienza was concerned, this desire for light may have been spiritual, reflecting the emphasis placed upon celestial luminosity in the preachings of San Bernardino of Siena, which had influenced the young Aeneas Silvius Piccolomini. One is also reminded of Abbot Suger's description (ca. 1150) of the choir of Saint Denis: "a circular string of chapels by virtue of which the whole would shine with the wonderful and uninterrupted light of most luminous beauty, pervading the interior beauty" and an anonymous poem (ca 1459) praising the old sacristy of San Lorenzo in Florence, "so marvellous and so joyful / that who attentively admires it seems to be

dazzled, / because throughout it seems the sun is there."[95] Certainly in Pius' cathedral, light is used as a metaphor for heaven, as an exercise in Neoplatonic metaphysics. The deep love of light which Pius demonstrated in his approval of this design also may have had more subconscious psychological grounds, a desire perhaps for warmth for his gouty limbs and a welcome relief from the cloudy skies of the north under which he had spent so many years. In any case, it is light that determined the form of the interior of this cathedral. Remembering the orientation of the Palazzo Piccolomini, one might even believe that the new positioning of the building along the north-south axis was dictated by similar concerns—southern light for both palace porticoes and church choir.

Pius' description of the cathedral is clear and precise. "As you enter the middle door the entire church with its chapels and altars is visible and is remarkable for the clarity and the brilliance of the whole edifice. There are three naves as they are called. The middle one is wider. All are the same height." The Cathedral of Pienza is, surprisingly, a hall church. The plan is simple and compact, the interior measuring eighteen by thirty-nine and a half meters, or two times as long as the width of the nave plus the depth of the choir chapel. The height of the vaults (sixteen meters) is slightly less than the width of the nave. "Eight columns, all of the same height and thickness, support the entire weight of the vaulting. The side naves are of the same width as far as the third column." Rectangular chapels extend from the projecting arms of the transept, "and the entire church ends in a semicircular apse. The further part, like a crowned head, is

20. Baptismal font from the Rossellino workshop in the Cappella di San Giovanni of the cathedral.

21. Interior of the cathedral.

divided into five small chapels [including those in the transept] which project from the rest of the structure." The *Commentarii* is emphatic about whose idea it was to build this sort of church: "This was according to the directions of Pius, who had seen the plan among the Germans in Austria."[96]

Basing their theories upon the testimony of the pope, both Heydenreich and Donin have sought direct prototypes for the Pienza cathedral north of the Alps. Heydenreich found the closest analogies in the *Hallenkirchen* built by Hans Stetheimer (ca. 1350–1432) in the Bavarian towns of Landshut, Straubing, and Wasserburg. Donin, on the other hand, has pointed to late medieval examples in Austria such as the Church of Saint Otmar in Mödling or the parish church of Gumpoldskirchen.[97] In all cases, these Bavarian and Tyrolean churches display remarkable similarities in plan and often in elevation to the Cathedral of Pienza. Pius, of course, had had ample opportunity to study these Germanic churches during his long career as an employee of the various church councils and as secretary and ambassador for Emperor Frederick III.

Why, it may be asked, would such a transalpine building be erected in Renaissance Tuscany at the express wish of a noted humanist? Heydenreich has suggested that Pius, because of his long absence from his native land, had little familiarity with the works and theories of Brunelleschi and Alberti.[98] In fact, however, the future pope had had sufficient opportunity to observe the new architecture during his several trips to Italy in the years preceding his entry into the clergy and, more recently, during the decade he had lived in Italy as bishop and cardinal. The style of the Piccolomini Palace (and the way Pius described it) and of the facade of the cathedral itself demonstrates the pope's acceptance of the most progressive tastes. That the interior of the cathedral was based upon German (and thus Gothic) prototypes can best be explained by the pope's almost claustrophobic love of bright, open spaces. Certainly, the Italian pope (whose writings reveal far less fascination with things German than Heydenreich maintained) would never have ordered the building of a Germanic church simply for the sake of its being German. Indeed, R. J. Mitchell, repeating the observation of Diether of Mainz "that 'The Italians do not hate the Turks so much as they hate us,'" declares: "The grain of truth that lay in Diether's fulminations was that Pius did indeed regard the Germans as barbarians. Individuals he could respect and admire, but generally speaking he felt a distaste for their civilization that the more intelligent were quick to appreciate."[99] It was, however, in the cold and cloudy north that Aeneas Silvius had acquired that desire for sunlight and brightness which not only permeated his writings but determined his architectural wishes at Pienza. He had noted the advantages of the *Hallenkirche* form and chose its style for his cathedral because it was functionally suited to admit the light necessary to his aesthetic and spiritual demands. Pius himself stated that he had selected the Germanic design because "it makes the church more graceful and lighter."[100]

Pius had ordered Bernardo Rossellino to build a church of a peculiar transalpine variety but the actual interpretation and execution rested in the architect's hands.[101] No doubt the pope gave him detailed descriptions, but Rossellino had no firsthand knowledge of northern architecture and certainly little personal inclination to design a church along Gothic lines. He could not ignore the papal instructions, but he tried to carry them out in accordance with Italian traditions and the new architectural spirit of which he was an important exponent. For native precedent in the mode of the hall church, he could have drawn upon such local examples as the Church of San Fortunato (thirteenth century) in Todi or the Cathedral of San Lorenzo (early fifteenth century) in Perugia, where, in both cases, nave and aisles are of equal height and light enters through high Gothic windows.[102] The shape of the polygonal apse at Pienza could well have been inspired, in part, by the unfinished tribune of Saint Peter's in Rome. That project had been carried out by Lombard stonemasons, who had been influenced (witness the Cathedral of Como) by the hall churches of neighboring Austria.[103] It also should be noted that the arrangement of the apse in Pienza is not unlike the tribunes of the Florence cathedral with which Rossellino was so very familiar.

Pius, as a lover of light, had long been an admirer of the Gothic tracery window. While traveling in England early in his career, he had marveled at York Cathedral, "notable in the whole world for its size and for a very brilliant chapel whose glass walls are held together by very slender columns."[104] In 1459 he ordered "a window of exceptional brilliance behind the high altar to be filled with glass" for the Cathedral of San Lorenzo in Perugia.[105] It was to be expected that the Gothic window would find a favored position in his own cathedral in Pienza. "Every chapel," he wrote, "has a high and broad window cunningly wrought with little columns and stone flowers and filled with the glass called crystal. At the ends of the naves were four similar windows which, when the sun shines, admit so much light that worshippers in the church think that they are not in a house of stone but of glass.[106] The combination of high aisles and great windows produced a luminosity unique in the churches of central Italy.

The windows in the chapels of the cathedral, with their flowing tracery and elaborate cusping, seem quite foreign to Rossellino's architectural vocabulary. Yet there is nothing hesitant in their design or execution; they are extremely sophisticated examples of their type. It must be assumed that Rossellino was guided by someone (a Lombard mason or glazier, perhaps) who was familiar with such windows or that he was given access to an appropriate pattern book. Despite the "old-fashioned" character of the windows, there is something about the restrained execution and clarity of form that bespeaks the new aesthetic structure of the Renaissance. The windows in the nave seem more in keeping with Rossellino's own manner. Here the Gothic decorativeness is compromised by a more disciplined treatment of the framework. These windows are a variation on the bifora-cross motif and are descended from the architect's window for the Badia Fiorentina of ca. 1438 (Plate 22). They are also clearly related to the windows of the Palazzo Piccolomini.

The "eight columns" supporting the vaulting of the cathedral are in actuality square piers with half columns attached to their four faces. Their design was

22. Detail of the eastern flank of the cathedral showing the visual relationship between its windows and those of the Palazzo Piccolomini.

probably an adaptation of the piers found in the Cathedral of Siena, and they also resemble the piers used in the old Church of Santa Maria, which this cathedral was built to replace. Attached columns articulate the side walls. The capitals used might best be described as a decorated Tuscan Doric, whose design relates to the colonnette capitals of Donatello's *cantoria* for the Florence cathedral. Generally, the capital bell is fluted and a bold egg-and-dart design appears on the echinus. In some cases, the egg and dart are replaced by a honeysuckle anthemion or an arrangement of the ubiquitous Piccolomini crescents. In a single case (an attached column flanking the door to the stairs of the campanile) a winged head decorates the bell of the capital (Plate 23).[107] One wonders what significance, if any, its use might have had. It is a most unusual device and, in terms of contemporary treatments, might best be compared to the anthropomorphic decorations Alberti used on the capitals of the facade of San Francesco in Rimini or those sculpted by Donatello on his *Annunciation Tabernacle* in Santa Croce in Florence. The ultimate source is found in certain late Roman capitals of Near Eastern inspiration, one of which may have been familiar to Rossellino from his stay in Rome.[108]

An all but unique feature in the architecture of the cathedral is the insertion of tall entablature blocks between the capitals of the piers and columns and the spring points of the vaults. Pius would have us believe that they resulted from the builder's miscalculations. "After the bases of the columns were in place and the columns with four semi-circular faces had been set upon them and crowned with capitals, the architect saw that they were not going to be high enough. He, therefore, placed above the capitals square columns seven feet high with a second set of capitals to support the arches of the vaulting. It was a happy mistake which added charm by its novelty."[109] Heydenreich, however (I think rightly), insisting that such a mistake was inconceivable for an architect of Bernardo Rossellino's caliber, thought the pope's explanation was only a fanciful story.[110] These entablature inserts represent, instead, the resolution of an aesthetic problem that confronted the architect. The hall-church design necessitated piers of a height incompatible with the proportional relationships demanded by an architect working *nel modo antico*. Rossellino used the "insert" as a compromise to preserve a reasonable mathematical harmony for the shafts of the piers, while providing the additional height needed in such a hall church and a stabilizing horizontal emphasis to balance the general vertical thrust. Precedent could be found in the piers of the choir of the Siena cathedral, where the identical feature appears.

Colorful decorations complemented the novel architecture and brilliant interior of the church. In the vaults of the chapels "are fastened gold stars and they are painted the color of the sky to imitate the heavens. The vaulting of the naves was painted in various colors and the columns, which we have said were added together with their capitals to correct an error, contributed the colors of porphyry and other precious marbles. The lower columns were left in the natural white stone. The walls of the church and all the rest of the building gleam with a wondrous white luster."[111]

Although the ceilings were richly

23. The third eastern bay of the cathedral with winged head in the capital of the pier on the right.

painted, the decoration of the cathedral was carefully held in check. This restraint echoes the new Renaissance appreciation of "decorum," practiced, for instance, by Brunelleschi in the interiors of both San Lorenzo and Santo Spirito and seen in the more moderate dress of the day. The emphasis was on quality, not opulent display. The classical emphasis on moderation joined with an increased religious sobriety. "In the central chapel," wrote the pope, "were the episcopal throne and the canons' seats, made of precious wood decorated with sculpture and designs in the work called intarsia. In the other four chapels were altars adorned with paintings by illustrious Sienese artists. In the second to the left of the throne was the repository for the Host, of finely carved white marble" (Plate 24).[112] This handsome freestanding ciborium, the Tabernacle of Saint Andrew, is the most significant piece of liturgical furniture in the cathedral, and if not an autograph work by Bernardo Rossellino, it certainly came from his Florentine workshop. The large Renaissance tabernacle rises from a high dado. The compartment designed for the host is set within an ornate frieze with rope, foliate, and egg-and-dart moldings. The bronze door is topped by a lunette containing a cockleshell. Paired but separated fluted pilasters with composite capitals are placed on either side of this central area. The spaces between the pilasters are decorated with "disciplined" acanthus and palmette plants growing out of urns, a motif that suggests the architectural sgraffiti of Rossellino's Palazzo Spinelli in Florence and, especially, that of the communal Palace in Pienza.[113] The four pilasters carry a large entablature surmounted by a lunette. An anthemion is used in the frieze of the entablature, and two angels supporting a miniature ciborium are sculpted in the lunette. The altar table upon which the tabernacle rests is apparently of modern manufacture. The closest parallel to this great freestanding tabernacle was executed by Andrea Cavalcanti (Il Buggiano) at the Cathedral of Florence, perhaps for the Rossellino shop.

Pius described other elements still to be seen today: "On the two columns nearest the door are two fonts, the work of no mean genius, from which those who enter sprinkle themselves with holy water. The high altar stands between the last two columns and is ascended by four steps. . . . In the body of the church are two other altars to serve the congregation."[114] The holy-water fonts are of handsome simplicity, with gracefully curving basins mounted on tapering fluted bases. The main altar table is largely a reconstruction, as are the altars in the surrounding chapels.[115]

In designing the interior of the cathedral, Rossellino was forced, and it may be supposed somewhat against his will, to adhere closely to the peculiar wishes of his employer. In planning the facade, however, the architect exercised his own will. "It was modeled," said Pius, "on those of ancient temples and richly decorated with columns and arches and semicircular niches designed to hold statues."[116] The Gothic *Hallenkirche* interior actually permitted Bernardo Rossellino to use a "temple" front for the exterior; the problem of the basilican profile, which constantly plagued Alberti and other classically minded architects of the Renaissance, did not exist.[117]

Pius has left the following description of the facade of his cathedral:

24. Tabernacle of Saint Andrew.

Three steps of hard stone [now two] ran the width of the church facade. By these you ascend to the church which was entered through an open space fifteen feet wide instead of a vestibule. The facade itself is 72 feet high, made of stone resembling the Tiburtine, white and shining as marble. . . . It had three beautifully proportioned doors, the center one larger than the others, and a great eye like that of the Cyclops. It displayed the arms of the Piccolomini, above them the papal fillet wreathed about the triple crown, and the keys of the Church between. The facade is of the same breadth all the way from the foundation to the roof. From there to its top it had the form of a pyramid decorated with charming cornices.[118]

The basic motif is easily grasped: a rectangle surmounted by a triangular pediment. Buttresslike pilaster strips resting upon tall pedestals divide the rectangular portion into three sections. Set within these three bays are two tiers of columns. The lower tier supports a cornice that divides the facade into two major stories. Arches spring from the upper columns. The crowns of these three arches touch the upper cornice. The even heights of the arches reflect the hall-church character of the interior. Three portals, the center one almost twice the size of those flanking it, are located in the lower bays (Plate 25). Semicircular tympanum arches rest on the cornices of the elegant and simple doorframes.

The oculus Pius described as a "great eye like that of the Cyclops" pierces the central bay of the upper level of the facade. Elaborately framed aediculae fill the outer bays of this story. Recessed horizontal panels, perhaps inspired by those adorning the Arch of Titus in Rome, decorate the surfaces of the wall above the two side portals and below the oculus, and this motif echoes the panels on the front of the pedestals that support the pilaster strips.

The vertical thrust of the pilaster strips that flank the central bay is continued into the triangular pediment, but there the severity and buttresslike quality yields to a more decorative treatment. The pilaster strips of the pediment are ornamented with reliefs of antique candelabra, and they flank a large plaque surrounded by a garland which displays the coat of arms of Pius II. Actually this is a broken pediment, since the raking cornice projects over the four pilaster strips of the facade, perhaps the first such pediment in the Renaissance.

It is quite possible to reconcile the facade of the Piccolomini Palace with the evolution of Rossellino's style. The facade of the palace represents a logical outgrowth of the approach to architecture which the master had first displayed in Arezzo a quarter of a century earlier and which was now disciplined by lessons taught by his experiences in Rome and his work with Alberti. The facade of the Cathedral of Pienza, on the other hand, seems to stand apart from this process of stylistic development. It is, of course, difficult to evaluate Rossellino's approach to the designing of church facades. As far as is known, the project at Pienza marked his first and only experience in planning the exterior of a church. Given his usual procedure in formulating a design, one might imagine that he drew upon examples previously executed by his teachers and contemporaries.

Actually, the Renaissance prototypes from which Bernardo could have profited were few. As Richard Goldthwaite

25. View through the west doorway to the tabernacle on the Altar of Saint Andrew.

has commented, "Despite the demand for chapels that occasioned the rebuilding of most of the city's [Florence's] churches, church facades got little attention and stood prominently incomplete on their squares."[119] Both of Brunelleschi's great churches in Florence remained facadeless, and although several theories have been proposed, nothing definite concerning the master's intentions for San Lorenzo and Santo Spirito is known. Only the unfinished portico of the Pazzi Chapel provides some indication of Brunelleschi's ideas about church facades, and clearly, even if the projected pediment had been executed, the exterior of the Pazzi Chapel would have been totally different from that of the cathedral in Pienza.[120] The linear treatment of the second story of the Pazzi Chapel is actually much more akin to the facade of the Piccolomini Palace.

Examples from the circle of Michelozzo are not quite so sparse. The single example of an early quattrocento church facade in Florence, that of San Felice, was probably designed by Michelozzo or by someone in his workshop.[121] This front was added to the single-nave church by a Mariotto Dinazzo Stephani de Lippis ca. 1457. It is stylistically linked to the Michelozzian church of Santa Maria delle Grazie (1452) in Pistoia (often attributed to the local builder Ventura Vitoni).[122] Both of these church facades are simple and rather severe. Their design represents (typically for Michelozzo) an updated version of the standard medieval parish church of Tuscany, and Bernardo's effort owes little to them. A closer relationship—probably a definite one—exists between the Pienza cathedral and the Michelozzian church of San Agostino (ca. 1450) in nearby Montepulciano, with which Rossellino must have been familiar.[123] The tripartite arrangement of its facade may have helped to determine his design for the Cathedral of Pienza. Yet the two churches resemble one another most closely in the upper stories and in the pediments, and these parts of San Agostino were not finished until 1508; it is, therefore, impossible to determine whether this work represents a continuation of the original plan, with which Rossellino might have been acquainted, or is itself an adaptation from the design of the Cathedral of Pienza.

Perhaps the closest parallel exists not in a Renaissance church but in examples dating, curiously enough, from the Romanesque and Gothic periods. The Church of San Rufino in Assisi (begun by Giovanni da Gubbio in 1140) has a facade that despite its medieval proportions and details, resembles that of the Cathedral of Pienza. So, too, does that of the Church of San Pietro (completed in 1268) in the same town; the resemblance to San Pietro was even more pronounced before that church lost its crowning pediment. Points of similarity include the general shapes of the buildings, the mathematical schemes that seem to have been used, the division of the facades into two stories, and the use of pilaster strips to divide the fronts into three bays. In many respects the Cathedral of Pienza gives the impression of being a modernized San Rufino or San Pietro.[124]

The marked "classicism" shown by the facade of the Pienza cathedral raises, once more, the question of Alberti's involvement. Admittedly, the facade might be called Albertian, yet Alberti's two contemporary facade designs, for Santa Maria Novella in Florence (begun in 1458) and San Sebastiano in Mantua (started in 1460), are quite different. At Santa Maria Novella, although the use of projecting entablatures and the pairing of columns with pillars may be connected to motifs found on the Pienza cathedral, the overall treatment is two-dimensional. Two-dimensionality is even more apparent at San Sebastiano. The strongly three-dimensional statement of the facade of the cathedral in Pienza most resembles Alberti's Church of San Francesco (the so-called Tempio Malatestiano) in Rimini, which dates to around 1450, and the similarity between the two projects may be significant. At the same time Alberti was designing the facade for San Francesco, he and Rossellino may have been preparing a design for the front of a new Saint Peter's, and it is possible that the facade of Pius' cathedral was based, in part, upon that never-realized proposal. One of the most notable elements of the Pienza church, the use of blind arches springing from the columns, also figures in the scheme for the campanile of the cathedral in Ferrara, which is most often attributed to Alberti. Since it is dated to the mid-1440s, the tower reinforces the notion of an Albertian influence but no direct participation by the humanist architect.

Alberti's personal involvement in the designing of the facade of the cathedral is also refuted by other factors. Despite the fact that the cathedral stands "somewhat raised above the level of the rest of the town," as Alberti recommended for such buildings, and though its facade is, as the pope said, "modeled on those of ancient temples," there are several features in the facade which are inconsistent with the Albertian approach as shown at San Francesco and the later churches in Florence and Mantua and with the recommendations in the *De re aedificatoria*.[125] The most obvious point is the oculus. Alberti appears to have been quite opposed to this sort of medieval holdover. In a letter to Matteo de' Pasti, 18 November 1454, he wrote, "You will never, never find, in any building praised by those who understand what nobody understands today, any round window at all."[126] In remodeling the church of San Andrea in Mantua in 1470, Alberti was careful to mask the original medieval round window of the facade with a curious "hood," thereby showing his continued displeasure with a form that he felt admitted too much uncontrolled light.[127] The proper functions for columns and piers were carefully preserved at San Francesco, but in the Pienza facade Bernardo Rossellino allowed the arcading of the second story to spring from columns. Alberti (if he was, indeed, the man responsible) had done the same thing at the campanile in Ferrara, but by the time he wrote his architectural treatise, he had rejected the anachronism. Nor are the precise proportional relationships Alberti was wont to employ— at Santa Maria Novella, for instance—to be found in Rossellino's design.[128] Furthermore, the direct antique allusions, archaeological interests, and profuse sculptural decorations apparent at the Rimini church are absent from Rossellino's cathedral in Pienza. Despite a detectable Albertian flavor, therefore, the facade of the Cathedral of Pienza is no more due to Alberti than the front of Rossellino's Misericordia Palace in Arezzo was due to Michelozzo or the Spinelli Cloister to Brunelleschi. Assuredly, the Palazzo Piccolomini has more of Alberti in it than does the town's cathedral.

Although not perfect by purely Albertian standards, and thus somewhat maligned by that master's partisans, the facade of the Cathedral of Pienza certainly must rank among the most successful church designs of the fifteenth century. Part of its virtue lies in the harmonious ordonnance of its members. A variety of geometric shapes—circles, arcs, rectangles, squares, triangles, both real and implicit—were used in establishing the design. These forms reappear throughout the height and breadth of the surface. The triangle of the gable is echoed in the broken pediments of the aediculae as well as in certain visual triangles, such as the one linking the three inset panels over the entrances. Curving and circular shapes are repeated in the columns, arches, *tondi* of the *stemma* and oculus, lunette arches over the doors and "shell niches." In the portals, pedestals, panels, pilaster strips, and the general shape of the bays of each story, rectangular forms provide stabilizing forces. The entire facade is tied together with interlocking and well-balanced vertical and horizontal thrusts. Despite the several factors of which Alberti would have disapproved, Bernardo Rossellino's facade does seem a valid demonstration of Alberti's definition of beauty as "a harmony of all the parts . . . fitted together with such proportion and connection, that nothing could be added, diminished or altered, but for the worse."[129] The syncretism of the classicizing facade and the Gothic interior was very much in keeping with the harmonious ideal of Alberti, who followed much the same procedure in Florence when he completed the facade of Santa Maria Novella.

Another feature that makes the facade of the Cathedral of Pienza so attractive is the way it relates to the neighboring facade of the Piccolomini Palace (Plate 26). A sympathetic bond joins the two surfaces into a complementary harmony. The buildings are visually united through their systems of trabeation, and the proportions of the stories of the church's facade echo those of the palace. Subtle relationships such as those existing between the doorways and between the roundheaded windows of the palace and the arcuation of the cathedral also appear. All these factors, of course, point to the overall mood of classicism which is the chief connecting link between the two neighboring buildings. Rossellino clearly intended for the eye to appreciate the similarities, but he allowed the facade of the cathedral to make the more forceful impact.[130] The great mass of the palace seems like a low-relief grid compared to the shadow-catching plasticity of the front of the cathedral. Moreover, the facade of the church stands out through its coloration. Whereas the palace is constructed of brownish blocks of sandstone, which glow golden in the evening light, the cathedral's facade is built of a gleaming white travertine, which immediately becomes the focus of attention for anyone standing in the piazza.

"The other [exterior] walls," wrote the pope, "are of less precious material [sandstone] but the stones are squared and well polished with projections like ribs interspersed at regular intervals to strengthen the fabric."[131] In his handling of the sides and rear of the cathedral,

26. View from the tower of the Palazzo Comunale with the cathedral and the Palazzo Piccolomini.

Bernardo struck a balance between the "classical" appearance of the facade and the Gothic character of the interior. The framework of the facade, based upon a grid of pilaster strips and cornices, is repeated on the external walls along the flanks of the cathedral but the elements are given a Gothic twist. The pilaster strips are transformed into real pier buttresses and the cornices serve as string courses with the middle band functioning as a hoodmold over the round- and pointed-arched windows. Heydenreich has compared this external treatment with that of such Gothic churches in Germany as the hospital church of Landshut or Sankt Nicholas in Neuötting, but a parallel can also be drawn with the unfinished tribune of Saint Peter's in Rome.[132] The clasping buttresses seen on the plan of the tribune and in several sixteenth-century views seem to be echoed on the exterior of the apse of the Cathedral of Pienza.

On the left side of the church, an attached campanile rises above the gable of the stubby transept (Plate 27). On his 1462 visit, Pius noted that "a third of this was still unfinished," but the tower "was to be 160 feet high."[133] Apparently, when the pope saw the tower, it had risen to the level of the cornice below the bell chamber. So far the expenditures for the tower had been included in the general appropriations for the construction of the cathedral. On 4 October 1462, after work on the cathedral proper had been completed, a new commission was given to "master Bernardo and associates who have undertaken to make at their own risk the bell tower of the church at Pienza and the Palace of the Commune of Pienza" (Appendix 2, Doc. 50). Among the members of Bernardo

Rossellino's atelier was his grand nephew Puccio di Paolo whose name appears often in subsequent entries together with that of his uncle. Puccio, identified as a *maestro* in the documents, evidently served as second-in-command of the Rossellino workshop in Pienza.

The Rossellino shop was to receive 2,700 ducats from the papal treasury for work done on both the tower and the Communal Palace. It is impossible to determine how much of this total amount was allocated specifically to complete the tower. According to the entry of 4 October, the payments were to be made in four parts of 675 ducats each. The first two parts of the total sum were paid in four separate installments— 200 ducats on 4 October 1462, 475 ducats on 24 December 1462, 200 ducats on 30 March 1463, and 475 ducats on 10 April 1463. (Appendix 3, Docs. 50, 55, 58, 59). The remaining payments of 675 ducats each were given to the Rossellino firm on 7 July and 17 August 1463 (Appendix 2, Docs. 72, 77).

The lower portion of the campanile is integrated into the body of the cathedral. The treatment is quite clever: seen from the piazza, the structure retains its identity as a tower throughout its elevation, but observed from the side, the lower part merges with the fabric of the transept. Above the level of the upper cornice of the church, the tower continues as a square block to the height of the ridge of the roof. At this point the appearance of the campanile is transformed in both color and form. Below this point the tower is built of the same brown sandstone used in the adjoining walls of the church, but above the level of the roof the campanile is faced with the same white travertine blocks used on the fa-

27. View along the Via del Casello (Ciglio Quarter) of the eastern flank of the cathedral with the campanile. The Palazzo Canonica is on the right.

cade. Seen from a distance the sandstone portion of the tower is obscured by the facade and the impression is that the entire tower is constructed of the same more elegant material as the facade. This treatment saved a considerable amount of money (the travertine had to be quarried with greater labor and transported from several kilometers away) at no loss to aesthetics.

A chamfered base resting upon the square platform of the lower portion of the tower provides a transition to the octagonal form of the upper stories of the campanile.[134] There are two such stories separated by a string course resting upon mock machicolations. Bent pilaster strips define the corners of the octagonal tower. A cornice supported by modillions (repeating the motif of the raking cornice of the facade) projects above the second story. The campanile terminates in an octagonal spire decorated with gables about its base and crockets along the ribs (Plate 28).

Richard Donin related the cathedral's campanile to Austrian bell towers like the one found at the church of Sankt Johann im Mauertale, Wachau, or to the Heidenturm of the Stephansdom in Vienna. The campanile of the Modena cathedral also has been suggested as a possible prototype.[135] Bernardo Rossellino did not have to look that far away to find his inspiration, however. Like the cathedral, itself, this campanile was his first solo encounter with ecclesiastical designing, and he selected as his model a bell tower with which he had long been familiar, the campanile of the Badia Fiorentina which was built ca. 1310 after the design, it is supposed, of Arnolfo di Cambio; the spire was an addition of ca. 1330.[136]

It should not be surprising that Bernardo Rossellino derived the Pienza campanile from this tower. For twenty-five years his workshop had been almost literally in its shadow—in the Via del Corso from 1435 to 1439 and then in the Via del Proconsolo, both very near the Badia.[137] Rossellino took this Gothic bell tower as his model but simplified it and rearranged the design in keeping with his modern concepts. Thus, the campanile, like the cathedral itself, is a classicized Gothic structure. In making his revisions, Bernardo was probably influenced by his present experience as the *capomaestro* in charge of completing Brunelleschi's lantern for the cupola of the Florence cathedral. Such features as the bent pilaster strips can be traced to this project. The great Filippo Brunelleschi, it should be added, had also found his inspiration in the tower of the Badia.

If Rossellino had borrowed ideas for his tower, it later served as a source for others. The campanile of San Pietro in Perugia was rebuilt between 1463 and 1468 after the pattern of the Pienza bell tower, a fact not too amazing since the relevant documents show that Bernardo Rossellino gave advice on it and members of his shop, including Puccio di Paolo, were involved in its construction.[138] A bit more surprising is the similarity between the campanile's spire and those of the *torrioni* of the ducal palace in Urbino. Those features can probably be attributed to Francesco di Giorgio, who integrated a number of Pientine elements into his style. Three-quarters of a century later, the influence of the Pienza campanile can still be found on the one completed bell tower of Antonio da Sangallo the Elder's pil-

28. The campanile of the cathedral wiith Mount Amiata in the distance.

grimage church of the Madonna di San Biagio at Montepulciano.[139]

The campanile of the Pienza cathedral, with its mixture of borrowings and clever adaptations, is exactly what might be expected from Bernardo Rossellino. As he had done throughout his career, he again created a most original and striking design through a careful process of distillation. His bell tower in Pienza displayed a very personal combination of Gothic and Renaissance elements and supplied the perfect complement to the Gothic/Renaissance church over which it presides.

The Piazza Pio II

The construction of the Cathedral of the Blessed Mary Ever a Virgin and the Piccolomini Palace were the two principal projects the pope had first entrusted to his chief architect, Bernardo Rossellino. Pope Pius seems to have been pleasantly surprised with the speed with which the work had been executed, for he noted that "all these buildings except the bell tower which was still unfinished were completed from foundation to roof in three years." Also nearly completed by the time of his visit in 1462 were the piazza-parvis in front of the cathedral and the handsome public well in that square (Plate 29), and the pope wrote quite precisely about them.[140]

The area about which Rossellino grouped the principal buildings of Pienza is extremely cramped. Indeed, its dimensions are no larger than those of the *cortile* within the Palazzo Piccolomini.[141] Rossellino managed to gain some much-needed space by pushing the cathedral as far to the south as he could. Projecting almost half of the church out over the hillside left a distance of about twenty-five meters between the facade of the cathedral and the buildings that faced it along the northern side of the main thoroughfare.

It was impossible to fit a rectangular piazza into this space for several reasons: the street entered and exited the area at differing angles; the old Priors' Palace (the future Palazzo Vescovile) was set at an angle of eighty rather than ninety degrees; and the Palazzo Piccolomini had to be placed at a seventy-five-degree angle if it was to remain parallel to the Church of San Francesco and in alignment with the street. The cathederal piazza, thus, quite naturally assumed the shape of a slightly irregular trapezoid.

Bernardo Rossellino accepted the dictates of the physical situation and then proceeded to exploit them. The street connecting the present Piazza del Mercato (di Spagna) and the Piazza Pio II, the Via G. Marconi, was selected as the primary point from which to view the complex of buildings set about the square. The central portal of the cathedral is on a direct axis with the spot at which this street enters the square. The inverted perspective of the trapezoidal piazza actually produces a salutary result, creating an open space at either side of the cathedral. The buildings facing onto the piazza are harmoniously unified, but this free space on both sides of the cathedral permits the church and the palaces flanking it to maintain their individual architectural integrity. The small area of the square, coupled with the confining walls of the palaces to the left and right, forces the visitor toward the inviting facade of the cathedral. Yet there is the opportunity to escape the architec-

29. The Piazza Pio II with the cathedral and the Palazzo Piccolomini as seen from the loggia of the Palazzo Comunale.

tural surroundings through the open areas at either side of the building. There, the visitor is granted deep views of the Orcia Valley and Mount Amiata beyond. Furthermore, these open areas prevent the monumental facade of the cathedral from oppressively dominating the square. The human scale of the piazza is preserved.

The impression is different when the visitor stands at the entrance to the cathedral and faces north to the opposite line of buildings. The converging lines of the perspective are now accentuated by the trapezoidal shape of the piazza. Seen from this point, the area diminishes rapidly toward the little street leading to the Piazza del Mercato. Unconsciously, perhaps, Rossellino had established a psychological system of crowd control which would ensure the rapid emptying of the square following services or celebrations in the cathedral. The effect is not dissimilar to the perspective illusion he had introduced in the entrance corridor of the Palazzo Spinelli in Florence.[142]

Despite the fact that other buildings were soon to be built or remodeled around the northern and eastern sides of the area, the Piazza Pio II had been not only laid out by the time of the pope's arrival in the summer of 1462 but also, according to Pius, "paved with bricks laid on their sides in mortar."[143] There is some debate among modern scholars as to the precise nature of the original paving. It is not known, for instance, whether the grid pattern that today is such a fundamental feature of the piazza was used in Pius' day. This grid system makes the square seem at once larger and more regular in plan, visually reducing any disturbing effect worked by the trap-

ezoidal shape of the piazza. Old nineteenth-century views show the strips, but some would still argue that this paving scheme is of comparatively recent date. The travertine bands that separate the brick paving into rectangles of approximately 6.5 × 4 meters so beautifully reiterate the vertical articulation of the neighboring cathedral and papal palace that one hopes they were part of the original design. Yet no mention of such a distinctive feature appeared in the *Commentarii,* and the question may finally be settled only through excavation. In the meantime, it should be pointed out that precedent for such a rectangular pattern is to be found in medieval Florence where just such a design was used in the Piazza della Signoria in the fourteenth century.[144] A similar paving scheme is also represented in Piero della Francesca's painting *The Flagellation* (ca. 1460), now in Urbino, as well as in any number of paintings of the period. In the painting the square sections of paving help establish an atmosphere of rationality that convinces us of the intellectuality of the three figures in the foreground. The same is true in Pienza. We can imagine men like Piero's discoursing there.[145]

Another question concerning the Piazza Pio II is raised by the pope's specific statement that "three steps of hard stone ran the width of the church facade.[146] Clearly this is not the case today; the platform upon which the cathedral stands is only two steps high. Either Pius miscounted or the level of the piazza has been raised since his day. If the piazza was raised at some point, it would mean, of course, that originally one would have had to step down into the piazza from the adjoining Piccolomini and Bishop's palaces. There is another possibility, questionable certainly, yet intriguing. Perhaps the pope counted the entire piazza as the first step, which would mean that the piazza was elevated above the original level of the *corso*. Today the paving of street and Piazza is contiguous, but just when the street was first paved is unclear. It is shown paved in nineteenth-century views,[147] but from the *Commentarii* we gain the impression that it was a simple dirt street when Pius paid his 1462 visit. On the Feast of Saint Matthew (21 September), Pius watched races run through the town "from a very high window," perhaps a window of his palace. The racecourse, part of which presumably was the appropriately named *corso*, he described as slippery from a recent rain, and he said the participants were "seen to slip and fall and roll on the ground and mud," unable to "shake their feet clear of the sticky clay."[148] If the pope was describing the condition of the *corso*, then the street would probably have been lower than the paved piazza. The idea that the piazza-parvis was raised above the level of the passing street like a stage is a delightful thought.[149] If true, then it and its principal religious and signorial buildings would have been set even more apart from (or above) the everyday life of the community, and those deliberately entering onto the space would truly have enacted their roles as players in the pope's grand architectural drama. A subtle yet definite line would have been drawn between the mundane communal activity of Pienza and the more elevated and ennobling arena of religious and hierarchical experience.

One of the most attractive features of the Piazza Pio II is the public well located next to the east entrance of the Palazzo Piccolomini (Plate 30). In his *Commen-*

tarii, Pius wrote: "In the square before the palace was a deep well of living water, the mouth of which was decorated with very beautiful marble columns supporting an entablature artistically sculpted."[150] This *pozzo* is one of the finest examples of Bernardo Rossellino's architectural sculpture and recalls the refined treatment he had accorded the ciborium in the cathedral and the font in the baptistery below. The design is derived from such medieval wellheads as that in the Piazza della Cisterna of the town of San Gimignano (1346) but here in Pienza this basic post-and-lintel framework was transformed into a design suitable to the antiquarian taste of the Renaissance.[151]

The two unfluted columns that flank the well support a beautifully sculpted entablature, which bears the inscription PIVS PPII MCCCCLXII and the escutcheon of the Piccolomini. The latter device is carved in a fashion similar to that of the stemmae above the doors within the adjoining palace. The architrave has two fascia, the lower one smooth and the upper fluted. The cyma reversa uses the egg-and-dart motif. The design of the architrave is identical to that used for the capitals of the piers of the cathedral. The frieze contains a strigil design, and the entire entablature is capped by a distinctive cornice. This framework rests upon a two-stepped circular podium and frames a multipart basin decorated with fluting and cable molding.

A wellhead identical in form to this one but which substituted Ionic for Composite capitals formerly stood in the main piazza of the town of San Giovanni Val d'Arno.[152] San Giovanni was the hometown of Rossellino's wife, and he

30. The well in the Piazza Pio II.

had been busily buying up property there for a number of years.[153] The logical assumption is that either Bernardo Rossellino designed the well in San Giovanni or it came from one of his close associates (Puccio di Paolo, perhaps).

The fact that the Pientine well is not centered in the piazza may seem a violation of the expected Renaissance norm of symmetry. In Rome, too, Pius had laid out the fountain to one side of the piazza at Saint Peter's Basilica, for such an "obstacle" before the main portal of a church would create liturgical difficulties. At Pienza in place of the well a travertine circle (original?) was traced in the middle of the piazza; it is as if the well had been transported from its "ideal" location, leaving behind a memorial of its intended site. Moreover, as is the case with any number of individual elements in Pienza, the communal well plays an additional aesthetic and iconographic role in the general scheme of things. Its trabeated design seems to advance the articulation of the background facade of the Palazzo Piccolomini onto the grid of the piazza and, at the same time, to lead the eye toward the palace. This latter effect is particularly noticeable when the well is viewed from the eastern stretch of the *corso*. Is it only accident that the well's location forces the citizen of Pienza to come to the Piccolomini Palace for his basic supply of water, and is the quality of that water somehow theologically enhanced by its proximity to the papal residence?

The Palazzo Canonica

Apparently also completed as part of the first phase of activity at Pienza was a house built diagonally across the square from the well and to the east of the cathedral along the southern edge of the hill (Plate 31). According to Pius, "The Pope built a house adjoining the church on the left where the bishop and the canons might be comfortably lodged, from which they would without interference pass to their duties by night or day through a little door let into the side of the church for their convenience."[154] Both in its external appearance and in its present internal arrangements, this lodging house resembles nothing other than a simple dormitory. Construction work on the Palazzo Canonica probably began sometime after 29 October 1460, the date on which the pope's *camerario apostolico* and then vice-treasurer Giliforte dei Buonconti paid forty ducats to the Commune of Pienza for two contiguous houses with an alleyway (or open space) in the *quartiere de la ripa al ciglio*.[155] Since this was not a personal purchase and since both description and location were appropriate to the site of the Palazzo Canonica, it would seem that it was for this building that Giliforte acquired the property.

The plain front of the Palazzo Canonica was divided into two stories by a narrow string course. An arched doorway, framed by smooth travertine blocks with a slightly projecting keystone, is asymmetrically placed on the left of the lower story. In the second story is a row of three evenly disposed round-headed windows. The third story was added at the turn of this century when the Canons' House was converted into a museum.[156] A change in the coloration of the stone just below the bases of these upper windows reveals the level of the original roof line, which can also be

31. The Palazzo Vescovile with the Palazzo Canonica on the right.

traced along the flanks of the building. The fabric of the Canons' House is a mix of local sandstone and brick covered with greyish-brown stucco. The stuccoed surface was originally decorated with sgraffito work, some of which, although badly worn, is still to be seen along the Vicolo della Canonica side of the building. The remaining traces are as simple as the design of the Palazzo Canonica—simulated stone blocks and a handsome frieze of anthemion below the string course.

How much the disposition of the present interior of the Palazzo Canonica preserves the original features is uncertain, for extensive renovations were undertaken prior to the opening of the museum. Today, one enters a vestibule from which a quarter-turn stairs with landing leads to the second floor. A hallway, off which the rooms open, runs down the center of the long building and gives to it the rather barracks-like effect already noted. Pius' description indicated that the Canons' House had been completed before his visit in the summer of 1462. Although it was probably erected under the general supervision of Bernardo Rossellino, there is nothing in its design to connect this architecturally undistinguished structure with his personal manner other than the sgraffito work, which was becoming a major decorative feature of his style. Apparently, the Palazzo Canonica was the product not of an actual architectural design but rather of the joining together and refurbishing of several older buildings, most likely including the two houses acquired from the Commune on Pius' behalf by his vice-treasurer Giliforte dei Buonconti in October of 1460.

With the construction of the cathedral and his great family palace and with the paving of the new piazza, the first phase of Pope Pius' dream for his birthplace had been realized. Much more was still to be done in the town, but Pius was clearly content with the progress he saw on his visit. Medieval Corsignano was fast disappearing and the new Pienza was truly becoming "as lasting as possible a memorial of his birth."

Chapter 3

The Second Phase

Other Public and Private Buildings

Standing in his newly laid out square before his handsome cathedral and palace, Pope Pius could not fail to have been pleased. He "inspected all the details and did not regret what he had spent, though he had laid out more than 50,000 ducats on the work. The beauty and dignity of the buildings made him forget his annoyance at the cost."[1] Pius noted that he "had received many insinuations against the architect: that he had cheated; that he had blundered in the construction; that he had spent more than 50,000 ducats when his estimate had been 18,000. The law of the Ephesians, according to Vitruvius, would have obliged him to make up the difference." Pius left the following description of the confrontation between patron and architect:

He was a Florentine named Bernardo, hateful to the Sienese from his mere nationality. In his absence everyone abused him. Pius, when he had inspected the work and examined everything, sent for the man. When he arrived after a few days in some apprehension, since he knew that many charges had been brought against him, Pius said, "You did

well, Bernardo, in lying to us about the expense involved in the work. If you had told the truth, you could never have induced us to spend so much money and neither this splendid palace nor this church, the finest in all Italy, would now be standing. Your deceit has built these glorious structures which are praised by all except the few who are consumed with envy. We thank you and think you deserve especial honor among all the architects of our time"—and he ordered full pay to be given him and in addition a present of 100 ducats and a scarlet robe. He bestowed on his son the grace he asked and charged him with new commissions. Bernardo, when he heard the Pope's words, burst into tears of joy.[2]

The pope's rather casual attitude about Rossellino's cost overruns quite likely was due to an auspicious piece of luck a few months earlier. Valuable deposits of alum, a chemical essential to the dyeing of cloth, had been discovered in the papal territory near the town of Tolfa. Previously, European merchants had had to import this material from the East through the hands of the Turks at an annual cost of some 300,000 ducats in tribute and considerable humiliation. Not only could Pius now look forward to a constant source of revenue, but he had the satisfaction of knowing that the subsidy to the sultanate from Christian Europe would cease.[3] Pius took the alum discovery as a sure sign of divine blessing both for his great crusading venture and for the architectural labors at his birthplace. Without the mines, the cost of his proposed expedition against the sultan would surely have curtailed his building projects, but with an assured income from the sale of alum, he could afford to be generous to Rossellino and could authorize not only the completion of his original plans for Pienza but also a new phase of building activity.

The Palazzo Vescovile

One of the new commissions with which Pius charged his architect involved the construction of a residence for the new bishop of Pienza (Plate 32). Although Bishop Cinughi was for a time "comfortably lodged" in the Canons' House, those simple quarters were intended to be only temporary until a more suitable episcopal palace could be provided. "Across the square from the [Piccolomini] palace was an old house where the prior and other magistrates of the town were accustomed to live. This Pius bought and handed over to the Vice-Chancellor [Cardinal Rodrigo Borgia] on condition that he should build on the site an episcopal palace and present it to the Blessed Virgin Mary."[4] What exactly Borgia (the future Pope Alexander VI) was to have gained from this agreement is hard to imagine, other

than lodging when he was in Pienza and the pope's favor.

The acquisition of the medieval priors' palace was recorded on 1 September 1462 in the *gabella dei contratti* of Siena, which stated that the pope had received a palace valued at 480 ducats "in exchange" (for the promise to build a new town hall?) from the Commune of Pienza.[5] On the day Pius left Pienza (28 September 1462), he authorized the payment of fifty ducats to Bishop Cinughi to pay the builder Pietro Paolo dal Porrina, "who buys implements for the Bishop's Palace" (Appendix 2, Doc. 49). These "implements" are not further identified but may well have been items of construction equipment. Porrina was a Piccolomini in-law, an architectural contractor from Siena who was also responsible, as we will see, for the remodeling or building of several houses in Pienza as well as for the actual construction of the Piccolomini-Todeschini Palace in Siena, the design for which had been furnished by Bernardo Rossellino.[6] Porrina probably operated in Pienza as an independent builder connected with and under the overall supervision of the Rossellino firm. The appearance of his name in the only existing document that seems to pertain to work done on the Palazzo Vescovile does not mean that he was responsible for its design. Its general appearance as well the specifics of its detailing points more convincingly to Rossellino.

The Bishop's Palace is a nearly cubical block measuring approximately eighteen meters along each side and fourteen meters in height.[7] The main facade faces the Palazzo Piccolomini across the Piazza Pio II. Simple travertine string courses

32. View eastward from the Palazzo Piccolomini across the Piazza Pio II and along the Corso il Rossellino. The Palazzo Comunale is on the immediate left, and the Palazzo Vescovile on the right.

divide the building into three stories of diminishing heights. The richly treated doorframe is an almost exact reproduction of the main portal of the Piccolomini Palace but executed in travertine rather than sandstone. The doorway, strangely positioned off center, is flanked by stone benches that run the length of the main facade. Three small square windows topped by travertine lintels are let into the ground story, two to the right and one to the left. The second and third stories of this west facade both contain a row of four travertine-framed cross windows, vertically aligned but irregularly spaced. A similar arrangement, minus doorway, runs down the Corso il Rossellino side of the palace (Plate 33).

The plain fabric of the palace consists of rectangular blocks of sandstone accented by the white travertine details of door and window frames and the string courses. Although there is no evidence of it today, sgraffito work may have been planned for the surface of the palace. Architecturally appropriate sgraffito decoration of the kind used on the neighboring communal and Canons' palaces and elsewhere throughout the town would have concealed the awkwardly visible arches above door and window frames and would have brought the palace into better harmony with the piazza and the other buildings surrounding it. Yet though the present unarticulated facade of the Bishop's Palace contrasts with the treatment of the Piccolomini Palace on the other side of the piazza, there are certain architectural details that tie the two buildings together. Among these elements are the similar division of the elevations into three stories that progressively decrease in height, the use of

cross windows, and the similarity of the entrance portals.

From the entrance way a long barrel-vaulted corridor leads to the rear of the building. At the end of the hallway is a door, past which is a narrow room ending in another door, through which one enters a courtyard at the rear of the palace. It has previously been assumed that this *cortile* formed part of the original Bishop's Palace, but according to Monsignor Aldo Franci, the door is a recent addition. Apparently, the courtyard once belonged to the old hospital building bought by Jean Jouffroy and added to his palace. There is, thus, no interior courtyard in the Palazzo Vescovile. Three rooms open off each side of the hallway; all have cross vaults, save the room at the northwestern corner, which has lunette vaults springing from composite corbels similar to those used in the Piccolomini Palace. Midway down the corridor, a doorway gives access to a flight of stairs leading to the piano nobile. There, and on the third level, the layout of rooms corresponds to that of the ground floor but the ceilings are wooden rather than vaulted.

Despite the testimony and wishes of the pope, the Bishop's Palace may not have been built upon the site of the medieval Priors' Palace but actually may have been nothing but a modernization of that older building. Several features seem to support this conclusion, including the asymmetrical placement of the portal, the outlines of Gothic-looking pointed arches visible above the window frames in the piano nobile, and the clear traces above the Renaissance portal of the arch of what might have been the original doorway. Variations in wall thicknesses and floor levels also point to an

33. View along the Corso il Rossellino to the Piazza Pio II and the Palazzo Vescovile. The Palazzo Piccolomini is on the right, and the Palazzo Ammannati to the left.

agglutinative history, as do the many putlog holes along the piazza and Corso il Rossellino facades, which may indicate the presence of *sporti* connected with the old Priors' Palace. Again, the second-story window to the right of the entrance, which is smaller than its fellows and has a flatter arch, may point to a pre-Renaissance fabric. Vice-Chancellor Borgia apparently had no intention of investing more than was absolutely necessary to satisfy the passion of his pope. If indeed he did simply remake the old Priors' residence, work would have been restricted to dressing up the exterior with new door and window frames, raising the third story of the building (distinguishable through a change in the color and texture of the stonework two courses below the upper story), and vaulting some ground floor rooms.

Until recently this was the interpretation given to the physical evidence presented by the building. Several authorities now have begun to doubt this thesis.[8] They prefer to see the arches above the door and windows as structural and not residual, pointing to Sienese building practices (even if Rossellino were the designer, the actual builders would have been masons from the Sienese region, e.g., Porrina). These scholars attribute the arches to the workmen's lack of experience in handling the new trabeated window frames. According to this view, the exterior of the palace dates from the time of Pope Pius and the change in fabric in the upper story is explained by positing two phases of quattrocento construction.

Certainly, dating the Palazzo Vescovile entirely to the Pientine intervention has certain advantages. It would allow for the existence of a smaller medieval Priors' Palace, which would not have impinged upon the rear of an east-west oriented Romanesque church on the site of the present cathedral. It also would allow us to attribute the irregularly disposed windows of the piazza facade not to some haphazard Gothic arrangement but to deliberate plan. Their positioning, with increasing distance placed between them, produces distinct perspectival effects.[9] When the building is viewed from the western entrance to the piazza, the disposition of the windows visually forces the building back upon an imaginary line that "corrects" its actual oblique alignment. Seen from the southwest corner of the piazza or from the doors of the cathedral, the diminishing march of windows has the effect of lengthening the front of the building. If this perspectival interpretation is more fact than fancy or accident, then such a sophisticated scheme would complement the vertical perspectives noted in the Piccolomini Palace and in the Bishop's Palace itself. The systems of architectural perspective applied to both palaces, furthermore, would seem to echo Bernardo Rossellino's extraordinary use of perspective in the entrance passage of the Palazzo Spinelli in Florence.[10] These several instances point to the architect's unusual interest in rather advanced techniques of illusionism, most visibly displayed in the layout of the cathedral square in Pienza.

The Palazzo Comunale

In his *Commentarii,* Pius said that "he bought also other houses of the citizens on the side of the square opposite the church and gave orders that they should be razed and a third palace erected with a portico, a great hall, chambers, store-rooms, a tower with bells and a clock, and a prison. He intended this to be the residence of the magistrates of the city and a meeting place for councils of the citizens. He himself hired the workmen and contributed a large part of the expense, wishing the square to be surrounded by four noble buildings (Plate 34)."[11]

Although the actual commission for the Communal Palace was not given until the pope's visit in 1462, the new civic center was probably part of the original project proposal. The papal expense accounts reveal that the first purchase of property to that end was made on 12 August 1462, when a barber named Matteo was given payment "for his house sold to His Holiness in order to construct the house for the Commune of Pienza." On 2 September of the same year a Ser Tommaso da Terni received a sum "for a house sold to Our Lord at Pienza for the mayor and magistrates and the [town] chamberlain." Another "house located in Pienza," was bought on 23 September, "in order to make the place of the Commune."[12] These three houses were the ones that, according to the pope, were to be razed to make way for the city hall.

It would appear that the Communal Palace was constructed as an isolated block, for those structures abutting it to the east seem to be of comparatively modern date. In its former freestanding state, the Palazzo Comunale would have assumed a more pivotal role between the civic space of the Piazza del Mercato (the modern Piazza di Spagna) and the ecclesiastical and hierarchical parvis of the Piazza Pio II. If we think of the building

as standing in the middle of a single spatial area formed by the combination of the two squares, then the similarly sited Palazzo Pretorio in San Giovanni Val d' Arno, so familiar to Rossellino through family and business ties, comes immediately to mind.

Documents previously cited which included payments for both the campanile of the cathedral and the Communal Palace prove that the Rossellino workshop was responsible for the construction of this new "palace of the Commune of Pienza." According to these accounts, the commission was given on 2 September 1462 and the construction work continued until mid August 1463. Two entries in the account books of the Vatican, dated 5 and 19 February 1464, show that the pope's desire to have a clock installed in the tower of the Palazzo Comunale was also realized.[13] The clock was apparently bought in Rome for fifteen ducats, and a certain Arigo de Anfordia was sent with it to Pienza to supervise the installation.

The Communal Palace is a rectangular building two stories in height with a pitched roof. A square tower is attached to its southeastern corner.[14] The facade faces onto the cathedral square and is divided into four bays. In the first story, three of these bays are given over to an open loggia whose arches spring from squat, unfluted Ionic columns with an exaggerated entasis. The degree of swelling is unusual for the Renaissance and, of course, entasis is in itself improper in the Ionic order. Its use here is deliberate, however, and not naive, for the energy it suggests announces the active life of communal government and echoes the dynamics of the trapezoid of the adjacent piazza. The bold sculpting

34. The Palazzo Comunale. The house formerly associated with Gregorio Lolli is on the left, and a corner of the Palazzo Vescovile at the right.

of the capitals matches the almost "archaic" proportions of the column shafts. The left-hand column of the first bay and the corresponding column of the return arch are set against a pier at the corner of the loggia. This pier provides a structural and visual support at the angle of the building, and its combination with the columns of the arcade marks one of the first attempts to solve the "corner-support" problem that had marred the effectiveness of such earlier Renaissance courtyard and cloister designs as Michelozzo's *cortile* in the Palazzo Medici and Rossellino's own Spinelli Cloister at Santa Croce. The L-shaped corner support used for the Palazzo Comunale in Pienza reappeared in a more integrated form with attached half columns at the Loggia Rucellai in Florence (also possibly associated with the Rossellino shop) and, then, in even more sophisticated fashion in the *cortile* of the Palazzo Ducale at Urbino and the Castello di San Giorgio at Mantua and in a host of later Renaissance cloisters and courtyards.

Two roundheaded doorways open off the cross-vaulted loggia, one leading into a room on the ground floor and the other, by means of a dogleg staircase, to the piano nobile. Above the mezzanine landing of this staircase is a lunette vault that springs from plain triangular corbels. The *sala di consiglio* (town council chambers), built above the loggia and overlooking the piazza and the dominating presence of the cathedral, is the principal room on this main floor. A strange optical effect can be noticed by those sitting beneath the wood-beamed ceiling of this chamber. The great pontifical Piccolomini crest sculpted in the pediment of the cathedral seems to loom

larger than life just outside the windows although it is in reality some thirty meters distant (Plate 35). Any magistrate or council member who happened to glance out the room's *bifore* saw not blue sky but the clear and constant presence of Pienza's *padrone;* it was borne in upon the council that decisions were to be made in accordance with Piccolomini wishes. On the north wall of the chamber is a fresco *Madonna and Child with Saints Vito, Modesto, Sano, and Matteo,* by a Sienese artist in the circle of Vecchietta. In its position across from the bulk of the cathedral, it seems almost a projection of that building's holy patroness into the seat of civic authority. The council members would have sat flanked by images of the town's spiritual protectors and the *stemma* of its present overlords.

A wide entablature separates the facade of the Communal Palace into two stories. The architrave is reduced to a simple flat band and the cornice to a thin projection. Twin-lighted windows framed in travertine occupy the four bays of the upper story. The details of these windows are typical of other windows Rossellino had designed throughout his career. The colonnettes have capitals of the type found in the Spinelli Cloister and associated with the Rossellino shop from midcentury on.

The facade of this stone and brick building was stuccoed and richly decorated with sgraffiti.[15] These decorations are not fanciful but complement the architectural features of the palace. The surface of the wall is treated with a simulated rustication, and imitation voussoirs follow the arcading of the loggia. The entablature frieze that separates the stories is decorated with simulated festoons draped from candelabra. In the

35. View through a window of the Council Chamber of the Palazzo Comunale.

upper story, the bays are divided by sgraffito pilaster strips in a manner reminiscent of Brunelleschi's intended treatment for the front of the Hospital of the Innocents.[16] The space within each of the mock pilasters is filled with a stylized acanthus plant sprouting from an urn. Another frieze, this time displaying an anthemion motif, completes the facade just below the roofline. In its richness, this decoration recalls the classically florid style used by Alberti at the Tempio Malatestiano and later at San Andrea. How much of the sgraffito work on the Palazzo Comunale is original is unclear, since the facade and its decoration were restored in 1900.[17]

The bell tower grows out of the core of the building in much the same fashion as does the campanile of the cathedral across the way. Above the line of the roof as the tower ascends, there are two cornices: one encircles the tower below the windows of the bell chamber and the other serves as a visual impost for the arches of those windows. The tower originally terminated in a strongly projecting battlement; the set-back tower that now tops the structure was not added until 1599.[18] Sources for the design of the tower of the Palazzo Comunale can be found in that of nearby Buonconvento and in Michelozzo's tower (completed in May 1459 by Checho di Meo) for the town hall in Montepulciano.[19] It would seem more probable, however, that Rossellino had the tower of the Bargello in Florence in mind. As in the case of the campanile of Pienza's cathedral, Rossellino had selected a model with which he had had almost daily familiarity, and in fact, the juxtaposition of the two towers in Pienza is

not unlike the visual relationship between the towers of the Bargello and the Badia in Florence.

The Palazzo Comunale of Pienza shares stylistic traits with a number of medieval city halls in Tuscany: those of Monticiano, Montalcino, and Buonconvento, for instance. This link to Italian tradition serves to integrate the town's new governmental center with the continuity of civic life in Corsignano/Pienza. There is, however, an abundance of new concepts and features at work here, as well, including the Ionic columns, the corner support for the loggia, and the lushly antiquizing sgraffito decoration of the facade. It is this combination of many separate elements which gives the building its distinction. Furthermore, as in Montalcino, San Gimignano, and Montepulciano, and in Florence itself, these elements often had been present as part of the civic statement, but the loggia either had been a detached structure (Montalcino, Montepulciano, Florence) or positioned in clear architectural separation (San Gimignano). At Pienza, loggia and palace are united and this unity, coupled with the more obvious decorative features, gives to the Palazzo Comunale of Pienza its characteristic Renaissance harmony.[20]

With the construction of the Palazzo Comunale and the commitment of the vice-chancellor to build the Palazzo Vescovile, Pius II realized his wish of having his new piazza at Pienza "surrounded by four noble buildings." The pope's ambitions for his native town were not at an end, however. Cathedral and family palace had been built, and work on the splendid square and the other principal civic and ecclesiastic buildings adjoining it was well in hand; Pius now turned his attention to the rebuilding of other portions of the community.

"Other magnificent houses," Pope Pius tells us in the *Commentarii*, "were built in the city. The Cardinal of Arras erected a large and lofty palace behind the Vice-Chancellor's. Next to him the treasurer and after him Gregorio Lolli laid their foundations. First of all the Cardinal of Pavia built a most convenient and beautiful square house, covering an entire block. The Cardinal of Mantua bought a lot with a view to building as did also Tommaso, a papal official, and [other] officials of the court, and many of the townspeople tore down old houses and built new ones, so that nowhere did the aspect of the town remain unchanged."[21] As was noted in Chapter 1, these plans may have been set into motion as early as two summers before. Among the most energetic in complying with the pope's wishes was his trusted confidant, Giacomo (Jacopo) Ammannati, the cardinal of Pavia (called della Papiense).

The Palazzo Ammannati

Giacomo Ammannati (1422–1479) of Lucca was a member of Pope Pius' inner circle of close friends and advisers. The pope described him in the *Commentarii* as "a Lucchese by birth but a Sienese by courtesy, adopted into the Piccolomini family by the Pope himself, who had been charmed by his cleverness."[22] Ammannati's humanist credentials were impeccable, for he had been a pupil of Guarino Veronese at Ferrara and was later schooled in Florence under Leonardo Bruni and Carlo Marsuppini.[23] Like

Pius, Ammannati had found employment as a secretary to Cardinal Domenico Capranica. His service brought him to Rome in the 1450s and to eventual appointment as an apostolic secretary under Pope Calixtus III. Ammannati continued in that position under Pope Pius until his elevation to the purple in December of 1461. In his interests and his humanist background, Ammannati was a kindred spirit to his papal patron. He shared the Piccolomini pope's delight in the simple joys of country living and the bucolic surroundings of Pienza.[24] Unlike the other cardinals, Giacomo Ammannati truly enjoyed the little Italian hill town and continued to return there long after Pius' death. Ammannati's rustic tastes are confirmed in a delightful letter written 12 August 1468 to another of the late pope's intimates, Gregorio Lolli. Ammannati speaks of his resolve in "foresaking all other places, to delight in Pienza alone," and he vividly describes the community, the pastoral setting of the Val d'Orcia, and the scenic wonders of the place. More to our point, Ammannati also gives Lolli a brief description of his residence in Pienza: "There I have built two beautiful lodgings. One is for myself and for my few close friends; the other is used by my household. Both of these have the widest view around and are beautifully planned for the delights of summer weather."[25] This passage from Ammannati's own hand, coupled with the record in the Sienese *gabelle* of his purchase of property in 1460 and Pope Pius' description of the cardinal's palace in the *Commentarii*, provides us with valuable insight with which to analyze the Palazzo Ammannati today.

The cardinal's "most convenient and

beautiful square house, covering an entire block," was erected on the Corso il Rossellino opposite the main entrance to the Palazzo Piccolomini (Plate 36). Its location symbolized the Cardinal's close relationship to his papal benefactor. Ammannati laid his plans for the building very early on, demonstrating an intention that perhaps encouraged the pope to award him the cardinal's hat a year later. On 18 September 1460, on the occasion of Pope Pius' return to Corsignano/Pienza, Ammannati purchased two adjoining houses and a garden to their rear from the brothers Paolo and Francesco di Domenico Richa, another house from a carpenter from Montefolonico named Magio d'Agnolo, and yet another house from a Leonardo di Francesco.[26] According to the sums paid, about twenty-five ducats each, all four houses must have been of about the same size and condition. Apparently, construction of Ammannati's residence kept pace with the building of the papal palace across the street. Pius tells us in the *Commentarii* that Ammannati's palace was the first of the curial residences to be built in Pienza, and that statement is supported in a letter of 19 August 1462 written by the young Cardinal Francesco Gonzaga of Mantua, in which Gonzaga mentions "the most reverend monsignor of Pavia who already has built his house."[27]

The Palazzo Ammannati appears to have been constructed in two distinct stages, the first being the "square house, covering an entire block" mentioned by Pius, which the cardinal had said was reserved for his personal use and for that of his closest friends, and the second stage being a neighboring building built sometime between 1462 and 1468 and

intended to house the members of the cardinal's household. The first structure, whose squareness matches Pius' description probably incorporated the sites (and, perhaps, the actual buildings) of the two houses of Paolo and Francesco di Domenico; the present *cortile* of the Palazzo Ammannati probably corresponds to the garden located behind their two houses. This portion of the palace, the corners of which are defined by sandstone quoins, has a facade along the Corso il Rossellino some 15-1/4 meters long and 14 meters high. Simple string courses divide the elevation into three stories that, typically for Pienza, diminish in height upwards. A single travertine-framed arched doorway is set in the center of the ground floor (the two flanking shop entrances may be of more recent date). Stone benches running along the front of the palace provide seating for passersby and a visual base for the building. The second and third stories both contain a row of evenly spaced cross windows (the mullions and transoms of those in the second story have been removed to permit more modern glazing). Single cross windows are set in the two upper stories of the side of the palace which fronts the cathedral square.

As in the case of the Palazzo Vescovile, which this part of the facade so much resembles, there is no actual articulation of the wall surface. The facade of the Palazzo Ammannati was enlivened, however, through the extensive use of sgraffiti, which provide a rich fictive membering. Simulated channeled rustication adds an apparent texture to the surface of the wall, and the facade is divided into three bays by paired (but widely separated) pilaster strips, also executed in sgraffito. These pilasters, much

36. The Palazzo Ammannati as seen from the Piazza Pio II.

like the sgraffito pilasters at the Spinelli Palace in Florence, are decorated with entwined acanthus tendrils. Sgraffito friezes appear beneath the two cornices separating the stories. The lower frieze contains a continuous garland motif, and that below the upper cornice makes use of an anthemion of palmette and acanthus blossoms. A third frieze runs across the top of the windows of the third story carrying an anthemion of palmette and lotus blossoms. In the lower story, a band of *opus reticulatum*, also done in sgraffito, provides a podium above the benches. Although it runs, as it were, behind the pilasters, this unusual motif links the design of this palace with that of the Palazzo Piccolomini across the way. A stone block bearing the papal shield was set above the entrance portal, and Ammannati's own crest appears in each of the flanking bays of the first story.

From the entrance portal, a barrel-vaulted corridor leads to an irregularly shaped little *cortile* at the rear of the palace (Plate 37). An arcade runs around two sides of this courtyard. The arches rest upon Ionic columns, one of the capitals of which bears the arms of the Piccolomini, another reminder of Ammannati's adoptive affiliation with that family and with his patron. The variety of the corbels supporting the cross vaults of the loggias points to the possible medieval origins of the *cortile* as well as to the heterogeneous sources used in the Renaissance remodeling. Two of the corbels are of the old-fashioned shield type; three are triangular; another is Ionic; and yet another is of the Composite sort used in the Piccolomini Palace and may well be an "extra" from that project. Traces of sgraffito masonry

show how the walls surrounding the courtyard were treated in the Renaissance conversion of this garden area. The original presence of an upper gallery is indicated by a walled up Ionic column visible above the western arcade.

The front rooms opening off the passage leading to the *cortile* have lunette vaults springing from corbels with flat profiles and fluted necks above triangular calathoi. They are identical to the variety used in a house along Pienza's "Curial Row," identified here as having been built for the papal treasurer.[28] The upper stories of the Palazzo Ammannati have wooden ceilings, the beams of which have subsequently been repainted. A fireplace in the room at the southeast corner of the piano nobile is of especial interest. It is handsomely carved from what appears to be the gray Florentine sandstone called *pietra serena*. Across its lintel runs the inscription, in bold classical lettering: ENEAS · PICOLOMINEVS. Below is a shield bearing the coat of arms of Giacomo Ammannati.

As already noted, today's Palazzo Ammannati is not the simple square house described by Pope Pius, for it is conjoined by a tall belvedere tower. The most striking feature of the present building, this tower extends the palace westward eleven meters to the corner of the Via Condotti and then nineteen meters back down that street to the north. That this portion of the palace was an addition to the building as built between 1460 and 1462 is confirmed not only by the testimony of the papal memoirs and the cardinal's letter to Lolli in 1468 but also by a number of structural features. The ground plan of the palace shows a long barrel-vaulted cor-

37. The *cortile* of the Palazzo Ammannati.

ridor snaking like a reversed **S** through the palace, bisecting the building and marking the division between the older and newer parts. This corridor was, in fact, at one time an alleyway, a continuation of the present Vicolo San Pasquale, which ran from the Via della Mura to the Corso il Rossellino and perhaps even continued to the Via Gozzante through the site upon which was built the Palazzo Piccolomini. That this passage once was a public way, open to the sky, is demonstrated by a number of physical peculiarities still detectable today. First, although cellars exist beneath the "original" palace and the tower, they are interrupted by the line of the corridor, which has no such basement. Second, the western flank of the older unit originally was given a coating of sgraffito masonry, extensive traces of which are to be seen in the staircase to the belvedere loggia; this decoration would have been appropriate only in an exposed location. Third, a decisive break in the fabric runs down the front of the palace between the two sections of the building and another vertical line runs parallel to it at a distance of about two and a half meters to the left. The space between these two divisions marks the width of the old alleyway and the palace corridor that came to replace it (Plate 38). Evidently Ammannati secured permission to extend the upper stories of his residence across the old alley sometime between 1462 and 1468 but, as is clearly shown by an immured arch in the lower story, it continued to function as a vaulted public passage for some years thereafter. A similar tunnel can be observed in modern Pienza where the Via Chiocarella enters the Corso il Rossellino. Finally, it also should be noted that there is no trace on the tower portion of the Palazzo Ammannati of the sgraffito work with which the core of the building was so lavishly decorated, nor is the line of stone seats continued across the front of the tower.

What does bind the two units of the Palazzo Ammannati together is the continuation of the string courses across the facade and the use of cross windows, two in each of the upper stories, matching those in the older part of the building. Of the two round-arched doorways in the tower, the one opening into the alleyway/corridor is probably new; the one at the corner appears to be original, although the present frame is of relatively recent date.

There is little agreement about how to date the belvedere story of the tower, which rises some seven meters above the third-floor level of the palace. Across the top of the tower are four arcades that spring from brick piers (and not the more common columns of the Florentine *altana*) distinguished by the use of moldings to define Tuscan-style pseudo-capitals. This arcading continues along the flanks of the tower with a line of six arched openings running down the western side. The severely classical character of this belvedere seems oddly out of place in mid-fifteenth-century Tuscany, so much so that later datings ranging from the sixteenth to the eighteenth century have been suggested. Admittedly, belvederes of this type were foreign to central Italy at the time of Pienza's rebuilding but so too were cross windows.[29] Both motifs were, in fact, importations from the Roman region.

Connections with the architectural vernacular of fifteenth-century Rome are emphatic.[30] Among easily recognizable

38. Detail of the facade of the Palazzo Ammannati showing the position of the original alleyway.

possible sources for the belvedere loggia of the Palazzo Ammannati are the palace of Cardinal d'Estouteville at the Church of Sant' Apollinare of ca. 1440–1450; that of Cardinal Capranica of about the same date; the palace of Cardinal Pietro Barbo of ca. 1455, which was greatly enlarged into the Palazzo Venezia from 1465; and the Borgia Tower, whose presence may have been included in Nicholas V's plans for the papal palace in the Vatican.[31] The incorporation of such a tower-with-a-view in the Palazzo Ammannati could suggest a role for Bernardo Rossellino in the building's design even though he probably would have been dead before its execution. Such features as the belvedere and the cross window would have been familiar to him but not necessarily to local Sienese stonemasons or building contractors such as Porrina. Rossellino would have been quite familiar with the corner tower and loggia from his work in Rome in the 1450s. The loping line of severe arcades in the belvedere of the Palazzo Ammannati is also reminiscent of the arcades employed by Alberti along the sides of the Tempio Malatestiano in Rimini. Again, a connection with Rossellino is indicated.

That Roman architectural ideas such as cross windows and belvederes should have appeared in Tuscan Pienza was both natural and to be expected. Pienza, after all, was a city rebuilt by papal decree by members of the Roman Curia who carried to the little hill town many of the concepts of the big city. The use of the belvedere was also a feature that would have offered Ammannati, who had an expressed love of nature, a vantage point above the powerful bulk of the Palazzo Piccolomini from which to enjoy many a splendid sunset. The cardinal's enjoy-

ment of his Pientine palace is well expressed in a letter he sent to Cardinal Francesco Gonzaga in 1468: "I have come to Pienza and am in my house which was built at one time in honor of Pius and now offers me the most agreeable sojourn. . . . If you ask me what I do, I'll quickly tell you: I am wrapped up in my books; I read and write and take walks. I contemplate the blessed remembrances of Pius which are impressed all over the hillside."[32]

The Curial Row

Stretched out in a line behind the Palazzo Vescovile are three palaces alluded to by Pope Pius in his *Commentarii*. These buildings, together with the Palazzo Vescovile, constitute what might be termed the "Curial Row" of Pienza (Plate 39). If we accept Pius' description at face value and assume that he listed these "other magnificent houses" in their physical order and not according to *when* they were constructed, a few of their original owners can be identified with some confidence. The first of these residences is even designated by the coat of arms of its builder, Jean Jouffroy (1412–1473), the cardinal of Arras (or Atrebatense in Italian) and Albi.[33]

The Palazzo Jouffroy

The Palazzo Jouffroy, or Atrebatense, was constructed for a Frenchman whom Vespasiano da Bisticci characterized as "highly learned in theology and in the seven liberal arts and most eloquent" but whom Pope Pius was later to describe as having "an ingrained hatred of the Italian race" and who "had long been hostile to

39. View of the Ciglio Quarter from the tower of the Palazzo Comunale along the rooftops of the Curial Row. The Palazzo Jouffroy is at the lower right; the Treasurer's Palace is in the middle; and the Palazzo Lolli lies beyond.

the Pope." He was, according to Pius, a man "whose distinguished gifts of learning, intellect, and almost superhuman memory were sullied by avarice, ambition, and inconstancy."[34] Despite, and perhaps because of, some of these less than noble traits, Jouffroy was persuaded to erect "a large and lofty palace behind the Vice-Chancellor's."[35]

Aside from the *Commentarii,* there are two documentary references that would seem to pertain to the construction of the Palazzo Jouffroy. The most significant of these appeared in the deliberations of that great Sienese charitable institution, the Hospital of Santa Maria della Scala, 12 July 1462. The entry, concerning the disposition of the institution's hospital building in Pienza states that the French cardinal, "having in the city of Pienza . . . begun a beautiful and noble building," wished to purchase the adjoining hospital building belonging to Santa Maria della Scala. Presumably, Jouffroy needed the site for part of the palace he was having constructed. The hospital committee decided, in consideration of the pope's desires to beautify Pienza and because their hospital building there was now "much crowded by the buildings newly made in the same place at one side or the other," to sell their property to the cardinal. In return, Jouffroy was to pay Santa Maria della Scala one hundred florins and provide a suitable site in Pienza for a new hospital.[36]

The exact location of the Palazzo Jouffroy has been the subject of some debate. In the past, Pius' testimony that Jouffroy "post vicecancellarium . . . aedificavit" was interpreted as a reference to when and not to where the palace was built. Jouffroy's residence, accordingly, used to be identified with a house across from the Palazzo Piccolomini located on the northeast corner of the Via Condotti, perhaps because that building has the only "Gothic" windows in Pienza, windows that could be said to "look French."[37] That building, now most often associated with the name of Salomone Piccolomini, will be discussed later.

Although the July deliberations of the Hospital of Santa Maria della Scala had been published previously in connection with the Palazzo Jouffroy, Armando Schiavo was the first to draw attention to the passage that referred to the old hospital as being crowded from more than one side. This description, according to Schiavo, was incompatable with a building situated on a corner and he rejected the older designation. He preferred, instead, to identify Jouffroy's palace with a row house located along the Corso il Rossellino between the Bishop's Palace and the building at the corner of the Corso and the Via della Fortuna, generally called the Palazzo Gonzaga.[38] Enzo Carli, tentatively accepting Schiavo's argument, pointed out that the passage in the hospital's deliberations referred specifically to the crowding of the hospital building in Pienza and not to Jouffroy's palace, which he thought the cardinal already had completed.[39]

The problem is resolved by a more careful examination of the properties involved and their physical characteristics. Schiavo's map of Pienza shows three palaces (the Palazzi Vescovile, Jouffroy, and Gonzaga) in the block between the Piazza Pio II and the Via della Fortuna.[40] This reconstruction assumed, as did all historians of the town, that the Bishop's Palace extended farther along the Corso il Rossellino than it actually did.[41] The mistake is understandable because the string courses of the Bishop's Palace continue across the facade of the building to its rear. This latter structure, however, was not originally connected with the Bishop's Palace. It was, in fact, the Palace of Cardinal Jean Jouffroy (Plate 40).[42]

The two-phase construction of this palace, indicated in the 12 July 1462 deliberations can be seen in both the external and internal features of the building. The facade along the Corso il Rossellino is twenty meters long and is composed of regular blocks of local sandstone. String courses, continued from the adjoining Palazzo Vescovile, divide the facade into three stories of decreasing height. A round-arched doorway, set at the extreme right-hand side of the lower story, probably served as the original entrance of the palace as completed. The other three doorways seem to be of recent date as do three of the windows in the lower story. The remaining two windows, larger in size and with beveled sides, may be original. A row of five aligned windows appears in each of the two upper stories. Here the original break between the two buildings composing the present palace is evidenced by the wider spaces between the second and third windows from the left. Evidently the house on which Jouffroy had begun work was two windows wide (about eight meters); the property received from the Sienese hospital allowed him to expand his new palace three additional window bays westward to abut the rear of the Palazzo Vescovile. Certainly this western part of the Palazzo Jouffroy meets the description of a building crowded "at one side or the other."

While all five windows of the third story are roundheaded. the distinction between the two parts of the palace is preserved, inadvertently perhaps, in the window types of the piano nobile. The three western windows are roundheaded but the two windows to the east are cross windows, the assumption being that these cross windows were in the "beautiful and noble building" first built by the cardinal. Actually, traces of arches run above and behind the frames of these cross windows, indicating that all the windows on this and the floor above were roundheaded at first and that Jouffroy, at some later point, decided to harmonize his windows with those of the Palazzo Vescovile; it was an intention carried out only in part. Curiously, the easternmost cross window is of sandstone while its neighbor is made of travertine. It is on the travertine lintel that the coat of arms of the building's owner appears. In his final plans for the facade, with the unifying effect of continued string courses and the projected use of cross windows, Jouffroy obviously intended to blend his palace visually with that of the vice-chancellor. Along the base of the palace, the fabric shows traces of what once might have been a continuous bench. It was perhaps planned to continue all of these common motifs along the length of the Curial Row, thereby converting individual palaces into a disciplined line of elegant row houses displaying hierarchically subordinated features associated with the great papal palace that visually terminates the western end of the Corso il Rossellino.

One would expect a hospital of the period, even one in such a provincial location, to have had a service courtyard or at least a portico. The *cortile* of the Palazzo Jouffroy, long considered part of

40. View westward along the Corso il Rossellino toward the Palazzo Piccolomini. On the immediate left is the corner of the palace of the papal treasurer, followed by the palace of Cardinal Jouffroy, and then the flank of the Palazzo Vescovile.

the Palazzo Vescovile, seems to have been reworked from just such a feature (Plate 41).[43] In fact some its architectural elements may have survived from its originally more public role.

It is a rather unusual feature of this building that the *cortile* is not reached by a passageway but, instead, through a large hall set, like the courtyard, along a transverse axis. Its three cross vaults are supported by corbels typical of the Renaissance structures in Pienza, either Composite, like those used in the Palazzo Piccolomini, or the more florid type introduced by Bernardo Rossellino at the Palazzo Spinelli in Florence and found in Pienza in the Palazzo Vescovile and on the well in the Piazza Pio II. The far side of this room opens onto the courtyard through arcades supported by two columns in the innovative Tuscan Doric order also used to frame the passages of the papal palace. The Tuscan Doric is used again at the ends of this arcade, but strangely enough, the capitals rest here upon old-fashioned attached octagonal columns. The courtyard, in which stands an octagonal wellhead, is defined on its northern and southern sides by three arcades and on the western end by a single arched opening. The southern loggia is quite narrow, functioning more as an internal portico for the two vaulted rooms lying behind it. Along the walls of this loggia, the narrow cross vaults spring from simple triangular corbels that may predate the Palazzo Jouffroy. The two responding columns in the arcade have rather curious capitals, allied in their medieval proportions but differing in design. One of them is a flattened out rendition of the Ionic, and its companion is distinctly archaizing in character with a ball and leaf at the corners. This capital might be thought a holdover from the old hospital were it not for the lily that adorns it.[44] The lily suggests a more modern date, contemporary with Jouffroy's project, for here in Pienza it is far more likely to signify the fleur-de-lis of the palace's French occupant than the *giglio* of Florence.

A door in the eastern wall of the *cortile* leads into the earlier section of the palace and the principal staircase. The midlevel turning of the stairs is cross vaulted, its three vaults springing from decidedly old-fashioned *foglia d'acqua* corbels and an attached column from whose smooth-leaf capital stare down little medieval heads. Whether these elements are original, relocated, or from a later period of revival is uncertain. What is clear is that the hodgepodge of motifs throughout the palace, ranging from the medievally *retardataire* to the classically progressive seems well suited to the tastes of a French cardinal living in the midst of the Italian Renaissance.

The Treasurer's Palace

The name of the papal official for whom the next palace (at 38 Corso il Rossellino and now the property of the Simonelli family) in the Curial Row was built is not at all certain.[45] Unfortunately, Pius' choice of words in his description of this and the next palace—"diende thesaurarius post eum Gregorius Lollius fundamenta iecit"—is rather vague. This phrase can be interpreted in two ways, either sequentially, as "next the treasurer [and] after him Gregorio Lolli laid his foundation," or spatially, as "from that place [the Palazzo Jouffroy] the treasurer [and] after him Gregorio Lolli laid his foundation." The difference in possible

41. The courtyard of the Palazzo Jouffroy.

meaning allows us to think either that the papal treasurer began building his residence after Jouffroy had started work on his or that the treasurer's palace was built next door to Jouffroy's. Now that it is clear that four palaces rather than three made up the block between the Piazza Pio II and the Via della Fortuna, Pius' words can be taken in the more literal sense and the better interpretation would seem to be the spatial one.

But who was the treasurer of whom Pius spoke? Despite the fact that his was an official position of considerable importance within the Vatican hierarchy, he has not been easy to identify. The names of both Ambrogio Spannocchi and Niccolò Forteguerri da Pistoia have been suggested.[46] The Sienese banker Spannocchi was, however, one of the pope's personal financial administrators and not the treasurer of the church.[47] Forteguerri, whose name has recently been put forward, is a viable alternative.[48] He was a distant maternal relative of Pius and a powerful figure in the Curia. Holding the bishoprics of both Teano and Santa Cecilia, he was elevated to a cardinalate in March 1460 and served as captain general of the papal forces. More to the point, he also held the office of vice-treasurer from November 1458 to 1460. He never became treasurer, however, and had laid down all financial responsibilities before the time in question. Logically, he could not have been the *thesaurarius* described in the *Commentarii* of Pope Pius.

Additional possibles include other members of the pope's actual and adoptive family: Niccolò Picoluomo de Piccolomini, whose name is on the pope's crusade accounts of 1463–1464 as one of three private treasurers, and Alessandro de Mirabelli-Piccolomini da Napoli.[49] Mirabelli would seem a good possibility, for he was Pius' majordomo and served him as a private treasurer as well. In 1458 he was given control of the *Tesoreria di Roma* and the *Depositeria della Camera*. Pius held Mirabelli in such high regard that he even adopted him into his family and appointed him prefect of Frascati. Yet neither Niccolò Picoluomo nor Mirabelli ever held the official title of *thesaurarius*. In any case, one would have expected Pius to have identified Forteguerri, Niccolò Picoluomo, or Mirabelli—Piccolomini family members all— by name.

Instead, two lesser-known individuals present themselves as more plausible candidates. One is Giliforte dei Buonconti da Pisa, who held the position of *camerario apostolico del papa* from 1448 and who succeeded Forteguerri as vice-treasurer in 1460.[50] Buonconti, in fact, was advanced to the position of treasurer in September 1461 and held the title until 12 August 1462. Consequently, he was *thesaurarius* during much of the time Pius was in Pienza on his protracted inspection tour. Why he left the office is not known. I hope, for his own sake and for the sake of my argument, it was not death that relieved him of his duties. The other possibility is, of course, Buonconti's successor, a certain Antonio Laziosi da Forli.[51] Laziosi had been a member of the *clerici camerae apostolicae* and was given the post of *officium thesaurarius regens* on 26 September 1462. After 1 October 1462, he is identified in the records as *pape generalis thesaurarius*. Thus both Buonconti and Laziosi held the post of treasurer during part of the period in question. Which of the two did the pope mean? The balance tilts toward Giliforte

Buonconti because Laziosi was not given the title of treasurer until the end of September and because Buonconti's name appears in the records of the Sienese *gabelle* as the purchaser of property in Pienza, and Laziosi's does not.[52]

As shown in the preceding chapter, the houses bought by Buonconti for Pope Pius in 1460 probably occupied the site of the future Palazzo Canonica. At the same time, however, Buonconti also bought for his own use at the cost of seventy-two ducats a house in the same *quartiere dela ripa al Ciglio*.[53] The specified location would nicely fit that of the palace of the treasurer, and so Giliforte dei Buonconti da Pisa can tentatively but with some degree of confidence be identified as the builder of the treasurer's palace.[54]

Actually, the Palazzo Buonconti, as we may now call it, probably represents more a remodeling of an existing structure than an entirely new construction (Plate 42). The palace is some two meters higher than the adjoining Palazzo Jouffroy and is in line with the elevation of the building to its east. Compared to its immediate neighbors, the exterior of this row house appears rather undistinguished and even incomplete.

Unlike the Palazzo Jouffroy, which was built of sandstone blocks, the fabric of the Palazzo Buonconti is brick and stone rubble unenlivened by either string courses or cross windows. Traces of stucco upon which was drawn a pattern of sgraffito masonry do reveal, however, that the front of the building once looked far more finished than it does today. Four unframed rectangular windows are set in alignment in each of the two upper stories. The ground story contains the facade's one notable element, a hand-

some rectangular travertine doorframe placed at the extreme left-hand side of the palace. Its typically "progressive" *quattrocentesco* design features a wide cyma bordered by a fillet that turns in at the base and a torus band that follows the inner perimeter of jambs and lintel. A large hall lies immediately beyond the entrance. The lunette vaults of this room rest upon corbels with flat profiles and fluted necks similar to those in the ground-floor chambers of the Palazzo Ammannati. Across the hall from the entrance, a staircase gives access to the upper stories, and a barrel-vaulted passageway on the right leads to the rear of the palace. On the western side of the Palazzo Buonconti two rooms abut the party wall of the Palazzo Jouffroy. Between them is a tiny *cortile*, really more light well than courtyard. Behind the palace a walled garden was laid out overlooking the city wall and the Orcia Valley below, perhaps a miniaturized imitation of the *giardino pensile* of the Palazzo Piccolomini. Today, the Palazzo Buonconti is united with the building to its east and so are their gardens; one assumes a wall once separated the two garden areas.

The Palazzo Lolli

The building at the corner of the Via della Fortuna (38A Corso il Rossellino, now part of the Simonelli residence), which terminates the Curial Row has long been identified with the palace of the young Cardinal Francesco Gonzaga of Mantua (Plate 42).[55] While tradition should never be lightly dismissed, there is good reason to doubt this association. The identification was recently challenged by Giancarlo Cataldi, who point-

42. View looking west along the Corso il Rossellino from the corner of the Via della Fortuna toward the Palazzo Piccolomini. Buildings in the Curial Row shown from left to right are the Palazzo Lolli (note the place of the original doorway in the light patch of masonry below the modern balcony), the Treasurer's Palace, and the Palazzo Jouffroy.

ed to the description given in the *Commentarii*, which, if taken spatially, places the palace of Gregorio Lolli next to that of the treasurer (here identified as Giliforte Buonconti).[56] In fact, the phrase used by Pius ("post eum Gregorius Lolli fundamenta iecit") parallels the one he used to describe the verified location of the Palazzo Jouffroy ("Cardinalis Atrebatensis post vicecancellarium . . . aedes aedificavit"). The word *post,* in both cases, would seem to have denoted place and not time. Just as this palace has been traditionally associated with that of Gonzaga, so the little brick house on the Piazza Pio II across from the Cathedral has been linked to Lolli (Plate 34). The existing documentation would appear to argue against this attribution, however, and to support Cataldi's conclusion that this house belonged to Tommaso del Testa Piccolomini. The appearance of this two-story house, certainly, conflicts with Lodrisio Crivelli's contemporary description of Lolli's palace: "Here your lofty building shines, . . . the highest glory of the holy home" (Appendix 1, Doc. 4). Nor does it fit with Porcellio Pandoni's description of Lolli's "palace of gold and Parian marble" (Appendix 1, Doc. 3).

On 31 August 1462 the Sienese *gabelle* recorded Lolli's purchase of two houses, one for seventy ducats from a Nanni di Piero Piccolomini and the other for thirty-two ducats from a Mariano di Thomme Menicucci. One of these properties was identified as lying in the *ciglio* quarter of Pienza, and the other was even more specifically located *al ciglio et in loco decto la ripa*. Later, on 21 October 1463, Lolli bought a cultivated field *in loco dicto il quartiere de la ripa* from a Jacopo di Niccolò Cecco di Matteo.[57] Clearly the brick house on the Piazza Pio II could not have been so described and just as clearly Lolli made his purchases in the part of town lying along the escarpment (*ripa*) in the southeastern part of town. This information, coupled with the testimony of Pius would seem to securely connect Lolli's name with the handsome building at the corner of the Via della Fortuna. We may assume, consequently, that this palace was constructed on the site of the two houses bought in August 1462, with the field acquired in October of the next year being used for its garden.

Gregorio Lolli (d. 1478) was the son of Pope Pius' maternal aunt Bartolommea, with whom the future pope had stayed during his student days in Siena.[58] Following the pursuits of a scholar, Lolli had entered papal service as a *secretario apostolico* and, along with Giacomo Ammannati, acted as confidential secretary to Pope Pius. He enjoyed the special favor of his uncle and was regarded as a papal intimate and one of the most powerful men in the Curia. Yet even for one in his position, building this palace in Pienza must have been a considerable financial burden. In the *Commentarii,* only the foundations of the building (as well as that of Giliforte dei Buonconti) are said to have been laid. The fact that property for the *giardino pensile* behind the palace was not acquired until the Autumn of 1463 attests to the slow pace of construction. Whether Lolli ever saw the project to completion, or even spent much time in Pienza, is open to question. Ammannati's letters to Lolli over the next several years are filled with descriptions of Pienza and its environs and are devoted to extolling the virtues of the place. One gets the decided impression that Lolli had little familiarity with Pienza and that Ammannati was seeking to talk his humanist colleague into trying out the rustic life.[59]

The house built for Gregorio Lolli at the corner of the Via della Fortuna balances the mass of the Palazzo Vescovile at the other end of the Curial Row. The facade on the Corso il Rossellino is divided into three stories by string courses. Three handsome cross windows, resting on the lower string course, are set at the level of the piano nobile. The middle window has since been recut to serve as the doorway to a little balcony. The three aligned windows in the upper story are small and unremarkable. Two small windows with beveled frames flanked a large doorway originally located in the middle of the ground story. This doorway has been closed up and its frame removed but its presence is revealed in the fabric. Like Buonconti's palace, Lolli's was built of brick and masonry and may have been stuccoed. Sandstone quoins define the corner of the palace. Down the line of the Via della Fortuna there are traces of several stone-framed and round-arched windows. Similar windows are also to be seen in the rear of the building.

From the original doorway of the Palazzo Lolli, a barrel-vaulted corridor led straight through the building to its rear and to the garden beyond.[60] The remains of windows in the walls of this passageway indicate its probably medieval role as an alleyway between the two houses purchased by Lolli and united into the present palace. To the east of this corridor are three rooms: that in front has a wooden ceiling; the next is cross vaulted; that in the rear has lunette vaults. On the other side of the corridor, between the front and rear rooms, was a little *cortile* with a well built against its northern wall. The walls around this former *cortile* show traces of sgraffito masonry. Since there is no staircase in the present palace, it is likely that there once was a wooden staircase with hanging balconies built against the southern wall of the courtyard. On the piano nobile, a most unusual ceiling was recently revealed in the northeast corner room. This brightly polychrome wooden-beamed ceiling boasts imaginatively carved consoles that take the forms of beasts and grotesque heads. The carvings (not yet fully authenticated) seem decidedly un-Italian and far more medievally transalpine than one would expect in Renaissance Pienza. They are rather strange characters to have once looked down upon the secretarial activities of a humanist scholar. They certainly seem to contradict the style of decoration which would have been approved by Pope Pius, who had once deplored this sort of medieval manner in which "you would find only the shapes of beasts and monsters and not of men."[61]

The Palazzo Gonzaga

With Gregorio Lolli now identified as the builder of the last of the houses in the Curial Row, Cardinal Francesco Gonzaga is left temporarily "homeless." Yet his residence in Pienza would seem to be, in many ways, the most solidly documented of all the cardinals' palaces. Not only is it mentioned in the *Commentarii,* but it is also discussed, over and over again, in the preserved correspondence of the young cardinal, his family, and his associates.[62] Additionally, purchases of property for the site have been found by Nicolas Adams in the *gabella dei contratti* of Siena.[63]

Francesco Gonzaga (1444–1483), son of the marchese Lodovico of Mantua and Barbara von Brandenburg, was presented with a cardinal's hat in December 1461 at the same time that Pope Pius also elevated Giacomo Ammannati, Bartolommeo Roverella of Ravenna, Jean Jouffroy, Louis d'Albret, and Jaime of Cardona.[64] The pope described Gonzaga as a youth "who was not yet twenty years old but looked much older and had almost the dignity and wisdom of an old man."[65] Gonzaga was having serious problems obtaining a permanent residence in Rome and probably should have avoided accompanying the papal entourage on its journey to Pienza in the summer of 1462, for his housing difficulties were only to be exacerbated.[66]

In the *Commentarii*, Pope Pius reported that the "Cardinal of Mantua bought a lot with a view to building." As seems to have been the case with all of those coming to Pienza with the pope, Gonzaga had been subjected to the papal enthusiasm and told to begin building a palace in the town immediately. As early as 19 August 1462, the young cardinal was writing to his mother of the pope's urgings and of his own protestations about the cost and his inability to bear this additional burden to his finances. Gonzaga said that Pius had requested commitments to build from both Cardinal Borgia and himself; Ammannati was quick to join the pope in pressing the issue. Cardinal Ammannati, who according to Gonzaga, had already built his house, brushed aside all claims of poverty by pointing to the reputed fortune of the young cardinal's father as the logical source of funding. Pius told Gonzaga

that no more than a thousand ducats would have to be spent and that in return he would receive the first lucrative bishopric available. Pius, Gonzaga added, expressed the wish that work should begin quickly so that he might inspect the palace the following year.[67] Giacomo d'Arezzo, the cardinal's law instructor, wrote to Gonzaga's parents three days later to express the opinion that both Borgia and Cardinal Francesco would have to acquiesce in the pope's desires, and on 26 August, the cardinal's majordomo, Bartolommeo Marasca, wrote his master's mother that Messer Thomeo [probably Tommaso del Testa Piccolomini] had told him it was the pope's intention to give the promised benefice to another unless construction on the palace got underway soon.[68] The cardinal himself wrote the same thing to his father two days later, requesting financial assistance for the project.[69]

The papal threat was at least initially effective, for Marasca traveled to Pienza on 2 September from the nearby monastery of Sant'Anna in Camprena, where Gonzaga and his retinue had been billeted. Marasca came to acquire the property upon which Gonzaga was to erect his palace. In a letter to Barbara von Brandenburg the very same day, the cardinal's majordomo said that "despite great trouble and outcry of the poor men who do not wish to sell their homes, I have obtained a block with four houses, three of them costing 178 ducats and 15 soldi. The fourth little house was given to his Reverence the Monsignor by her magnificence, my lady Laudomia, sister of the Pope, valued at 14 ducats."[70] The three actual purchases were recorded in the Sienese *gabelle*, one of the houses being described as situated *el ciglio*.[71]

That description in the Sienese records, of a house bought from a Niccolò Diedi, is the only sure documented indication of the location of the Palazzo Gonzaga, except for the logical surmise that Laudomia's house was the one she bought in August 1460, described at that time as situated in the *quartiere di castelnuovo al ciglio*. In another letter to Gonzaga's mother that day, Marasca repeated the comments of other members of the Curia that the Gonzagas were so rich that building the palace would not present a problem and that the cardinal really had no need of additional benefices. He also noted that the pope was harping on the cardinal's failure to follow through on the palace.[72]

Two days later, the cardinal wrote to his father that he was proceeding with the palace in Pienza and that he needed his parents' help with the finances. From Mantua, Marchese Lodovico wrote his son that money was in tight supply and that patience would be required. In response, the cardinal, in a letter of 18 September, wrote that work on the palace would not begin until funds were received, but at the same time, he asked his father to send him "one of your engineers to make the plans whenever the work will be commenced."[73]

Fortunately for the cardinal, papal pressure eased for a time as the pope's troubles with Sigismondo Malatesta of Rimini increased, but with the new year, Pius grew insistent once again. In a letter to his mother from Rome on 26 February 1463, the cardinal reminded her that, encouraged by promises (?) of support from his father, he had told the pope that work on the palace would be underway by spring. He again asked that a builder be sent to him from Mantua to superintend the project. Despite his assurances

to Pius, nothing was being done, as we learn in a letter dated 18 March from Marasca to Barbara von Brandenburg. Marasca reported that the pope had refused to grant Gonzaga a much-needed residence in Rome because of his increasing ire over the delays in the Pienza project. Finally, in June, Gonzaga presented the pope with plans (or a model) for the proposed house in Pienza, as we learn in a letter of 29 June 1463 to the marchesa from her faithful correspondent Marasca, who later noted, in a letter of 11 July 1463, that the pope would be much more forthcoming to her son once he was certain that work was indeed beginning "at the house in Pienza." He told her that the pope's approval of the design had been sent via Giacomo Piccolomini, one of the Pius' nephews. Marasca added that Niccolò Piccolomini had remarked, "Fine, and that house, when will it be begun?" To Marasca's promises, Niccolò responded: "Up to this point you have spoken only words; we want action. At least you can make the foundations but not a bit of building equipment is yet to be seen."[74]

Separate letters from Marasca and Giacomo d'Arezzo on 31 July indicated that the pope had grown so perturbed with Gonzaga's delays that he even thought to bar the cardinal from his presence. Clearly, something positive had to be done and in his letter Marasca reported that on the next day someone would be sent to Pienza with two hundred ducats so that the project could be begun. Cynically, Marasca suggested that costs could be held down if convicts were employed and merely paid in bread and wine.[75]

A letter from Marasca on 11 August 1463 described the pleasure with which Pope Pius had received Cardinal

Gonzaga and the news that work on the palace had started at long last. The cardinal promised the pope that he would secure another five hundred ducats and that all would be finished by the following April (1464). Marasca concluded by voicing his own opinion that "these were words which will be wanting deeds." At the end of the month (28 August), the cardinal himself wrote to his mother, "I sent someone to Pienza to begin on that house and to make provisions for doing the work." Whether anything was ever really accomplished is uncertain, for mention of the Pienza project was not made again, nor did Cardinal Francesco, so far as is known, ever return to the town. Pius died on 15 August 1464 and the pressure was off. We last hear of the Palazzo Gonzaga in December 1468, when Marchese Lodovico wrote to his son concerning the transfer of ownership of the property to Cardinal Ammannati, and again on 18 February 1469, when Lodovico protested to Ammannati that no thanks were necessary for that "beginning of the house in Pienza." The Gonzaga, apparently, were more than happy to be quit of it.[76]

If it were not for the two references in the Sienese *gabelle* locating two of the old houses acquired by Gonzaga either *el ciglio* or in the *quartiere di castelnuovo al ciglio,* one could easily suspect that the cardinal of Mantua's property was identical with the belvedere annex to the Palazzo Ammannati. In addition, Marasca's statement in September of 1462 that he had obtained four houses for Gonzaga which together formed a block (*isola*) indicates a piece of self-contained property surrounded by streets. Giancarlo Cataldi has used this description to identify with the Palazzo Gonzaga a building across the Via della Fortuna from the Palazzo Lolli. This house, at 10–44 Corso il Rossellino, betrays, however, not a trace of fifteenth-century origin either externally or internally.[77] This should not be too surprising, for all the available information indicates that Gonzaga had, at best, the good intention of building in Pienza and that he saw to completion no more than the foundations of the plans furnished him by his father's unidentified Mantuan architect. What Cardinal Ammannati did with the property once it was passed on to him is unknown. Despite the attractiveness of Cataldi's proposal, which would extend the line of the Curial Row along the hillside toward the Porta al Ciglio, the evidence points in another direction, across the Corso il Rossellino to the northeastern part of town. All of the buildings of the Curial Row are described as being located in the *quartiere della ripa al ciglio,* yet the little house Laudomia Todeschini-Piccolomini donated to Gonzaga in September 1462 was described when she bought it two years earlier as being in the *castelnuovo al ciglio* district, the northeastern part of Pienza on the other side of the Corso il Rossellino. One would like to imagine that Gonzaga had found a site for his future palace which shared a view over the Orcia Valley with his curial associates, but that seems not to have been the case. Several isolated buildings in the Castelnuovo quarter might be suggested as the site for the proposed palace of Cardinal Francesco Gonzaga, but at present, there is no way of making any sort of firm determination.

The Palazzo di Salomone Piccolomini (?)

Its architectural features make a three-story building in the northwestern (or murello) quarter of the town one of the most interesting of the lesser palazzi in Pienza (Plate 43).[78] This house, at the corner of the Corso il Rossellino and the Via Condotti, displays architectural elements that clearly seem datable to the fourteenth century or, at the very latest, to the early years of the fifteenth century. There are doorways whose voussoirs form ogee arches; one of these doors, in fact, has a medieval shouldered arch. The two bifore with pointed arches and trefoil lights are also patently Gothic. Colonnettes (that on the left is a replacement) topped by Gothic capitals serve as the mullions of these windows. The sgraffito work that covers the facade is, however, of the type associated with the Renaissance face-lifting of Pienza. The stories, separated by simple string courses, are covered with the usual simulated channeled rustication. A curious sgraffito frieze of repeated cusped "windows" runs below the upper string course. Equally unusual but far more classical in spirit is the line of swags suspended from bucrania which decorates the frieze below the lower cornice. Although the plaster has peeled away today, a large stemma of the Piccolomini family once occupied the center of the second story between the Gothic bifore.[79] All these surface decorations show up quite clearly in old photographs, so clearly, in fact, that their authenticity might be doubted, for they might well be the result of a nineteenth-century refurbishing.

The location of this palace, across the Via Condotti from the Palazzo Ammannati and facing the great bulk of the Palazzo Piccolomini, as well as the nature of its ornamentation (if original), would seem to indicate its use by one of Pope Pius' family or intimates. Traditionally,

as we have noted in our discussion of the Palazzo Jouffroy, the building has been associated with the name of Cardinal Jean Jouffroy and identified accordingly in the literature as the Palazzo Atrebatense. In 1942 this tradition was challenged by Armando Schiavo, who correctly identified the palace to the rear of the Palazzo Vescovile as that of Jouffroy and posited the name of Salomone Piccolomini (probably to be identified with Salomone di Niccolò di Spinello di Salomone di Bartolommeo di Guglielmo Piccolomini [b. 1396]) as owner of this building.[80] This new attribution receives some support in one of the papal entries, which shows that on the day of his departure from Pienza (28 September 1462), the pope authorized a gift of one hundred ducats for Salomone "because he is redoing the facade of his house in Pienza" (Appendix 2, Doc. 48). Such a description might well correspond to a modernization of the facade of the palace at the corner of the Corso il Rossellino and the Via Condotti. I seconded Schiavo's identification in 1972, and Giancarlo Cataldi and others have also agreed to it, but the gabelle of Siena throw this hypothesis into doubt.[81] These records of sale show that Salomone bought a house in Pienza (then Corsignano) in June 1460 from a certain Matteo di Antonio Guglielmo (probably to replace those three houses bought from him by the pope in September 1459) and that in May, two years later, he exchanged a house in castelnuovo al murello with a Giovanni Jacopo Lombardo for one in the castelnuovo al ciglio. In April 1463 Salomone apparently enlarged his property with the addition of "a house with open space" acquired from a Jacopo da Mariano for twelve ducats.[82] It

43. House attributed to Salomone Piccolomini (left) and the belvedere tower of the Palazzo Ammannati.

would seem, therefore, that although Salomone may initially have purchased a house in the northwestern part of Pienza, the building whose remodeling was supported by the pope was in the northeastern quarter, in the area of town in which the cardinals, other members of the Curia, and Piccolomini relatives were concentrating their building activities. Although the Palazzo di Salomone Piccolomini cannot be identified as yet, it was probably located somewhere along the northern side of the Corso il Rossellino, perhaps across from the Curial Row. The refurbished Gothic palace at the corner of the Corso il Rossellino and the Via Condotti, as we shall see, might have belonged to Cardinal Bessarion, but for the present, the building cannot be assigned to anyone with any certainty.

The Palazzo di Tommaso del Testa Piccolomini

In his memoirs, Pope Pius says that a papal official named Tommaso had "bought a lot with a view to building." The Tommaso in question is not further described but in all likelihood he was Tommaso del Testa Piccolomini.[83] It might seem strange that the pope would choose to identify a member of his family so tersely, giving only his Christian name and a notation of his position, yet no other Tommaso held high office at the Vatican during Pius' reign. Tommaso del Testa was a distant relative of Pius and one of the clerks of the Apostolic Chamber. He also served as one of the pope's secret treasurers and in the Crusade Account Book was listed, with Niccolò and Gasparre Piccolomini, as a bursar. He probably is identical with the Thomas of Siena whom Platina recorded as holding the position of personal chamberlain to the pope together with Niccolò Piccolomini and Francesco Tergestino.[84] He was given the Piccolomini name on 3 March 1460 and maintained a close connection to Pienza, for he served, from 1470 to his death in 1482, as the second bishop of the new diocese.

Although Pius claimed that Tommaso had bought a building site, it was actually the pope who had done so. The Vatican accounts show that on 2 September 1462, Pius paid seventeen ducats to the brothers Bartolommeo and Giovanni di Pietro di Leonardo for a house to be given to Tome Piccolomini for building purposes (Appendix 2, Doc. 27). In an entry made four days later in the *gabelle* of Siena, its location is given as the *castelnuovo* quarter of town.[85] That Tommaso del Testa did proceed with construction is evident from Marasca's mention of Messer Thomeo as one of those urging Cardinal Gonzaga to start work on his palace.[86] One assumes that Tomasso did his prodding with a clear conscience.

Now that the little brick building on the Piazza Pio II has been freed from its long association with Gregorio Lolli, Giancarlo Cataldi has proposed it as the house of Tommaso Piccolomini (Plate 34).[87] Although there is no proof, either documentary or otherwise, to substantiate Cataldi's suggestion, it is an attractive hypothesis since it would resolve the dilemma of what to do with this prominently positioned building and would place Tommaso Piccolomini's residence close to that of the pope and hard by that of Cardinal Giacomo Ammannati. While the documented location of Tommaso's palace in the *quartiere di castelnuovo* might better describe a site farther to the east, it is sufficiently vague (called neither the *quartiere di castelnuovo al ciglio* nor the *quartiere di castelnuovo al murello*) to fit this building site.

The use of string courses to divide the facade into three graduated stories repeats the familiar architectural refrain of most of Pienza's new and renewed palaces.[88] The red-brick fabric, along with the use of boldly recessed arches over the doorway and the three asymmetrically disposed windows in the two upper stories, strikes a different note, however. Unlike the grander palaces of the town, which are constructed of stone or are covered with sgraffito decoration and mock masonry, this building appears far more Sienese than Roman or Florentine. Its nearest local relative is the monastic building at the side of the Church of San Francesco. The projecting *sporti* along the Via Marconi are probably of later date.

So modest is this little building (it has neither courtyard nor internal stairs) that if it were not for its conspicuous location, one would logically take it for the home of a prosperous craftsman, not one of the pope's own family and a high-ranking Vatican official. Interestingly enough, there does exist one piece of documentary information that could be used to support just such a conclusion. On 3 September 1462 the carpenter Magio d'Agnolo da Montefalonico was loaned a sum of sixty ducats at the orders of the pope "to make a house" in Pienza (Appendix 2, Doc. 33). The corresponding entry in the Sienese *gabelle* locates this house "by the side of the house where Magio dwells." In 1460 Magio

had sold Giacomo Ammannati one of the houses later incorporated into the cardinal's palace.[89] It is possible that all three of Magio's properties were in the same area and, if so, also possible that the splendidly situated brick house on the Piazza Pio II may have been home to a tradesman and not to a member of the papal aristocracy. Arguing against this conclusion is a rather confusing passage in Crivelli's poem (Appendix 1, Doc. 4) which seems to imply that Tommaso Piccolomini built his house near the papal palace; such a location would be appropriate for the residence in question.

Other Palaces of the Piccolomini

Salomone and Tommaso Piccolomini were not the only relatives of Pope Pius to participate in the renewal of Pienza, nor were they the only members of his extensive family to enjoy the considerable resources of the papal treasury in their building activities. Pope Pius apparently intended that his birthplace become not only a secondary seat for the papacy and a refuge from plague-ridden Rome but also an honored home and distinguished retreat for the entire Piccolomini clan.[90] Fear of financial nepotism proved no hindrance to the papal plans.

Although the Piccolomini had been granted the right to return to Siena from their rustic exile, Pius wished to maintain their high profile in Pienza. To that end, the pope purchased a vineyard for his nephews Giacomo and Andrea Todeschini-Piccolomini on 23 September 1462 (Appendix 2, Doc. 46), and on 19 July 1463, as has been mentioned, he deeded to them and their brother Antonio ownership of his newly completed palace. Even before this important event, Giacomo and Andrea had embarked on a rather significant and costly building project in Pienza. On 27 May 1463 the *Tesoreria segreta* recorded the transfer of 1,600 ducats from Pope Pius to Goro and Meo Massaini as part payment for a property on which the two Piccolomini brothers were to build (Appendix 2, Doc. 65). The total cost of the purchase was set at the extraordinary sum of 4,585 Sienese florins. Goro Massaini, it should be noted, had been *gonfaloniere* of Siena in 1461 and might well have benefited from an insider's information about papal plans for Pienza. Twice in June, additional sums of 300 ducats were paid out to the Massaini in what apparently was an agreed–upon system of payments (Docs. 70–71). The Massaini brothers received another 300 ducats at the beginning of August, but this time the entry stated that the payment was being made not on behalf of Giacomo and Andrea but for their mother Laudomia (Doc. 75). Such was also the case with the 600 ducats transferred at the end of the month to cover sums owed for September and October and with the final payment of 422 ducats made on 18 November (Docs. 78, 82). The latter entry noted that Laudomia had also been sold an additional house and garden by Goro Massaini. It would seem that Laudomia's two sons had the intention of constructing a grand palace in Pienza for their branch of the family and began their effort with considerable subvention from their uncle. After Pius gave them title to the great Palazzo Piccolomini, they quite naturally withdrew from this project and their mother then assumed the "mortgage."[91]

Laudomia Todeschini-Piccolomini had already bought a little house in the *castelnuovo al ciglio* quarter of Pienza in August 1460 from Matteo di Antonio Guglielmo (a relative of her brother-in-law?).[92] Purchased at a price of only twelve ducats, this structure certainly would have been too small for the pope's sister and it was given to Cardinal Francesco Gonzaga in September 1462. In the meantime, Laudomia had found herself in possession of what must have been one of the largest pieces of real estate in Pienza. Unfortunately, not one of the documentary references in the Vatican accounts gives any hint of just where in Pienza her extensive holdings were, and the *gabelle* of Siena are totally silent about the transactions. Nor is there any record of how much work actually was begun on what we might call the Palazzo Todeschini-Piccolomini, though Crivelli praised Laudomia, "for your buildings shine among these in the city" (Appendix 1, Doc. 4). This "palace," by the way, was not the only property then owned by Laudomia in Pienza; sometime in 1463 the Vatican treasury paid out two hundred ducats to her son Andrea for his mother to use "in repairing the houses which they have on their land outside of Pienza."[93]

Pope Pius' other sister, Caterina Guglielmi-Piccolomini also benefited from the financial support of her brother. For her in the spring of 1463 the pope authorized payments from the papal treasury totaling 620 ducats to be made to his majordomo and adopted kinsman Alessandro de Mirabelli-Piccolomini for a house owned by him in Pienza.[94] As in the case of Laudomia's "palace," there is no evidence to indicate where the house was located. Several houses along the north side of the Corso il Rossellino might be suggested.[95] One of these (79 Corso il Rossellino) at the corner of the Via Chiocarella even preserves traces on its facade of the Piccolomini coat of arms executed in sgraffito. Although it seems that most of the new housing was concentrated in the eastern part of Pienza, attention should also be directed to the sgraffito-embellished facades of two palazzi in the southwestern quarter along the Via Elisa. One of these buildings, at numbers 8–10, has the Piccolomini shield, single Piccolomini crescents, and an as-yet-unidentified coat of arms on its facade (Plate 44). A larger palace across from it at 11 Via Elisa displays traces of elaborate sgraffito decoration in which appear figures in what may may be scenes from Roman history. Dating is difficult because the decoration is deteriorating, but the period 1465–1490 might be suggested. Another building, at 6–8 Via del Giglio in the northwestern quarter, appears to be one of the more significant Pientine palazzi. Here the building is topped by an *altana* whose three arched openings relate to the belvedere of the Palazzo Ammannati.

About the other members of the Piccolomini family both the *Commentarii* of Pius and the official records in Rome and Siena are silent. Whether such Piccolomini as Laudomia's other son, Cardinal Francesco of Siena (the future Pope Pius III) or Niccolò Forteguerri or Niccolò Piccolomini or Alessandro de Mirabelli-Piccolomini ever really intended to build palaces in Pienza is unknown, though Crivelli does address Mirabelli, "Your threshold follows your distinctions and you . . . are considered a fellow citizen of Pius" (Appendix 1, Doc. 4). Equally uncertain are the possible roles played in Pienza by such close

associates of Pius as Agostino Patrizzi. Inasmuch as Patrizzi was the third bishop of Pienza (1482–1495), one might assume that he established a residence in the town, but what of many prominent members of the Curia—for instance, the powerful Cardinal Guillaume d'Estouteville who built palaces in Rome, Ostia, and his native France?[96] What of Cardinals Carafa, Roverella, Calandrini, Eroli, and the others?[97] Did they remain immune to papal pressure?

Lodrisio Crivelli cryptically mentions *Barbate* ("Bearded One") as building in Pienza. This may be a punning allusion to Cardinal Pietro Barbo, later Pope Paul II, or, more likely, a descriptive identification of Greek Cardinal Bessarion, whose whiskered visage is depicted on Pope Pius' funeral monument and in several illuminated manuscripts. Bessarion, as far as is known, was the only member of Pius' court to wear a beard, and it seems to have been almost emblematic of the great humanist.[98] Crivelli, after describing the cathedral and papal palace, says, "Next is your palace, Bearded One, with its metal transformed, for the mass of lead suggests gold" (Appendix 1, Doc. 4). Crivelli says that "farther on" are the palaces of Tommaso and of Rodrigo Borgia. Contextually, therefore, Barbate's palace could be the building now associated with Salomone Piccolomini at the corner of Corso il Rossellino and Via Condotti. The "mass of lead" that "suggests gold" could be a reference to its remodeling, which transformed it from an old-fashioned to a modern residence.

In the *Commentarii*, Pope Pius said that "plumbi ministri" were planning to build in Pienza, and certainly the known documentary evidence tells only part of

44. Detail of sgraffiti on the facade of an unidentified house on Via Elisa.

the story of the extensive involvement of the papal court in the town.[99] Only recently, for example, Nicholas Adams discovered a curious document in the State Archives of Siena which records the construction in July 1462 of five houses in Pienza "for courtiers."[100] The available evidence points to the concentration of building activity in the eastern part of town, but as we have noted, several decorative and physical elements demonstrate that the western district also shared in the general renewal.

Other Urban Modifications

Old Corsignano, as was the case with many of the communities of the Sienese *contado,* had a little hospital of its own, a branch of the great and powerful Spedale della Santa Maria della Scala of Siena. Cardinal Jouffroy's new palace had displaced the facility, but Jouffroy had been required to promise to secure the site for a new hospital.[101] The *gabelle* of Siena record the cardinal's purchase of a house from Alessandro de Mirabelli-Piccolomini for 147 ducats. Since this transaction was made on 6 September 1462, after the property for the Palazzo Jouffroy had been acquired, it probably represents the cardinal's fulfillment of his pledge to the *spedale.* Whether or not this house was identical with the "house with a courtyard" bought in December of 1459 by Mirabelli for 139 ducats from a Gherardo di Mariano da Monterchi is not clear.[102] Be that as it may, the site of the new hospital of Santa Maria della Scala in Pienza remains unknown. The emblem of that institution with its telltale ladder has not been noted on any building in the community. That work on the new hospital was actually begun is confirmed by

an entry in the papal accounts, which recorded the payment of fifty ducats to a Fra Giovanni di Maestro Martino of the Hospital of Siena on 9 June 1463 "for the hospital which they are building in Pienza" (Appendix 2, Doc. 69).

One of the "public" projects for the new Pienza with which Pope Pius was involved was the creation of an inn.[103] Such an establishment clearly was a necessity for a town that could expect the frequent visits of the pope and his prelates. Suitable accommodations were in short supply, as Cardinal Francesco Gonzaga could have attested when he was quartered three miles distant at the Monastery of Sant'Anna during Pius' summer visit of 1462.[104] On 3 September of that year, the pope ordered a loan of one hundred ducats to the potter Domenico di Antonio, nicknamed Riccio, "in order to make an inn" (Appendix 2, Doc. 31). This entry in the account books of the Vatican was repeated in the Sienese *gabelle,* which added that the loan was for the purpose "of raising and elevating in height his house for use as guests' lodgings."[105] The loan was to be repaid at the rate of four ducats a year to the parish of Pienza. Another hundred ducats were advanced to Riccio on the same conditions on 28 April 1463 (Doc. 63). Only a few days later, 5 May 1463, however, a *gabella* entry recorded that Riccio had sold a house to the cathedral.[106] The sale is also noted in the records of the diocese, and the property is said to be located in the *castelnuovo* quarter of Pienza.[107] It is not certain if this transaction involved the house Riccio hoped to convert into an inn, but from that point until early in 1464 the records are silent about both Riccio and his project.[108] Then on 3 March, less than three weeks after Pope Pius' brief stopover in Pienza on his way to Ancona, 248 ducats were paid "for an unfinished house bought from Riccio of Pienza and bought for the *opera* of the church of Pienza" (Doc. 88). A day later, the Sienese builder Pietro Porrina, whose major activity in Pienza will be considered shortly, was given two ducats to pay a Master Pietro del Abbacio "for estimating the house of Riccio" (Doc. 89). Riccio evidently had failed to follow through on his intentions and was in the process of negotiating the sale of his property, for on the next day, the papal treasury gave him 264 ducats for "an unfinished house with roofed and unroofed open spaces."[109] That the pope had every intention of having his inn is apparent in an entry in the papal accounts of 29 March, which authorized 333 ducats to be given to a Master Antonio Lombardo (likely a builder) "to do the house formerly of Riccio at Pienza which his Holiness is making into an inn for the institution of the church" (Doc. 90). It would seem that the pope had decided to take control of the moribund project and to assign the property to the bishopric. The transfer took place less than five months before the pope's death in Ancona, and whether the inn ever opened its doors is unknown. The site of the intended inn is a mystery, too, especially if it was unrelated to the house sold by Riccio in 1463. Recently, Luciana Finelli and Sara Rossi have suggested, with little more than intuition as a guide, that it was located at the northern end of the Piazza del Mercato.[110] That setting in the heart of the business district and near the new papal buildings and the Curial Row would have been a good one for such an establishment. This building, however,

at least in its present condition, fails to meet the description of the 5 March 1464 document, for it lacks the courtyard alluded to in that entry. Certainly, it would have been necessary for an inn to have a courtyard and an adjoining area for the stabling of horses. A better site might be that of a house on the northeast corner of the Corso il Rossellino and the Via della Buca, at the other end of the block from the Gothic-style house traditionally identified with Salomone Piccolomini (Plate 45). This building, like the one Riccio sold in May 1463, is located in the *castelnuovo* district, at 29–35 Corso il Rossellino; it has a courtyard and an upper loggia overlooking it and actually adjoins the former Albergo Letizia, which served as Pienza's hotel until a few years ago.

In the *Commentarii,* we are given the impression of a Pienza engulfed in a flurry of building activity. "Many of the townspeople," wrote Pope Pius, "tore down old houses and built new ones, so that nowhere did the aspect of the town remain unchanged."[111] Much of the financial support for this civic face-lifting came from the pope, himself. Between 3 September 1462 and 5 September 1463, for instance, the Vatican Treasury was ordered to disburse 338 ducats to six of Pienza's citizens (Appendix 2, Docs. 32, 33, 57, 64, 79). In each case, the sums, which ranged from as little as twenty-five ducats to as much as a hundred, were lent "in order to make a house in Pienza." Those benefiting from these papal loans were tradesmen and included a smithy, a barber, an apothecary, and the carpenter Magio (a transaction perhaps involving the brick house associated with Lolli and Tommaso). As in the case of the town's would-be innkeeper, four

45. View westward along the Corso il Rossellino toward the Porto Murello. The building at the immediate right may have been the inn. On the left is the monastic building of San Francesco.

of the recipients were required to repay their debts with annual contributions to the cathedral or to "the canons" chapter of Pienza." Not only was Pius assisting the citizenry in modernizing their town, but he was also assuring the upkeep of his new cathedral.

Since the *gabelle* of Siena do not record the purchases of new properties by any of those receiving the loans, it is likely that the funds were used to remodel and refurbish old dwellings. It is, of course, possible that some of those involved, especially those receiving the larger amounts, actually did raze and rebuild, but it is far more probable that they were content to dress up the facades of their houses by adding cornices and sgraffiti and perhaps an extra story. Which houses and in what part of town they were cannot be said, but a line of dwellings along the south side of the Corso il Rossellino (nos. 70–76) between the Via Buia and the Vicolo Cieco might be judged typical of what was intended (Plate 46).[112] This block of contiguous houses is divided into three stories by cornice strips and the street corners are emphasized by the addition of sandstone quoins. The fabric is a conglomeration of brick and stone and must originally have been plastered. The use of cornices on these row houses is particularly noteworthy, for this element seems to have been an architectural leitmotif of the Pientine renewal. Cornices distinguish the facades many houses all over town. Well-preserved stretches of cornice-lined buildings can be noticed along the Via Elisa, the Via del Giglio, the Via della Rosa, and in the Piazza del Mercato, and, of course, all along the length of the Corso il Rossellino. It is also possible that some work was carried out in Pienza like that

the pope had decreed during his stay in Viterbo in the early summer of 1462.[113] There, in preparation for the procession of Corpus Christi, Pius "gave orders first of all that the street leading from the citadel through the city to the cathedral, which was cluttered with balconies and disfigured with wooden porticoes, should be cleared and restored to its original splendor. Everything that jutted out and obstructed the view of the next house was removed and everywhere the proper width of the street was restored. Whatever was removed was paid for from the public funds. No wall was allowed to project further than another and roof to overlap another."[114] The appearance of most of the houses lining the Corso il Rossellino and the general regularity of the street suggests that just such a project was carried out in Pienza.

One of the most interesting of all of the building programs associated with the creation of Renaissance Pienza took place in the northeastern section of town. There, in 1463 Pope Pius personally ordered the building of a series of row houses and paid for their construction out of the funds of the *Tesoreria segreta*.[115] Actually, preparations for this building campaign seem to have been made on 11 September 1462, while the pope was yet visiting in Pienza. On that day the brothers Giovanni and Deo Fortunato da Cotone were given 240 ducats for houses and property they owned in an area described as *loco dicto cretanuovole*.[116] Seven months later, on 14 April 1463, they were given another payment of 219 ducats for additional properties they owned in the same "new area."[117] This time, however, the purchase was made not only on the pope's behalf but on that of Antonio, Giacomo,

46. Row of houses along the Corso il Rossellino near the Porta al Ciglio.

and Andrea Todeschini-Piccolomini. Once sufficient land had been obtained, actual construction quickly followed suit. On 29 May 1463, the Sienese contractor Pietro Porrina was given 200 ducats as part payment for the building of "fifteen houses to be done for His Holiness at Pienza" (Appendix 2, Doc. 66). On the same day, Porrina was compensated with an additional 55 ducats "for open areas and houses bought for doing the said houses" (Doc. 67). Despite the fact that fifteen houses were specified initially, only "the twelve houses they are doing in Pienza on commission from Our Holiness" were mentioned when Porrina received 255 ducats on 20 July 1463 (Doc. 73). Evidently, the original contract had been reduced by three houses but on 25 July 300 ducats were allocated (not specifically to Porrina, however) "for more houses done for Pienza" (Doc. 74). On 4 August, the pope ordered 600 ducats to be given to Porrina for "the twelve houses" followed by another 400 ducats on 11 November for the same purpose (Docs. 76, 80). Also on 11 November, Porrina was given a separate sum of 100 ducats "for more houses [or things] remaining to be done at Pienza other than the twelve houses." (Doc. 81). A final settlement of some 43 ducats was made to Porrina on 19 February 1464 "for those things done at Pienza and his salary." (Doc. 85). From these records, it would appear that Pope Pius had spent about 514 ducats for the necessary building sites, 1,455 ducats for the twelve new houses, and some 400 more for the unspecified number of additional houses. Actual construction costs for each of the twelve individual units was about 120 ducats. These modest houses were, we

may suppose, intended to accommodate some of those dislodged by the large-scale property acquisitions of the Piccolomini, the cardinals, and the papal staff. In his letter to Barbara von Brandenburg of 2 September 1462, Cardinal Gonzaga's majordomo, Bartolommeo Marasca, had described "the outcry of the poor men who do not wish to sell their homes."[118] Pope Pius evidently had heard their complaints and was attempting to alleviate this severe problem.

What Pope Pius got for his money can still be seen in the partially restored line of twelve houses stretching westward from the *castelnuovo* along the aptly named Via delle Case Nuove (Plate 47). Originally a uniform two stories in height, all the row-house units feature a ground-floor workshop entrance flanked by an elevated residential doorway (the so-called *porta del morto* scheme) reached by a flight of steps. Immediately inside this latter doorway, a staircase leads up to living quarters on the second floor. In plan, each of the dwellings is a little over four meters wide and twelve meters deep, with two rooms arranged one behind the other on each of the two floors. The second-floor rooms were each lit by a single roundheaded window placed front and rear. The design corresponds to a type of house known as the *casa a schiera,* which has a long history in Italy traceable through the Middle Ages into Antiquity.[119] The extensive use of such housing and its importance in the development of concepts of city planning is only now being broadly recognized and evaluated.[120] In the history of urban typology, the twelve houses of the Via delle Case Nuove, so firmly documented and dated, may be every bit as important

47. Pietro Paolo da Porrina's twelve new houses. The houses at the end of the block show the condition prior to the recent restoration of most of the units; the houses in the middle show the approximate height of the original buildings. Differences in fabric may be due to rebuilding following the sixteenth-century earthquake, which severely damaged this section of Pienza.

48. Site of Pius' projected lake.

as the more massively assertive palaces of the Piccolomini and their aristocratic associates.

Most of the building that took place in Pius' Pienza was carried out over the course of five short years. Had the pope lived longer, one might have expected a continued transformation of the community, the completion of new curial palaces, the construction of additional *case nuove*, and a continued regularization of streets and house fronts. One also could have expected a different view across the Val d'Orcia. Both in the poems of Lodrisio Crivelli and Porcellio Pandoni and in the biography of Pius by Giannantonio Campano (Appendix 1, Docs. 3, 4, 6) we hear of the pope's intention to dam the Orcia River to create a great lake in the valley below Pienza (Plate 48).[121] Perhaps the idea came to Pius as he surveyed the scene from the porticoed terraces of his newly completed palace. In all likelihood, however, he had been toying with the notion for a while prior to his visit in the summer of 1462. On his way from Rome to Pienza that year, he had spent several weeks lodged at the Monastery of San Salvatore on the slopes of his beloved Monte Amiata with a clear view across the countryside to his birthplace. From there, he made several ex-cursions to seek the source of the nearby Vivo River and to inspect the courses of a number of tributaries of the Orcia. That these outings were not only pleasurable but purposeful is made clear in the *Commentarii:* "He carefully observed the configuration of the ground to see whether, as he had hoped, he could divert the river's course, turn it into the Orcia above Bagni di Vignoni, and thereby damming the stream, a project he had often planned, make a lake which should cover the more level regions and supply the province with fish as well as protect it from hostile invasion. It would be an expensive operation and need a pope with plenty of leisure."[122] Such a project would have been worthy of the Caesars, and though he possessed the alum-enriched revenues of the papal treasury, Pope Pius was not given the time. One would also expect that the Sienese would have opposed the inundation of their productive grain fields in the Orcia Valley. On the other hand, they might have been willing to sacrifice yield in grain for the promised harvest of fish; indeed, in a desire for fish they revived Pius' proposal in 1468 and began an effort to dam the Bruna River.[123] That project took twenty years of work, cost considerable money, and ended in failure.

Chapter 4

Pienza as an Urban Statement

PIENZA provides a splendid opportunity to look at a variety of building
traditions—those of Rome, of Florence,
of Siena—and a range of theoretical concepts all combined into an urban environment representing what might be
termed the "international architectural
style" of the early Renaissance. Its importance as an aesthetic proving ground
(witness, for example, Urbino) is substantial. Altogether, some forty buildings
are known to have been either built or
refurbished in Pienza between 1459 and
1464. Yet, despite the extent of this
considerable effort, the real importance
of Pienza to the history of architecture
and urban planning lies not in the
qualities of its individual elements but
rather in the entirety of its expression. In
this regard, the major buildings—the
cathedral, the Piccolomini Palace, the
Communal Palace—seem but key words
in a new and broad statement of Renaissance harmony. Throughout the town,
on buildings large and small, similar
architectural and decorative features provide unifying elements that give Pienza
an unusual sense of visual homogeneity.
What Leonardo Bruni wrote of Florence

in 1404 seems even more appropriate
applied to the Pienza created some six
decades later by Pope Pius and his architect: "For just as harpstrings . . . attuned
to each other so that, when they are
twanged, a single harmony arises from
all the different tones . . . this farsighted
city has so adapted all her parts to each
other that there results a harmony of the
total structure. . . . Nothing in this state
is ill-proportioned, nothing improper,
nothing incongruous, nothing left vague,
everything occupies its proper place
which is not only clearly defined but also
in the right relation to all others."[1] If
Bruni's description of the Florentine re-
public sounds not unlike Leone Battista
Alberti's definition of beauty as "a harmony of all the parts, in whatsoever
subject it appears, fitted together with
such proportion and connection, that
nothing could be added, diminished or
altered, but for the worse," we should
not be at all surprised.[2] Both humanists
shared the objectives of the age; so too
did Pope Pius and Bernardo Rossellino.
Pienza, like Bruni's vision of Florence,
was intended to express the ideals of
civic virtue—its architectural monu-

ments standing as the outward signs of the inward spiritual grace inherent in the life of a Renaissance commune.

The focal point of this rejuvenated community was the handsome Piazza Pio II. It was around this square, at once cathedral parvis and civic center, that the most important religious, communal, and domestic buildings of Pienza were situated. The functional relationships existing between these various units were expressed through common decorative leitmotifs (pilasters, cross windows, doorframes) and in the organization of the piazza, which brings the separated architectural units into a cohesive totality.

A half century ago, Ludwig Heydenreich drew attention to the great differences between the Renaissance piazza of Pienza and those common to most medieval Italian towns.[3] Previously, according to Heydenreich, the arrangement of town squares in Italy had been limited to two primary types. Either several entirely unconnected and widely separated buildings were grouped together within a large open area (e.g., the Piazza dei Miracoli in Pisa or the Piazza del Duomo in Florence) or the buildings were closely strung together in a wall-like fashion about the main square (e.g., the Piazza del Comune in Assisi, the Piazza dei Priori in Volterra, the Piazza del Campo in Siena). Heydenreich saw Rossellino's design for the main square of Pienza as a complete break with these medieval traditions.

Heydenreich's analysis has recently been refined by urban historian Raymond Curran, who has contrasted the "closed order" of the medieval approach to town planning to the "structured order" of the Renaissance. The closed order, writes Curran, "is generally characterized by a dense and apparently spontaneous disposition of buildings and an informal system of streets, etc." Curran adds that "in typical examples of medieval cities, public spaces were small and intimate in scale, providing a strong sense of enclosure . . . [and] a very passive urban organization . . . both expressive and supportive of a very intense public life." Curran sees growing commercial activity and burgeoning humanistic interests, beginning in the fourteenth century, as contributing to a change in European urban patterns. The result was what he calls the structured order, "expressed not only in more easily negotiated systems of access but in a much greater sense of clarity in the organization of the public domain . . . [typified by] broad avenues and large squares, organized in highly structured plans [which] expressed both a greater control over nature and a desire for a greater sense of interaction with it . . . at once uplifting and much less personal. Public spaces geared for movement and show," Curran continues, "often lacked the supportive intimacy of earlier eras."[4]

Actually, the structured-order type of planning, seen by Curran as a manifestation of the Renaissance spirit, had been a part of the urban scene of Europe since well back into the Middle Ages. Communities with generally rectangular perimeters and a gridiron pattern of streets simultaneously began to appear during the thirteenth and fourteenth centuries in several regions.[5] These "new towns" were most often border outposts or colonial settlements, indicative of the growth in medieval populations, and they seem to have revived or inherited many of the formal concepts of the ancient Roman *castrum*. A number were founded by Teutonic knights in East Prussia; in France, where they were called *bastides,* several, such as Monpazier, were associated with the continental claims of Edward I of England. Italy boasts a variety of these regularly formulated new towns.[6] In central Italy, some splendid examples are found in the Florentine *terre nuove* (e.g., Lastra a Signa, Scarperia, Firenzuola, Castelfranco di Sopra, Terranuova-Bracciolini, San Giovanni Val d' Arno) as well as in the territories of Lucca (Pietrasanta), Pisa (e.g., Cascina, Bietina), Arezzo (Montevarchi), and Siena (e.g., Staggia, Castelnuovo Beradenga, Paganico, Buonconvento).

Many of these medieval new towns would have been familiar to both Pius II and Rossellino. The pope would have passed through a number of them on his travels, including the Sienese town of Paganico only a few miles from his favored spa at Petriolo.[7] As secretary to Emperor Frederick III in the 1440s, Pius had also spent considerable time in an Austrian new town, Wiener Neustadt, which served as the imperial capital.[8] Rossellino would have known San Giovanni very well, for it was the hometown of his wife and he had been buying property there for the past several years.[9] Buonconvento, which is a superb model of such a planned community, lies only a few miles north of Pienza on the road to Siena; both Pius and Rossellino would have gone through it repeatedly.[10]

Yet, Pienza presents few, if any, points of similarity to these models of urban design. Pienza, after all, was not a virgin site; it was not built but rebuilt, not founded but reborn, and its basic layout was dictated by the naturally evolving fabric of medieval Corsignano. Thus, it could not have been to the rigidly organized medieval new towns that Rossellino looked for his inspiration. Their lessons pointed more in the direction of those "ideal" cities visualized in the treatises of Antonio Filarete and Francesco di Giorgio and realized, in part, in the Vigevano of Bramante, the "Herculean Addition" to Ferrara of Biagio Rossetti, and a whole host of sixteenth-century towns that clearly conformed to a structured order.[11]

Instead, Rossellino and his patron would have looked to other towns and cities where the desired architectural relationship among civic, secular, and religious components had been achieved more informally. The Piazza del Duomo in San Gimignano, the Piazza Grande in Montepulciano, and the Piazza Sordello of Mantua could have provided some help. It would have been more logical, however, for Rossellino to have looked to his native Florence for possible assistance, but there the civic and religious centers are separated.[12] The cathedral and its parvis are at one end of the Via dei Calzaiuoli and the town hall, loggia, and public square are at the other end with the guild headquarters of Orsanmichele situated midway along the street, acting as a sort of commercial fulcrum. All appears to have been more or less accidental. What would have interested Pienza's chief architect about Florence would have been the several proposals Brunelleschi is thought to have made concerning public squares in the city. Brunelleschi might have hoped to integrate his loggia of the Hospital of the Innocents into a redesigned Piazza Santissima Annunziata (actually realized in the next century), and he had given serious thought to laying out a new square in conjunction with his first proposal for reorienting and rebuilding the Church of Santo Spirito.[13] He also seems to have worked on a design for a piazza in front of San Lorenzo which would have linked that church to the nearby Medici Palace.[14] This design was especially applicable to the situation in Pienza, for it would have placed church, square, and patron's palace into a defined relationship.

Brunelleschi's unrealized projects in Florence could have been the stimuli for Rossellino in Pienza; so, too, could the ideas of his former mentor in Rome and his possible informal adviser at Pienza, Leone Battista Alberti. Actually, Alberti, although he expressed some decided opinions about the nature of streets in the *De re aedificatoria,* paid but little attention to town squares in his treatise. For the most part, his references to civic squares were unspecific. In his discussion of the ideal temple, however, he did remark that such a religious building "should have a spacious area in its front and be surrounded on every side with great streets, or rather with noble squares, so that you may have a beautiful view of it on every side."[15]

Although spatial constrictions made such a layout impossible for Pienza, there does exist a spiritual bond between Rossellino's Piazza Pio II and Alberti's concept. I do not mean to suggest that Rossellino attempted to reproduce Alberti's temple square, but, rather, that both the actual and theoretical examples were the natural products of a new Renaissance vision. It would seem that the haphazard or agglutinative approaches found in the normal medieval square had been replaced by an admiration for well-ordered and coherent spatial units that,

taken together, should be able to function as a perfect whole. Just as scientific perspective had replaced the empirical rendition of space in painting, so planning replaced chance in urban design.

Common sense, function, and convenience played a large role in such concepts. Alberti showed his interest in such considerations when, speaking of the practice of the ancients, he wrote: "They placed The Senate House in the middle of the city with the place for the administration of justice and the Temple nearby . . . that the city fathers might first pay their devotions in the Temple and, afterwards, repair immediately to the transaction of the public business."[16] Bernardo Rossellino's arrangement of the important civic and religious buildings around the "forum" square in Pienza reflects the reasoned approach to architecture he shared with Alberti. The piazza as forum was also in keeping with the way Pienza was seen by Pius and his circle; Flavio Biondo, after all, had compared his pope's project with that of Emperor Septimius Severus (Appendix 1, Doc. 2).

"For my part," wrote Alberti, "I would have a square twice as long as broad."[17] As noted in Chapter 2, the dimensions of the piazza Rossellino laid out in Pienza are quite different from those favored by Alberti, and much has been made of the unusual trapezoidal shape of Pienza's square. It has even been suggested as a forerunner of Michelangelo's design for the Capitoline Hill in Rome.[18] The resemblance is due, however, to the similar physical situations shaped by buildings already on the site. The same holds for the main piazza in Fabriano, which has occasionally been put forward as a prototype for the Piazza

Pio II.[19] Necessity dictated the form all three piazzas took.

Pius, like Pope Nicholas V before him, was a believer in the symbolic use of architecture. Clearly, he had paid attention to the great plans formulated by Nicholas and his advisers for the rebuilding of the Vatican and the Borgo district of Rome. Those plans had called for siting the palaces of many of the cardinals and other papal officials near the Vatican and in positions obviously related to the papal palace and the Basilica di San Pietro. It was this relationship that Pius transferred to his desires for Pienza. Both Pius and Nicholas remembered the words of Saint Augustine that "all doctrine concerns either things or signs but things are learned by signs."[20] Pius was well aware of the importance of establishing a visual dependency for his prelates and creating an architectural order that would reflect the actual organization of the Church's hierarchy. The "meaning" of Pienza is better understood in light of Pius' own description of a papal audience he witnessed in 1457 while a member of the court of Pope Calixtus III: "If you once saw the Pope celebrating Mass, or assisting in the Divine Office, you would confess that there is no order of pomp, or splendor save with the Roman pontiff. You would see the Pope sitting high upon his throne, the Cardinals on his right, and the great prelates on his left. Bishops, Abbots, Protonotaries, Ambassadors, all have their Place. Here are the Auditors, there the Clerks of the Camera; there the Procurators, there the Subdeacons and Acolytes. Below them are the multitude. Surely you would recognize that the Papal Court resembles the celestial hierarchy, where all is fair to the eye, and all

is done according to rule and law."[21] Practicality at Pienza, as in Nicholas' Rome, prevented the imposition of a specific residential ordering, but the general concept is there. The kind of hierarchy Pius saw in the structure of his court is expressed in the buildings of Pienza, from the bold statements of the cathedral and papal palace down through the residences of cardinals, officials, and family members to the simple statements of the Palazzo Canonica and the houses of the citizenry. The hierarchy imposed upon Pienza is expressed not only in the placement, size, and fabric of the buildings but also in their architectural articulation. Columns, for instance, with their shadow-casting plasticity, were reserved for the facade of the cathedral. Flatter, yet still three-dimensional pilasters defined the walls of the Palazzo Piccolomini. But such features on the houses of prelates and others were merely feigned in sgraffito.

In the piazza the paving scheme defines a visual rectangle upon which the Piccolomini and Bishop's palaces are positioned as if they are advancing outward from the cathedral, having received their motivating power from the Church, as do all, including pope and prelate. The travertine lines of the piazza also tie together the space and the surrounding buildings, thus constraining the space and giving it shape. Rudolf Arnheim notes that "dynamically . . . the reach of [a] square is determined not simply by its geometrical area but by the interplay between centrifugal expansion and surrounding constraint."[22] In Pienza the balance is fine-tuned by the vertical repetition of the grid of the piazza on the facade of the cathedral and surrounding palaces. One is reminded of the interior of Brunelleschi's churches of San Lorenzo and Santo Spirito. The Piazza Pio II achieves something of the quality of an external interior. The visitor coming up the Corso il Rossellino advances toward the authority of cathedral and papal palace; departing in the opposite direction, the visitor feels a part of the power that emanates from the pontifical presence.

That one moves on the Corso il Rossellino along a curving and not a straight path is an interesting curiosity of Pienza. This departure from the expected is in itself telling and clearly sets Pienza apart from the structured order associated with the Renaissance urban concepts of Filarete and Francesco di Giorgio, as well as from most of the medieval new towns. Interestingly enough, one of those fourteenth-century planned communities, nearby Buonconvento, does feature a curving main street, which seems related to the situation in Pienza; in both cases the streets apparently followed the course of earlier roadways.[23] The probable origin of the *corso*'s curve notwithstanding, its deviation from boring regularity would have appealed to the pope and Rossellino, whose own tastes reflected the sensible sensitivity of Alberti, who wrote, "But if it is only a small town, . . . it will be better . . . not for the streets to run straight to the gates. . . . For thus, besides that by appearing so much the longer, they will add to the idea of the greatness of the town, they will likewise conduce very much to beauty and convenience, and be a greater security against all accidents and emergencies. Moreover, this winding of the streets will make the passenger at every step discover a new structure . . . and whereas in larger towns even too much breadth is unhandsome and unhealthy, in a small one it will be both healthy and pleasant, to have such an open view from every house by means of the turn of the street." Alberti also saw a more climatic function in the bending of streets: "In our winding streets there will be no house but what in some part of the day will enjoy some sun; nor will they ever be without gentle breezes . . . and yet they will not be molested by stormy blasts, because such will be broken by the turning of the streets."[24] Rossellino would have had no desire to straighten the path of the town's principal thoroughfare. What he probably did do was to regularize its appearance by dressing up the facades of the buildings lining the *corso* with harmonizing cornices and sgraffito decorations and by removing the projecting structures ubiquitous in medieval Italian towns.[25]

Ivor De Wolfe has distinguished two fundamental types of urban design, the informal (organic) variety of the Middle Ages and the formal (gridiron) type associated with the Renaissance and later periods. He suggests that the medieval town was really more calculated in its spontaneity than we realize, but he can find little proof that spontaneity persisted in the more structured systems of the succeeding age. Was there, he asks, ever a balance achieved that would lend support to his suggestion?

To make a true appreciation one would need to find a ready-made, real-life town of the right period and analyse its effects in three dimensions on the spot, not an easy assignment obviously since ready-made towns of the right period do not grow on trees. And suppose that pattern turned out to combine the two kinds of logic, formal and pictur-

esque (the townscape eqivalent of Brunelleschi's San Spirito), then two
complementary conclusions could be justifia-
bly drawn. The men of the Renaissance could
be accepted as heirs of a living planning
tradition and the picturesque muddle of the
Middle Ages could be put down to more
deliberate purposes than "natural causes."
Concede the possibility of *picturesque planning*
and the whole situation changes. In place of
accidental muddle on the one hand and conscious townplanning on the other, a choice
could be made between two complementary
townscape approaches, formal and informal,
symmetrical and asymmetrical, regular and
irregular, classic and romantic, rational and
organic, free and formal. [26]

It is just such a situation, I believe, that
Pienza presents. Pienza is not the "ideal"
city of the gridiron-inspired Renaissance
planner; it does not adhere to the regularity of Antonio Filarete's *Sforzinda* or
to the calculated irregularity of the sixteenth-century Sabbioneta of Scamozzi.
It corresponds to the more sensitive and
sensible dictates of the Albertian aesthetic. [27] Pienza recognizes the inherently
antisocial nature of too much rigidity. In
fact, Pienza presents a far more "modern" concept of a type now being
favored by more advanced urbanists.
Thus, it may well permit a reevaluation
of the seemingly loose patterns of the
organic medieval town within the framework of De Wolfe's suggestion of picturesque planning. It also offers a refreshing
practical alternative to the monotonous
rigidity so often imposed with author-
itarian firmness upon the planned community.

In the number of its inhabitants,
Pienza remained in 1464 the town Corsignano had been five years earlier, but in
its atmosphere and appearance it had
taken on the character of a city, for it had
achieved a distillation of those ingre-
dients found in more cosmopolitan en-
vironments. These essential qualities are
compacted into the nucleus of great
buildings concentrated about the Piazza
Pio II and then flow out along the gently
curving Corso il Rossellino. The effect is
both urban and urbane.

Today, Pienza boasts two primary
centers of activity. One with a decidedly
more modern and extroverted personality is situated in the Piazza Aligheri
outside the Prato (formerly Murello)
Gate. It is of a type typical in any contemporary Italian community, an
area of bars, gasoline stations, auto-
mobiles, often noisy chatter, and ani-
mated gesture. The other, in the old
Piazza Pio II, has a quite different quality. It is an area frequented in the evening
hours by small groups or the solitary
stroller, a space committed to low conversation or silent introspection. On my
most recent visit to Pienza, as I sat in
front of the little brick cafe (once perhaps
the home of Pope Pius' kinsman Tommaso Piccolomini) and watched the Pien-
tines take their evening *passeggiata* about
the spacious piazza, I was struck by how
perfectly this setting related to those
moving about it. [28] I was reminded both
of the fourteenth-century French humanist Petrus Berchorius' observation that
"since piazzas are areas . . . arranged for
the purpose of providing space or set up
for the meetings of men, it should be
remarked that in general through piazzas
the condition of man in this world can be
known" and of Rudolf Arnheim's recent
reminder that "a work of architecture . . . acts as a symbolic statement
which conveys, through our senses, hu-

manly relevant qualities and situations."[29] The intimate space of this splendid piazza and the backdrop of elegant buildings set about it is a concrete illustration of the humanist principles of rational thought and reasoned living, designed both for individual reflection and group discourse. The piazza is the symbolic common ground, where those who functioned in the surrounding buildings could commune, whether their duties were clerical, civil, seigneurial, or purely plebeian; it represented the urban hierarchy. The relationship between the buildings and the people in the square is active, not passive, and the impact of this fifteenth-century architectural environment continues to be felt by those who live in Pienza today. A careful balance is established between the desire for individuality and the demands of communal life. Pienza strikes a happy medium between discipline and freedom; it is democratic and humane yet it is not a laissez-faire environment. Anarchy is no more encouraged here than is absolutism. Noble suggestions are subtly made by the noble space and the cincture of buildings. One's thoughts naturally aspire to a

higher plane. It is, thus, not remarkable that the citizens of Pienza seem different from those of other communities; they are the descendants of generations reared in these harmonious surroundings. The people of Pienza continue to display a sense of "decorum" unique even in the hill towns of Tuscany.

Recently, Raymond Curran has posed the problem confronting contemporary urbanists: "As the limitations and shortcomings of the modern tradition in city building have become more apparent in recent years," he writes, "a search for more meaningful criteria on which to base planning and design choices has become increasingly widespread. In essence, this search has largely focused on how to make cities less rigid and abstract, and on making them more supportive for people in their day-to-day experiences."[30] The concepts introduced by Pope Pius and Bernardo Rossellino in the creation of Renaissance Pienza offer, I believe, a lesson in the implementation of criteria important to the modern planner, and this, beyond her importance as an architectural and art historical document, is Pienza's lasting legacy.

Appendix 1

Fifteenth-Century Descriptions of Pienza,
with Translations by Catherine Castner

Pienza received immediate literary acclaim not only in the well-known memoirs of
its papal patron but also in the writings of several of his Vatican associates. The
Commentarii, itself, contains a laudatory verse composed in 1462 by Giannantonio
Campano, who some years later wrote another poem on Pienza and included a prose
description of the new city in his life of Pope Pius.[1] In 1464 a long poem devoted to
the glories of Pienza was dedicated to Pius by one of his humanist secretaries, Lodrisio
Crivelli.[2] About the same time, Porcellio Pandoni included a shorter, but interesting,
poetical passage describing Pienza in a work praising the accomplishments of the
pontiff.[3] A lengthy critique of the Pientine project was given by Flavio Biondo in the
addendum volume to his celebrated *Italia illustrata.*[4] These early sources expand upon
the pope's own report, given in Book 9 of the *Commentarii,* and provide valuable
information about later stages in the rebuilding of the community. These writings help
to flesh out the documentary evidence, and they also offer independent testimony
against which the veracity of Pius' own words can be judged. Considering the
importance of this material, it seems rather surprising that so little of it has been used
in previous discussions of the development of Renaissance Pienza. This appendix
brings together these fifteenth-century descriptions of Pienza and, for the first time,
renders them into English.[5]

Doc. 1. Poem in Praise of Pienza
by Giannantonio Campano (June 1462)

Quae nova sublimi surgo Pientia colle,
    Causa mei quae sit nominis ipsa loquar.
Me Pius ornatam templo murisque refertam
    Esse urbem voluit, quae fueram oppidulum.
Tecta suae gentis primis in moenibus aedes
    Tangere marmoreum sidera iussit opus.

> Addidit et nomen lectumque e more Senatum,
> Urbanos ritus et nova iura dedit.
> At vos, vicina quae surgitis oppida terra,
> Invidiae nihil est, nam genui ipsa Pium.[6]

I am Pienza, the city that rises, new-built, on the lofty hillside, and I myself shall tell the reason for my name. Pius wanted me to be a city decorated with a cathedral and filled with walls, I who had once been a small town. He ordered the marble construction, the covered house of the family in the first part of the fortifications, to touch the stars. He added my name, chosen according to the custom of the Senate, and he gave me ceremonies befitting a city and new laws. But you, towns that rise on the neighboring land, I envy you not a bit, for I myself gave birth to Pius.

Doc. 2. Extract from the *Additiones correctionesque Italiae illustratae* of Flavio Biondo (September 1462)

Sed quod in rebus contingit humanis, diversa ab ea quae Silvium olim Piccolomeum traxit fatorum series efficit, ut tua Beatitudo, causis intentissima christianae fidei et Ecclesiae, urbem Mantuam ad conventus habendos ab urbe Roma et propria pontificum maximorum sede petitura, recto per mediam Italiam itinere Corsignanum originis suae patriam repetere sit coacta; gratissimaque fuit non magis tibi quam ceteris, qui in celeberrimo comitatu tuo erant, cardinalibus praelatis nobilibus et aliis curiae Romanae praestantissimis viris tuorum decoratum natalium fortuna oppidum non inspicere magis quam aliquot diebus inhabitare; per quos dies nullus ingenii, nullus generosi inter nos animi, nullus vel mediocris ingenii fuit, qui non Corsignano amplas ornatissimasque et fortuna sua dignissimas optaverit aedes. Itum est inde Mantuam, et maior celebriorque ibi christianorum principum oratorum et populorum habitus est conventus ceteris omnibus quos nostra alibi per Italiam viderit aetas. Ad decimum inde mensem redeunti ad propria tecum Romanae curiae iter rectissimum per Corsignanum fuit, ubi alia et prima maior aedium tenuitatis oppidi illius quaerela passim inter nostros audita est, illudque ostensum a curialibus desiderium tuam movit Sanctitatem, ut quam omnibus exhibet genio quoque suo benignitatem impartiretur.

Postquam vero ibi a te destinatum est aedificium, fecisti quod non magis Iesu Christi vicarium et Petri Apostolorum principis successorem, quam omnes decet Christianos. A divinis namque incohans, destinatae basilicae, qualem Romani pontificis opus esse deceat, per diem martyris, Laurentii solemniis celebrem lapidem primum tu ipse manu tua fundamentis iecisti. Reditum est inde Romam, unde tertio post anno pestilentia nos dispersos abire coëgit; qua diversis in Etruriae locis debacchante, collegia Curiae et quandoque singulos curiales diversas habere et mutare sedes oportuit; sicque tuam Beatitudinem aliam saepius quam Corsignanum sedem habere oportuit. Ad diem vero apostoli Matthaei festo celebrem absolutam omnium opinione celerius basilicam dedicasti, eiusque Apostoli vocabulo insignisti, civitatem quoque de pontificatus nomine Pientiam et dici debere et haberi deinceps decrevisti, quod oppidum hactenus fuerat Corsignanum. Cui civitati cum episcopum dioecesimque dedisses, Ilcinium, quod oppidum tunc inhabitabamus, in civitatem Ilciniam Pientiae episcopatu sociam declarasti.

Ea die, primo cum absolutam inspicerem contemplaremque basilicam, assistentem lateri meo et singulis respondentem eius architectum infinitis prope quaestiunculis agitavi, quarum uni celeritatis perficiendi operis numquam potuisset facere satis, nisi subiecta oculis ipsa absolutio comprobasset. Quod vero Sanctitati tuae dixisse tunc memini, ea basilica multas in aliquibus Italiae urbibus habet magnitudine ipsi pares atque etiam ampliores, nonnullas habet marmorum crustamentis musivique operis pictura insigniores; sed nullam quis facile memorabit, quae Pientiae sancti Matthaei basilicae subterranei superiorisve totius aedificii proportione et partium inter se singularum convenientia aequetur. Palatium tuo natali cubiculo superaedificatum basilicam cui continet magnitudine superat, et, cum eiusdem architecti opificium sit, parem in singulis sui partibus proportionis et dimensionum gratiam prae se fert. Quam quidem gratiam cum architecto dicerem totam in operis summa minorem esse illa quam basilicae tribuebam, retulit ipse in tuos culpam, qui, quas passi principio non fuerant ab eo fieri particulas, perfecto iam operi addendas evicerint. Habet autem palatium et vestibulum et porticus et aulas triplices cubiculaque in utraque contigna-tione cum ampla tum ornatissima suis commodissima officinis, ut etiam qui auctorem ignoret vel habitatorem, si non omnino socors sit, utrumque munus in Romanum pontificem referat.

Ea nos, Pater sancte, ingentia pulcherrimaque opera inspexisse delectavit, non solum quia tali sumus animo geniti, ut saeculi nostri ornamenta amare non nequeamus, sed quia bono ea exemplo facta recognoscimus: optimos namque e principibus viris quosque scimus amorem suum, quo naturaliter abundarunt, in omnes passim, sed in suos et sua propensius ostendisse. Sic Severus Afer imperator Romanus doctrinae praesertim eloquentiae ingentis, morum gravitate continentia et bonitate meliores qui umquam fuerunt Romanos principes aut aequans aut superans, non dissimili tuae causa quae te Mantuam duxit, in Africam se contulit; qui, ad Leptim natalis sui soli locum perveniens, destinatas in accessu aedes, ibi rediens, extruere coepit, et Romae agens amplissimas perfici curavit. M. vero Antoninus Aurelius, philosophus, laudatissimae imperator probitatis, aedes in quibus natus educatusque est avitas apud Lateranensem nunc basilicam, orbis christiani primariam, adeo dilexit, ut eas postea imperator, quantum per occupationes licuit, libentius maioribus melioribusque palatiis aedibusque Romanis inhabitavit. Et e nostris pontificibus christianis Innocentius tertius, doctrina humanitate et ceteris virtutibus nulli paene pontificum Romanorum secundus, aedes paternas avitasque in quibus aut natus aut, quod indubitatum est, ab infantia nutritus erat, in excelsam amplamque extantem Romae turrim a gente sua Comitum dictam extruxit. Et si huius operis conditio volumenque pateretur, facile mihi fuerit principum et praestantissimorum hominum atque etiam pontificum Romanorum et eccle-siasticorum virorum mille in exemplum afferre, quibus pro posse et supra studium cura fuit opera extruere ingentia, quibus suam et suorum saeculi ac regionum virtutem et gloriam posterorum memoriae commendarent. Sed de his nunc satis.

Non sunt parvo Pientiae nostrae decori aedes iam multae in ea aedificatae, quales deceat magnos viros inhabitare. Quarum unam Iohannis Ioffridi Burgundionis cardinalis Atrebatensis, alteram Iacobi Lucensis cardinalis Papiensis vidimus absolutas, cum duas ab illustribus sororibus et alteras item geminas ab illustribus nepotibus tuis a nonnullisque alias audiverim destinatas.[7]

But insofar as human affairs are concerned, a series of events different from that which formerly drew Silvius Piccolomini, brought it about that your Holiness, very intent on the interests of the Christian faith and of the Church, was going to visit the city of Mantua in order to hold a conference far from the city of Rome and the particular abode of the greatest priests; and you were forced to travel, by a straight road through the middle of Italy, to Corsignano, the place of your birth. This was no less pleasing to the others in your throng of followers than it was to you, to the cardinals, prelates, nobles, and other outstanding men of the Roman curia who had the good fortune not to glimpse the honors of your birthplace more than to live in it for a few days; during those days no one among us who had any talent or was a gentleman or even had ordinary intelligence did not wish to have at Corsignano a palace, spacious and fully equipped and most worthy of his good fortune. From there the procession went to Mantua, and there was held a greater and more crowded congress of the Christian chiefs and speakers and people than all other congresses that our age has seen in any other place in all of Italy. Ten months from then, the Roman senate, returning to its property, took the most direct route, through Corsignano, where there arose among us another and the first major complaint that that town was poor in buildings.[8] This desire voiced by the senators caused your Holiness to share with his own family the kindness that he displays to everyone.

Indeed, after you had ordered the building to be built there, you did something that became the vicar of Christ and the successor of Peter, chief of the Apostles, no more than all Christian men. For you began with divine concerns and yourself laid with your own hand, on the feast day of Saint Lawrence, the famous cornerstone of the cathedral you had planned, an act that was fitting work for a Roman pope.[9] Then everyone returned to Rome. But three years later the plague forced us all to be separated by flight.[10] Since the plague was raging throughout the different areas of Etruria, it became necessary for the college of cardinals and individuals of the curia to find at some time or other new headquarters or abodes. And so it became necessary for your Holiness to have another home more often than Corsignano. On the feast day of the apostle Matthew you consecrated the cathedral, which had been completed more quickly than anyone had predicted, and you distinguished it with the name of that Apostle, and you decreed that what had until then been the town of Corsignano should henceforth be called and known as a city, Pienza, after the name of the Pope.[11] When you had given the city an episcopate and a diocese, you declared Montalcino, the town in which we were then living, as the town Montalcino, associated with Pienza through the common episcopate.

On that day, when I was examining the completed cathedral and was surveying it, its architect was present at my side, answering every one of the nearly numberless questions with which I harassed him. But he could never have given adequate answer to my question about the speed with which the work was accomplished if the completed building before my very eyes had not confirmed what he said. I remember that I said then to your Holiness that this cathedral had many equals in size in some of the Italian cities; and some cathedrals were even larger; and some were more distinguished with marble bas-reliefs and mosaics, but none would easily come to mind which are the equal of Pienza's cathedral of Saint Matthew [*sic*] in the proportion of the underground building or of the entire upper building and in the harmony of the individual parts with one another. The palace which is built over the room of your birth towers over the cathedral next to it, and, being the work of the same architect, displays the same charm in the individual details of its proportion and dimension. Indeed, when I told the architect that I thought that the charm of the whole work was inferior to that of the cathedral, he himself blamed your men for it, saying that they had not allowed him from the beginning to construct small sections but had persuaded him to add them to the already finished work. But the palace has on each of the two floors a forecourt and colonnade and triple halls and bedrooms not only spacious but also decorated most appropriately by its workshops, so that even he who might be unaware of the builder or the inhabitant, if he should not be completely stupid would attribute both functions to the Roman pope.

It pleased us, Holy Father, to have inspected these enormous and very beautiful works, not only because we are endowed with such a mind as is unable to admire the buildings of our own age, but because we recognize that they were built according to good example. For we know that each of the best of princes, according as he was greatest, has displayed his love, which he had by nature in great supply, toward all men in every direction, but he has been more inclined to display it toward his own people and possessions. In such a way Septimius Severus, a Roman emperor especially learned and eloquent, who either equalled or surpassed the best Roman princes who ever existed in dignity of character, self-control, and goodness, went to Africa for the same reason you went to Mantua. When he arrived at his birthplace, Leptis, returning there, he began to build a palace that had been planned when he acceded to the office, and while living at Rome saw to the completion of a very spacious palace. Indeed, Marcus Aurelius, the philosopher, an emperor renowned for his honesty, so cherished his ancestral house at the Lateran (now a basilica of the first rank in the Christian world) in which he had been born and brought up, that afterwards, when he was emperor, he lived in it, as much as his duties allowed him, more willingly than he lived in the greater and better-appointed palaces and buildings at Rome. And of our Christian popes, Innocent the Third, second almost to none of the Roman popes in learning, civilization, and the other virtues, built up the paternal and ancestral house in which he either had been born or, this much is certain, had been brought up from infancy, into a lofty tower still in existence at Rome, named after his family the Comites. And if the circumstances and scope of this work allowed, it would be easy for me to bring forward by way of example a thousand princes and most eminent men and even Roman popes and men of the church, who took pains to build, with exceeding zeal, enormous works with which they entrusted to memory their own merit, that of their time and their birthplaces, and the glory of their descendants. But enough of this topic.

The many houses already built there are no small glory for our city of Pienza, and are such as are appropriate for great men to live in. Of those already completed, I have seen one, that of Jean Jouffroy of Burgundy, cardinal of Arras; and a second, that of Jacob Ammannati, cardinal of the Pope. At the same time I heard that two palaces were planned by your distinguished sisters and two others likewise by your distinguished nephews, and that others had been planned by several other people.

Doc. 3. Extract from a Poem
by Porcellio Pandoni (1464?)

Quid memorem veterum patrum in natalibus arvis
    Quae posuit Matri templa dicata Deum.
Marmore Mygdonio et vivis caelata figuris
    Signa vides, auro limen et ara micant.
Ille suo hic urbem posuit de nomine, tellus
    Quaeque Pienta modo Corsiniana fuit.
Hic et praeclari posuere palatia patres
    Insignesque viri qui coluere pios.
Tum Maecenatis celebratur digna Tonante
    Inclyta vel Solis regia qualis erat.
Hunc Pius ante nigri decoravit honore galeri
    Moxque sacrum roseo cinxit honore caput,
Tanta erat ingenii et doctae facundia linguae,
    Virtutum et fidei gratia tanta fuit.
Te quoque in urbe Pia fundasse palatia, Lolli,
    Aurea et Pario marmore fama fuit.
At pius antistes, caput et decus urbis et orbis,
    Quique volens solvit crimina quique ligat,
Lustravit primum solido de marmore muros
    Et scrobibus cinxit moenia lata loci,
Fundavit mirasque aedes, monumenta nepotum,
    Quas ausim magni dicere tecta poli.
In caelum summi surgunt fastigia tecti
    Et centum frons est undique lata pedes,
Irradiantque auro centum fundata columnis
    Atria materiam nobile vincit opus.
Statque ingens totidem distincta coloribus aula
    Quam variis pinxit Zeuxis imaginibus.
Quales Roma refert Traiani Caesaris aedes
    Et Capitolino templa fuisse Iovi,
Tales ille domos posuit templumque sacravit
    Tale tibi, et Nati filia Virgo parens,
Instituitque lacum propter currentia rivis
    Balnea deque Pio nomen habere dedit.[12]

What should I recount about the temples that he placed in the native fields of the ancient father, consecrated to the mother of the gods? You can see the images of Mygdonian marble, chased with living figures; the threshold and altar shine with gold. That man built here a city named after him, the district which, now Pienza, was Corsignano. Here the famous fathers also built their palaces and the men who honored the illustrious pious ones. Then the royal house of Maecenas or of the Sun, worthy of Jove himself, comes in for celebration, such as it was.[13] Pius adorned this man before with the honor of the black skull-cap and soon he girded his holy head with the rose-colored mark of distinction, so great was the eloquence of his talent and his learned tongue, so great was the gratitude for his courage and trustworthiness. You too, Lolli, are said to have built in the city of Pienza a palace of gold and Parian marble. But the devoted priest, head and glory of the city and of the world, who both willingly nullifies and attaches accusations, first purified the walls built of solid marble and girded the place's wide ramparts with ditches. He laid the foundations of wondrous buildings, monuments for his descendants, buildings that I should dare to call the roof of the great heaven. The pediments of the highest buildings rise to the sky and the frontage is a hundred feet wide on all sides, and a hundred halls based on pillars shine with gold.[14] The noble work surpasses the material. An enormous palace stands there, decorated with just as many colors as Zeuxis painted in his different portraits.[15] That man has built a palace such as Rome reports Trajan's was, and the temple of Capitoline Jove; he dedicated just such a temple to you, Virgin daughter and mother of the Son, and he built a lake hard by the baths running with streams and allowed it to have a name derived from his own, Pius.[16]

Doc. 4. Poem Celebrating Pienza by Lodrisio Crivelli (Ash Wednesday, 15 February 1464)

Leodrisius Cribellus ad Polymniam Musam
in Laudem Pientiae Civitatis

Musa, tuum nobis memora decus ordine. Summi
    Namque Pii decus est principis omne tuum.
Incipe, dic quantis est aucta Pientia felix
    Civibus, ornatu splendida facta novo.
Annuit, et quoniam iusto tua corda tenentur
    Accipe quod carmen signet honore tuum.
"In summo positam vidisti collis aprici
    Urbem inter Senas Trasimenumque lacum
Atque inter calidas undanti gurgite venas
    Unde salutarem suscipit aeger opem.
Labitur inde liquor gemino de fonte perennis,
    Arridet facies purior ipsa Iovis.
Torrida non istic Zephyris spirantibus aestas
    Noxia corporibus vel gravis ulla venit.

Cedit apricanti vis hic quoque brumea soli,
    Glaeba est ad segetes fertilis atque pecus,
Fert oleam et dulcis gratissima dona Lyaei
    Divitibus mensis pocula digna dari.
Cum propius venies murorum annosa vetustas
    Quadratusque lapis non levis ambit honos.
Ingressus primum Divae venerabere Matris
    A dextris Mariae templa verenda piae.
Quisquis es, artifici concedes, Daedale, nostro,
    Vincit divitias ingeniosa manus.
Marmorea haec Christi genetrici convenit aedes
    Et constructori convenit ipsa Pio.
Nec solum tanto aspectu retinebere primo
    Mirum opus ostendent subdita templa tibi.
Hoc opus ingenii et manuum est, Pie papa, tuarum,
    Hoc videat quisquis nobile condit opus.
Hinc sunt Pontificis vicina palatia Summi,
    Et quis Romano principe digna neget?
Hunc, igitur, primum sibi dia Pientia civem
    Vindicat e prisca nobilitate Pium.
Delos et ut Phoebo, Smyrna illustratur Homero,
    Mantua Virgilio, Stagira Aristotele,
Sic de te exultat Tuscae telluris alumno,
    Qui prius Aeneas, terra paterna, Pie,
Deque tuo gaudet sumpsisse Pientia nomen
    Et Corsignani deposuisse sonum.
Hic illustrantes templa omnia et atria lunas
    Saphireae claudunt signa verenda crucis.
Proxima converso tua sunt, Barbate, metallo
    Atria, namque aurum plumbea massa refert.
Mirifico surgunt opere hic tibi protinus aedes,
    Piccolomineo nomine clare Thoma,
Quem plus quam gentis virtutis gratia pulchrae
    Pontifici assiduum cogit adesse Pio.
Concertant gravitas in te probitasque fidesque
    Et pudor et recti conscia vota sibi.
Urbe nova exultat hinc iam praetoria sedes,
    Ostendit medio seque superba foro.
Hinc quoque succedunt tua prima palatia templo
    Qui magnum in patribus fers, Rodorice, gradum.
In te magnanimi Calixti vivit imago
    Per quem sunt nostro sceptra relicta Pio.
Nec minus ex illo spes et praesagia magnae
    Huic sunt venturae tradita certa rei.

Illum devictis celebrat victoria Turcis
  Traxit sanguineas qua modo Savus aquas.
Astra suum potius perdent cum sole decorem
  Quam pereant tanto parta tropaea viro.
Fers animos patruo dignos et pectora tanto
  In Turcos classem qui, Rodorice, paras.
Struxit et ipse suas aedes et tecta Johannes
  Atrebatensis clarus in arce patrum,
Eloquio velox, audaci pectore, gressu
  Et lingua promptus, ingenioque ferox.
Fers tecum ad Gallos monumenta et pignus amici
  Grande Pii, pileo tempora tecte rubro.
Ipse novae pariter proles Gonzagia civem
  Sese Franciscus urbis amator agit.
Illustre exuperat proavorum moribus agmen
  Ingenuasque artes corde calente trahit.
Huius et aspicies fundata palatia clari
  Principis hospitium protinus esse sui,
Et debere Pio sentit crescentibus annis
  Quod teneat in summa Cardinis arce locum.
Tu quoque, magne pater, praesul Lebrete, minaris
  Et signas latis atria celsa locis.
Quid tamen in tantis, heros clarissime, differs
  Principibus fieri civis et ipse novus?
At vero tua iam faber alta palatia nullus,
  Magne Iacobe pater Piccolomine, struit.
Sed sunt ingenio, sunt consummata labore,
  Iam pridem ipsa frequens nobilis hospes habet.
Officio cunctos superasti et munere pulchro
  Nec studio quemquam passus es esse parem.
In te divinum est princeps miratus acumen
  Maximus et mentis captus odore tuae.
Iussit et excelsi conscendere rostra Senatus
  Tectum purpureo frontis honore caput
Deque tuo laudem nactus sibi munere sensit
  Omnibus ex illo se placuisse bonis.
Quod si non apicem summum tua fama teneret,
  Iret ab Anguigero laus quoque multa duce.
Hic tua celsa nitent, clarissime, tecta, Gregori
  Piccolomine, domus gloria summa sacrae.
Te sine iam tanto celebrata Pientia cive
  Audiret laudes non bene laeta suas.
Aeneae es nostro fidissimus alter Achates,
  Alter et Atridae Pylius ipse senex.

Pontificesque ideo populi regesque ducesque
  Et te praecipuo clerus honore colunt.
Divinas leges humanaque iussa tenaci
  Corde fovens omni laude canenda facis.
Quicquid et arcanum, quicquid grave rebus agendis
  Infracto peragis pectore, mente, manu.
Limina succedunt tua, Miraballe, decora
  Proque Giliforto civis habere Pii.
Dirigis imperiis insignem principis aulam,
  Quae venit ad nutus officiosa tuos.
Sed quibus ipsa mihi princeps dicere Camenis,
  Quae matronarum es, Laudomia, decus?
Namque tuae splendent aedes hos inter in urbe,
  Unde genus summa nobilitate trahis.
Ambiguum certe mater felicior utrum
  An soror; ad culmen nomen utrumque venit.
Silvius est idem pater et Victoria mater
  Qui summum nobis progenuere ducem.
Vidimus ante pedes fraternos sistere nuper
  Teque tuas cives, agmina longa, sequi,
Cum cinerem sacram patribus populoque viritim
  Principis inferret religiosa manus.
At tua iam soboles, clarissima pignora, paucis
  Carminibus non se sustinet ipsa capi.
Huic est purpureo frons insignita galero,
  Et summum Sacra nomen in Urbe tenet.
  Illum miles habet sumptis feliciter armis
  Campanaeque urbes, regia dona, ducem.
At reliquis omni cumulatis laude salutem
  Papa suam noctes credit et usque dies.
Felix una meo, felix e matribus una es
  Carmine; at es totiens ipsa beata soror.
Et dum tanta sequor, mihi ferme oblita Proseucha est;
  Struxit at hanc pietas ipsa colenda Pii.
Hinc iam profugium, miseri solamen egeni,
Accipit et requiem fessus, inopsque cibum.
Vos modo feliciter reditum deposcite, cives,
  Dirigit in Turcos qui sua signa, Pio
Quique mari classes et terris agmina totis
  Instruit intrepidus nec timet arma senex.
Excipiant reducem victrici classe fugatis
  Hostibus Italiae litora laeta suae.
Hoc eius pietas et religiosa meretur
  Canities nulla territa sorte gravi.

Ornamenta dabit tibi plura, Pientia, victor
Coget et hinc magnos forsitan ire lacus."
Pientiae, 15 Kalendas Martias 1464[17]

Lodrisio Crivelli to the Muse Polyhymnia
in Praise of the City of Pienza

Muse, remind us of your glory in order. For the glory of the most high prince Pius is all yours. Begin by telling how great are the citizens who have augmented the city of Pienza, which has been made splendid by a new embellishment. He nodded, and since your heart is held by a just honor, receive what your song signifies. [The muse replies.] "On the top of a sunny hill you have seen a city, located between Siena and Lake Trasimene, and streams hot with seething waters whence the sick man takes healthful aid. Thence the eternal water flows down from a twin fountain, whose appearance smiles clearer than that of Jove himself. To that place no morbid summer harmful to men's bodies, hot with blowing west winds, comes. Here the fog yields to the warm sun, and the earth is fertile for crops and herds, and it bears the olive tree and the very pleasant gifts of sweet Bacchus, cups worthy to be given to the tables of wealthy men. When you approach nearer, the ancient age of the walls and the squared dignity of the heavy stone extends around. As you enter on the right, you will worship the holy temple of the sacred divine Mother Mary.[18] Whoever you are, architect, you will yield to our workman, whose talented hand surpasses riches. This marble building is fitting for the mother of Christ and fitting too for its builder Pius. Not only will you be arrested at first by such a great sight, but the temples below will show you wonderful work.[19] This is the work of your talent and of your hands, Pope Pius; may whoever builds a noble work see this. Nearby is the summer palace of the supreme priest, and who would call it unworthy of a Roman prince? Divine Pienza claims for itself, then, its first citizen, Pius, from ancient nobility. And just as Delos is made illustrious by Apollo, Smyrna by Homer, Mantua by Virgil, and Stagira by Aristotle, so Pienza rejoices in you, Pius, previously called Aeneas, offspring of the Tuscan land. Pienza rejoices that she took her name from you and renounced the name of Corsignano. Here the holy sign of the sapphire-blue cross makes all the temples and public buildings bright, and encloses the crescent moons.[20] Next is your palace, Bearded One, with its metal transformed, for the mass of lead suggests gold. Farther on, your buildings rise here with marvelous work, Thomas, famous in the name Piccolomini, whom more than the grace of beautiful excellence of family impels to be continuously near the priest Pius. Dignity, honesty, and trustworthiness join forces in you, and decency and vows conscious in themselves of what is right. Henceforth now the praetor's palace rejoices in a new city, and shows itself proud in the middle of the square.[21] Here also your first palaces follow the temple, Rodrigo, you who walk mightily among the fathers. In you survives the spirit of great-souled Calixtus, through whom the power was left to our Pius. From him, too, was handed down to Pius the hope and sure predictions of a great future. After the defeat of the Turks, victory honors him where only recently the Savus' bloody waters flowed. Sooner will the stars and the sun lose their glory than will perish the victory won by such a great man. You Rodrigo, who ready the fleet against the Turks, possess soul and courage worthy of such a great uncle. The famous Cardinal Jouffroy of Arras built his own edifice and home in the citadel of the fathers, a man swift in eloquence, with a daring heart, ready in action and word, with a fierce nature. Your temples being covered with a red cap, you carry with you to the Gauls the written memorials and the lofty pledge of your friend Pius. Francesco himself, offspring of Gonzaga, a lover of the new city, comes as its citizen. He surpasses in good character the illustrious line of his ancestors, and his innate skills flow from a warm heart. Farther on, you will see that the well-founded palace of this famous man too is the guest chamber of his prince, and he perceives as the years pass that he owes to Pius the place of cardinal he holds in the high citadel. You also, great father, Cardinal d'Albret, put on an impressive display, and mark out the high public buildings in the wide places. But why, O most famous hero, do you, a citizen and a new one at that, delay your appointment among such great princes? But indeed no builder now constructs your high palaces, O great Jacob, father Piccolomini. They were on the other hand completed by talent and toil; for a long time now a noble guest has constantly had them at his disposal. You have surpassed all men in duty and excellent performance in public office; you have allowed no man to be your equal in devotion. The greatest prince marveled at your superhuman understanding and was charmed by the perfume of your mind. He ordered you to climb the platform of the high Senate, your forehead covered with the purple decoration of honor, and he obtained praise for himself as a result of your holding this office and therefrom perceived that he had pleased all the good men. And if your good reputation were not holding the highest honor, much renown would proceed as well from the duke Francesco Sforza.[22] Here your lofty building shines, most famous Gregory [Lolli] Piccolomini, the highest glory of the holy home. If not for you, her greatest citizen, the crowded city of Pienza would not now be listening happily to her own praise. A second Achates you are, most faithful to our Aeneas, and the old man himself is a second Nestor, most faithful to Agamemnon. To such an extent do priests, peoples, kings, leaders, and the clergy honor you also with an extraordinary honor. Cherishing with your steady heart divine law and human ordinance, you make them celebrated with all praise. And you accomplish with steady heart, mind, and hand whatever is hidden, whatever is serious in public business. Alessandro de' Mirabelli, your threshold follows your distinctions, and you instead of Giliforte are considered a fellow citizen of Pius. With your power you govern the famous court of the prince, which dutifully submits to your will. But with what Muses do you, Laudomia, who are yourself the chief glory of women, speak to me? For your buildings shine among these in the city, whence you trace your lineage from the highest nobility. It is uncertain whether you are more fortunate as mother or as sister, for each title arrives at the summit. The same Silvius is your father and Victoria your mother, who have borne for us the highest leader. We recently saw you stand before the feet of your brother, we saw your citizens follow you in a long line, when the prince's sacred hand was bringing the sacred ash man by man to the fathers and to the people. But now your offspring, most famous token of your love, does not allow

himself to be captured by a few poems.[23] His forehead is distinguished with a purple
cap, and he holds the highest title in the sacred city. The soldier is happy, when arms
have been taken up, to have him as a leader, and the cities of Campania, royal gifts, are
happy too.[24] But the Pope continuously during the nights and right up until the days
entrusts his own safety to the remaining men who are loaded with all praise.[25] You
alone of mothers are fortunate in my poem; but you yourself are as many times blessed
as sister. And while I sing of such great things, I almost have forgotten the hospice;
but Pius' devotion itself has built this and must be venerated. Here now there is a
refuge, the consolation of the needy wretch; the tired man receives rest, and the poor
man receives nourishment. But you, citizens, do you successfully demand the return of
him who directs his standards against the Turks, who draws up Pius' fleets on the sea
and troops in all the lands, the calm old man who does not fear weapons.[26] May his
own Italy's happy shores greet him as he returns with his victorious fleet after
vanquishing the enemy. This is the reward his devotion and conscientious old age,
terrified by no oppressive fate, deserve. The victor will give you more honors, Pienza,
and perhaps will force the great lakes to go from here. At Pienza, 15 February, 1464.

Doc. 5. A Poem Praising Pienza and its Patron by Giannantonio Campano (1468?)

Urbs nova deque Pio sortita Pientia nomen,
   Salve, Dii aspiciant moenia, Di homines.
Atque aedes salvete Pii fundataque templa
   Et sua siqua istis moenibus umbra vaga est.
Illi tu genialem solum, genialia tecta,
   Ille dedit nomen sceptraque prima tibi.
Hinc mihi communi succrevit gloria fato,
   Tuque Pio dederas, ut foret ille mihi.
Quae mihi nunc animo consurgunt gaudia cum te
   Aspicio, quanta est laetitia et lacrymae![27]

Hail, new city which has obtained the name Pienza from Pius; may the gods look
favorably on your walls and inhabitants. And hail also, palace of Pius and cathedral
built by him, and his shade, if any such thing is still wandering around those walls of
his. You gave him a native land, a family home; and he gave you a name and your first
royal authority. By a common fate, my fame has increased from this place, and you
had given it to Pius, so that he would be my own glory. What joys now rise up in my
soul when I catch sight of you, how great are both my happiness and my tears!

Doc. 6. Extract from the *Pii II vita* of Giannantonio Campano (before 1474)

Edificandi studium bella interceperunt. Caeterum in Vaticano cellas templi maximi
promiscue passim aedificatas dissici iussit, ac mox secundum parietis tractum collocari,

quo reddita est facies interior templi augustior et patentior. Addidit et cellam divi
Andreae ad primum angulum templi leva subeuntibus; ubi postea et sepeliri se iussit.
Scalas quoque instauravit pro foribus templi vetustate collapsas, stravitque aream
amplissimam, vestibulo palatii communito turri excubatoria. Incoatam supra scalas
marmoream porticum imperfectam reliquit. Est et ipsius arx Tyburtina opere tumul'
tuario confecta, quod non prohibuissent transitu et iuvissent comeatu hostes, et
recipere intra urbem ipsius praesidia recusassent; exprobravitque dubiam fidem et
diripi eorum agrum est passus. Fuitque et nostrum disticon:

> Tybur, habes arcem, quod non tibi creditur, hinc est:
> Aeneas Phryx est. Tybur es Argolicum.

Corsinianum ex oppido urbem Pientiam appellavit, designatis magistratibus urbanis in
speciem iuste civitatis; episcopio et pretorio edificatis, episcopum et triumviros
instituit, et certamina gymnica per gradus aetatis. Construxit et aedes gentilicias eximia
pulchritudine symmetria quadrangula, lapide suffusco extanti incrustatas ad digiti
crassitudinem, comissuris paulum recedentibus, duplici ordine fenestrarum, anulis et
cratibus ferreis. Addiditque porticum ad meridiem duplici concameratione, contigna-
tione insuper acclivi, et triclinia aestiva atque hiberna, et cellas promptuarias alte
suffossas, ortosque pensiles. Templum quoque egregia structura, et aream pro foribus,
et cellas in ambitum templi, aramque subterraneam; vetuitque in eo quenquam sepeliri
praeter sacerdotes et antistitem, quibus et tumulum seorsum assignavit; tum violari
parietem picturamque infingi, aut appendi iconias, aut cellas erigi, aut altaria preter-
quam quae ipse destinasset, et praedia in sumptus annuos coemit. Architecto ad
summam futurae impensae longe praementito, post perfectum opus addi centum iussit,
dicens desipere architectum qui de impensa quam nemo sit facturus ante praefiniat.
Fecit et Senae porticum gentiliciam conca'meratam, aedes quoque adiuncturus, quarum
iam aream straverat. Erexit et cellam ad phanum divi Francisci, et in ea sepulchrum
parentibus marmore ligustico, hoc inciso distico, quod ipse condiderat:

> Silvius hic iaceo, coniunx Victoria mecum est.
> Filius hoc clausit marmore Papa Pius.

Cogitaverat Anienem ad Tybur usque navigabilem reddere; portum quoque Traiani
repurgare, et in Pientino lacum facere, Orcia flumine occluso ac rivo ex Amiatae
radicibus eodem derivato.[28]

His [Pius'] enthusiasm for his building program was interrupted by wars. Moreover,
in the Vatican, he ordered the largest sanctuary's shrines, which had been built
indiscriminately here and there, to be laid in ruins, and soon afterwards ordered the
expanse of the wall to be laid out so that the temple's interior appearance was made
more majestic and more extensive.[29] He added a chapel to Saint Andrew at the
cathedral's first corner as you approach the left side and afterwards designated it as his
burial place. He also rebuilt in front of the temple doors the staircase, which had

collapsed from age, and he spread out a very spacious open area in the forecourt of the palace, a guard house with a fortified tower. He began, and left unfinished, a marble gallery above the staircase. At Tivoli a citadel also was completed, by Pius' own hastily improvised efforts, because they had not prevented the enemy from passing across and had even aided their free passage, and they had refused to receive Pius' own garrisons inside the city; he reproached their questionable fidelity and allowed their land to be pillaged. I have written a couplet about it:

> Tivoli, you have a citadel, and insofar as you are not
> trusted, it comes from this reason:
> Aeneas is Trojan; you, Tivoli, are Greek.

He called his city Pienza, which had been the town Corsignano, and the urban magistrates were elected for the purpose of the proper appearance of a city-state. He built a bishopric and a praetor's palace, established a bishop and triumvirs, and athletic contests according to age-group.[30] He also built an outstandingly beautiful family palace, squarely symmetrical; the palace was covered with dark stones which protruded to the thickness of a man's finger, as the joints were set back a little, with a double row of windows and with iron rings and gratings. To the south, he added a gallery, with a double-vaulted roof, with a constructed floor inclined upwards above, summer and winter dining rooms, and rooms for storing things ready for use, deeply excavated below, and hanging gardens. He also added a church, which was outstanding in its construction; and a courtyard in front of the doors, and chapels in the space around the church, and a subterranean altar. He forbade anyone to be buried in it except priests and bishops, to whom he assigned a separate tomb. Then he forbade the walls to be defaced, a painting to be drawn, or images to be hung up, or more chapels or altars to be built than those he himself had intended. He also bought land for the annual expenses. The architect had enormously underestimated the total of the eventual cost, but after the completion of the work Pius ordered a hundred ducats to be added to his pay, saying that an architect would be foolish if, in advance of a work's completion, he predicted the exact cost, when it was so large that no one would pay it. He also built at Siena a vaulted colonnade for his family, and intended too to join to it a palace, whose forecourt he already had laid. He also erected a chapel to the temple of Saint Francis, and in it a tomb of Ligurian marble for his parents, with this couplet of his own composition engraved upon it:

> I, Silvius, lie here, my wife Victoria by my side.
> Pope Pius, my son, covered me with this marble monument.

He had planned to make the Anio River navigable as far as Tivoli, and to free from obstructions the harbor of Trajan, and to create a lake in the territory of Pienza after damming the river Orcia and diverting the same stream at the base of Mount Amiata.

Appendix 2

Documentary Evidence for the Building of
Pienza from the Archivio di Stato, Rome

IN THIS appendix are published, for the first time, all the official documentation from the papal archives (now housed in the Archivio di Stato di Roma) pertaining to the architectural program carried out in Pienza under the patronage of Pope Pius II.[1] The majority of the entries are found in ASR, Camerale I: *Mandati camerale*, 834 (1458–60); *Tesoreria segreta*, 1288 (1461–62); and *Tesoreria segreta*, 1289 (1462–64).[2] Thirty-nine of the ninety documents presented here have never before been published or mentioned in the literature.[3] The remainder have been published or noted in Müntz, *Les Arts*, 1:301– 5; Borghese and Banchi, *Nuovi documenti per la storia dell'arte senese*, pp. 215–17; Pietro Rossi, "Pio II a Pienza," *Bullettino Senese di Storia Patria*, 8 (1901), 3–26; Tyskiewicz, *Bernardo Rossellino*, pp. 126–27; E. Casanova, "Un anno della vita privata di Pio II," *Bullettino Senese di Storia Patria*, 38 (1931), 30–33; and Mannucci, *Pienza*, pp. 90–92. The documents that have been previously published or cited are so indicated. I am indebted to Nicholas Adams for correcting some of my transcriptions and for his addition of Docs. 42–44 and 86 to the materials presented here.

A better understanding of the expenses incurred in the Renaissance modernization of Pienza might be had if the *ducati, grossi, bologni, fiorini*, and *soldi* in the documents could be given modern monetary values. This is not easily done, however, for the economy of fifteenth-century Italy was vastly different from that of today. Perhaps the best approach is to attempt to ascertain the "buying power" of Renaissance currency.[4] An examination of a variety of payment records of the period shows that a skilled worker in Rome—a building foreman or contractor, for instance—might earn around sixty ducats during a year of steady employment (estimated at about 260 days).[5] A papal ducat was about equal to a Florentine florin; both were worth about five Sienese lire. A third of that income would be spent on the basics of shelter, food, and clothing. Of those essentials, housing appears to have been the least costly, with simple quarters renting at an annual rate of under five ducats. Thus, the actual construction cost for each of the twelve *case nuove* built by Pietro Porrina in Pienza in 1463 was roughly equivalent to what a stonemason in a supervisory position might receive in two years' time, and Gregorio Lolli was able to purchase the smaller of the two houses on the site of his palace for about half the annual income of our hypothetical craftsman.

Doc. 1. 19 January 1459. Simili modo retineri faciatis summam florenorum auri de camera 600 videlicet de cameris pro 400 similibus florenis quos solvi feciatis in civitate Senarum sororibus sanctissimi domini nostri papae et pro 200 aliis similibus florenis quos solvi fecistis in castro Corsignani comitatus Senarum cuidem fratri Johanni de Corsignano ordinis sancti Francisci exponendos per eum in principio constructionis unius capellae. [ASR, *Mandati camerale,* 834, c. 80ᵛ (Müntz, p. 302)]

Doc. 2. 27 March 1459. Ludovicus etc. Reverendo . . . etc. mandatus. . . . Honorabilibus viris Ricardo de Sarracenis et sociis de Senis florenos auri de camera 325 quos ispsi solverunt Ser Cole de castro Plebe pro fabrica seu reparatione murorum palatii castri Corcigniani quos etc. [ASR, *Mandati camerale,* 834, c. 86ᵛ (Müntz, p. 302)]

Doc. 3. 28 December 1460. A detta Santita . . . duc. 1200 dati di comandamento di sua Santita a mirabelli per la frabica di corsignano. . . . [ASR, *Tesoreria segreta,* 1288, c. 73 (Tyszkiewicz, p. 126)]

Doc. 4. 23 January 1461. A detta Santita . . . duc. 1000 le quale di comandamento di Sua Santita a mirabelli per la frabica di corsignano. . . . [ASR, *Tesoreria segreta,* 1288, c. 74ᵛ (Tyszkiewicz, p. 126; cited in Müntz p. 301 n. 4)]

Doc. 5. 4 February 1461. A detta Santita . . . duc. 2000 dati di comandamento di Sua Santita al bancho di mirabelli per la frabica di corsignano e di siena per lo palazo. [ASR, *Tesoreria segreta,* 1288, c. 75 (Tyszkiewicz, p. 126; cited in Müntz, p. 301 n. 4)]

Doc. 6. 8 April 1461. A detta Santita . . . ducati 2000 dati di comandamento di Sua Santita al bancho danbruogio Spanocchi e conpagni per la frabica di corsignano. [ASR, *Tesoreria segreta,* 1288, c. 77 (Tyszkiewicz, p. 126; cited in Müntz p. 301 n. 4)]

Doc. 7. 1 May 1461. Alla Santita di N.S. . . . ducati 1200 dati di comandamento di Sua Santita a danbruogio Spanocchi e conpagni per la frabica di corsignano. . . . [ASR, *Tesoreria segreta,* 1288, c. 79 (Tyszkiewicz, p. 126; cited in Müntz, p. 301 n. 4)]

Doc. 8. 26 May 1461. A detta Santita . . . ducati 1500 dati di comandamento di Sua Santita al bancho danbruogio Spanocchi per la frabica di corsignano. . . . [ASR, *Tesoreria segreta,* 1288, c. 79ᵛ (Tyszkiewicz, p. 127; cited in Müntz, p. 301 n. 4)]

Doc. 9. 3 June 1461. Alla Santita di N.S. . . . ducati 1500 dati di comandamento di Sua Santita al bancho danbruogio Spanocchi per la frabica di corsignano. . . . [ASR, *Tesoreria segreta,* 1288, c. 80 (Tyszkiewicz, p. 127; cited in Müntz, p. 301 n. 4)]

Doc. 10. 9 July 1461. A detta Santita di detto ducati 1000 dati di comandamento di Sua Santita al bancho danbruogio Spanocchi e conpagni per la frabica di corsignano. . . . [ASR, *Tesoreria segreta,* 1288, c. 81 (Tyszkiewicz, p. 127; cited in Müntz, p. 301 n. 4)]

Doc. 11. 3 August 1461. Alla Santita di N.S. . . . ducati 800 dati di comandamento di Sua Santita al bancho danbruogio Spanocchi e conpagni per la frabica di corsignano. . . . [ASR, *Tesoreria segreta,* 1288, c. 83 (Tyszkiewicz, p. 127; cited in Müntz, p. 301 n. 4)]

Doc. 12. 5 September 1461. A detta Santita . . . ducati 600 dati di comandamento di Sua Santita al bancho danbruogio Spanocchi e conpagni per la frabica di corsignano. [ASR, *Tesoreria segreta,* 1288, c. 84 (Tyszkiewicz, p. 127; cited in Müntz, p. 301 n. 4)]

Doc. 13. 8 October 1461. A detta Santita . . . ducati 600 dati di comandamento di Sua Santita al bancho danbruogio Spanocchi e conpagni per la frabica di corsignano. [ASR, *Tesoreria segreta,* 1288, c. 86^v (cited in Müntz, p. 301 n. 4)]

Doc. 14. 2 November 1461. A detta Santita . . . ducati 1000 dati di comandamento di Sua Santita al bancho danbruogio Spanocchi e conpagni per la frabica di corsignano. [ASR, *Tesoreria segreta,* 1288, c. 87 (Tyszkiewicz, p. 127; cited in Müntz, p. 301 n. 4)]

Doc. 15. 4 December 1461. A detta Santita . . . ducati 1000 dati di comandamento di Sua Santita al bancho danbruogio Spanocchi e conpagni per la frabica di corsignano. [ASR, *Tesoreria segreta,* 1288, c. 91 (Tyszkiewicz, p. 127; cited in Müntz, p. 301 n. 4)]

Doc. 16. 2 January 1462. A detta Santita . . . ducati 1000 di camera pagati per comandamento di Sua Santita al bancho danbruogio Spanocchi e conpagni per la frabica di corsignano. [ASR, *Tesoreria segreta,* 1288, c. 94 (cited in Müntz, p. 301 n. 4)]

Doc. 17. 5 February 1462. Alla Santita di N.S. . . . ducati 1000 di camera dati di comandamento di Sua Santita al bancho danbruogio Spanocchi e conpagni li quale di per la frabicha di corsignano. . . . [ASR, *Tesoreria segreta,* 1288, c. 95 (cited in Müntz, p. 301 n. 4)]

Doc. 18. 7 March 1462. A detta Santita . . . ducati 1000 di camera li quale dati di comandamento di Sua Santita al bancho danbruogio Spanocchi e conpagni per la frabica di corsignano li quale ebbe agostantino loro contatore. [ASR, *Tesoreria segreta,* 1288, c. 96 (Tyszkiewicz, p. 127; cited in Müntz, p. 301 n. 4)]

Doc. 19. 7 April 1462. A detta Santita . . . ducati 1000 dati di comandamento di Sua Santita al bancho danbruogio Spanocchi e conpagni per la frabica di corsignano dati agostantino loro. . . . [ASR, *Tesoreria segreta,* 1288, c. 98 (Tyszkiewicz, p. 127; cited in Müntz, p. 301 n. 4)]

Doc. 20. 2 May 1462. A detta Santita . . . ducati 1000 di camera dati di comandamento di Sua Santita al bancho danbruogio Spanocchi per la frabica di corsignano porto contanti agostantino loro. [ASR, *Tesoreria segreta,* 1288, c. 100^v (Tyszkiewicz, p. 127; cited in Müntz, p. 301 n. 4)]

Doc. 21. 1 June 1462. A detta Santita . . . ducati 1000 di camera dati di comandamento di Sua Santita al bancho danbruogio Spanocchi e conpagni per la frabica di corsignano. [ASR, *Tesoreria segreta,* 1288, c. 103 (Tyszkiewicz, p. 127; cited in Müntz, p. 301 n. 4)]

Doc. 22. 19 June 1462. A detta Santita . . . ducati 1000 di camera dati di comandamento di Sua Santita al bancho danbruogio Spanocchi per la frabicha di pientia. . . .

[ASR, *Tesoreria segreta*, 1288, c. 104^v (Tyszkiewicz, p. 127; cited in Müntz, p. 301 n. 4)]

Doc. 23. 2 August 1462. A detta Santita . . . ducati 1000 di camera dati di comandamento di Sua Santita al bancho danbruogio Spanocchi e conpagni per la frabica di pientia liquali denari . . . per Stefano loro. . . . [ASR, *Tesoreria segreta*, 1288, c. 111 (Tyszkiewicz, p. 127; cited in Müntz, p. 301 n. 4)]

Doc. 24. 12 August 1462. A detta Santita . . . ducati 89, grossi 4 dati di comandamento di Sua Santita a matteo barbiere da pientia per la sua casa vende a Sua Santita per fare la casa del comuno di pientia. . . . [ASR, *Tesoreria segreta*, 1288, c. 113 (Casanova, p. 30)]

Doc. 25. 21 August 1462. A detta Santita . . . ducati 100 dati di comandamento di Sua Santita a M^o bernardo da fiorenza lo quale muro la chiesa e lo palazo di pientia li quali denari Sua Santita li dono. [ASR, *Tesoreria segreta*, 1288, c. 113^v (Tyszkiewicz, p. 127)]

Doc. 26. 1 September 1462. Alla Santita di N.S. . . . ducati 1000 li quali dati di comandamento di Sua Santita al bancho danbruogio Spanocchi e conpagni adi 27 pasato per la frabica di pientia. . . . [ASR, *Tesoreria segreta*, 1288, c. 115 (Tyszkiewicz, p. 127; cited in Müntz, p. 301 n. 4)]

Doc. 27. 2 September 1462. A detta Santita . . . ducati 17 dati di comandamento di Sua Santita a bartolomeo e M^o giovanni di pietro di leonardo da pientia per una casa vende a Sua Santita per donare a misser Tome Piccogluomini quale fa fare. [ASR, *Tesoreria segreta*, 1288, c. 115^v]

Doc. 28. 2 September 1462. A detta Santita . . . ducati 106 e grossi 8 dati di comandamento di Sua Santita a Ser Tomasso da Terni abitante a Radicofani li quali sono per una casa a venduta a N.S. a pientia lo quale casa se comprata per fare la casa a pientia per lo podesta e priori e camerlengho. [ASR, *Tesoreria segreta*, 1288, c. 115^v (Tyszkiewicz, p. 127; Casanova, p. 29)]

Doc. 29. 3 September 1462. A detta Santita . . . ducati 4 e grossi 6 dati di comandamento di Sua Santita a bongio dalegro duioltolina lombardo abitante a pientia li quali ebbe per una cantina con una piaza vende la rogato di Ser Franciescho dantonio di ciecho da Siena. [ASR, *Tesoreria segreta*, 1288, c. 116]

Doc. 30. 3 September 1462. A detta Santita . . . ducati 7 dati di comandamento di Sua Santita a marcho di nanni da pientia per una cantina con una piaza vende rogato il detto Ser Giovanni. . . . [ASR, *Tesoreria segreta*, 1288, c. 116]

Doc. 31. 3 September 1462. A detta Santita . . . ducati 100 dati di comandamento di Sua Santita a domenicho dantonio detto riccio habitante a Pientia li quali denari ebbe per fare uno abergho e rispondare l'anno ducati 4 alla chiesa di Pientia in perpetuo rogato Ser Tomasso da terni habitante a radicofani. [ASR, *Tesoreria segreta*, 1288, c. 116 (Casanova, p. 32)]

Doc. 32. 3 September 1462. A detta Santita . . . ducati 100 dati a M^o Quirico di cristofano da San Quirico habitante a Pientia li quali denari ebbe per fare una casa e rispondere in perpetuo alla chiesa ducati 4 l'anno rogato il detto Ser Giovanni. . . . [ASR, *Tesoreria segreta*, 1288, c. 116 (Casanova, p. 32)]

Doc. 33. 3 September 1462. A detta Santita . . . ducati 60 ne ebbe dati di comandamento di Sua Santita a M° Magio d'Agniolo dal monte a folonica habitante a Pientia li quali ebbe per fare una casa e pagare alla chiesa ducati 2 in perpetuo rogato Ser Tomasso da terni habitante a radicofani. [ASR, *Tesoreria segreta*, 1288, c. 116 (Casanova, p. 32)]

Doc. 34. 4 September 1462. A detta Santita . . . ducati 7 e bologni 4 dati di comandamento di Sua Santita a ser tibaldo canonico di Pientia e Ghelardo di Mariano suo fratello li quali ebbe per uno orto vende a Sua Santita rogato Ser Franciescho dantonio di ciecho da Siena. [ASR, *Tesoreria segreta*, 1288, c. 116ᵛ (Casanova, p. 30)]

Doc. 35. 4 September 1462. A detta Santita . . . ducati 12 e grossi 5 dati di comandamento di Sua Santita a Jacomo di Ser Nicolo di ciechi mattei per uno orto vende a Sua Santita rogato detto Ser Giovanni. [ASR, *Tesoreria segreta*, 1288, c. 116ᵛ]

Doc. 36. 5 September 1462. A detta Santita . . . ducati 6 e grossi 2 bologni 3 dati di comandamento di Sua Santita a pietro di nanni dugolino da pientia per uno orto comprato Sua Santita da lui rogato Ser Franciescho dantonio di checo da Siena notaio. [ASR, *Tesoreria segreta*, 1288, c. 117]

Doc. 37. 5 September 1462. A detta Santita . . . ducati 2 dati di comandamento di Sua Santita a Cristofano di mariano da pientia per uno orto vende a sua Santita rogato Ser Franciescho dantonio di ciecho da Siena notaro. [ASR, *Tesoreria segreta*, 1288, c. 117ᵛ]

Doc. 38. 5 September 1462. A detta Santita . . . ducati 2 dati di comandamento di Sua Santita a mino di Leonardo di nino da Pientia per uno orto vende a Sua Santita rogato il detto Ser Giovanni. [ASR, *Tesoreria segreta*, 1288, c. 117ᵛ]

Doc. 39. 5 September 1462. A detta Santita . . . ducati 4 e grossi 7 e bologni 2 dati di comandamento di Sua Santita a martino di Matteo da Pientia per uno orto vende a Sua Santita rogato il detto Ser Giovanni. [ASR, *Tesoreria segreta*, 1288, c. 117ᵛ]

Doc. 40. 5 September 1462. A detta Santita . . . ducati 6 e grossi 2 e bologni 2 dati di comandamento di Sua Santita a Jacomo di Leonardo di Franciescho per uno orto vende a Sua Santita in monie delle rede di Leonardo suo padre morte di poco et perche lui a due suoi altri fratelli pero disse lo contratto in nome delle rede rogato il detto Ser Giovanni. [ASR, *Tesoreria segreta*, 1288, c. 117ᵛ]

Doc. 41. 11 September 1462. A detto Santita . . . ducati 240 e grossi 8 e bologni 4 dati di comandamento di Sua Santita a detto giovanni di furtunato dal Cotono li quali sono per una casa posta in pientia e una pocisione in nella corte di pientia la quale anno venduta a Sua Santita rogato Ser Nicolo di Lorenzo da Siena. [ASR, *Tesoreria segreta*, 1288, c. 118ᵛ]

Doc. 42. 11 September 1462. A detta Santita . . . ducati 77 grossi 9 dati di comandamento di sua Santita a giovanni e rede di franciescho di furtunato dal cotono senesi li quali Sua Santita lo dona per limosina. . . . [ASR, *Tesoreria segreta*, 1288, c. 118ᵛ]

Doc. 43. 13 September 1462. A detta Santita . . . ducati 89 di camera e grossi 4 dati di comandamento di Sua Santita a matteo barbiere da pientia li quali furono per la sua casa vende a sua Santita per fare la casa del comuno di pientia rogato del contratto Ser Nicolo di lorenzo da Siena notaio. . . . [ASR, *Tesoreria segreta*, 1288, c. 119]

Doc. 44. 22 September 1462. A detta Santita . . . ducati 4 dati di comandamento di sua Santita ad andrea di nicolo di lolo per la sua partita di pientia. [ASR, *Tesoreria segreta*, 1288, c. 120]

Doc. 45. 22 September 1462. A detta Santita . . . ducati 100 dati di comandamento di Sua Santita a frate giovanni di M° Martino granciere dello spedaletto di val d'orcia li quali denari li o dati per fare uno spedale nella cipta di pientia lo quale spedale fa fare lo spedale di siena et per limosina Sua Santita fa quella limosina. [ASR, *Tesoreria segreta*, 1288, c. 120 (Rossi, p. 136; Casanova, p. 33)]

Doc. 46. 23 September 1462. A detta Santita . . . ducati 1359 e grossi 3 dati di comandamento di Sua Santita a orlando Saracini per comissione di Misser giovanni Saracini li quali sonno per una pocisione chiamata il castelletto et una casa posta in pientia per fare lo palazo del comuno et una vignia posta nella corte di Pientia le quali cose a vendute Jacomo di mino Piccogliuomini a Misser Giovanni Saracini per il Nipoti della Santita di N.S. [ASR, *Tesoreria segreta*, 1288, c. 120ᵛ (Müntz, p. 303)]

Doc. 47. 24 September 1462. A detta Santita . . . ducati 700 di camera dati di comandamento di Sua Santita al bancho danbruogio Spanocchi e conpagni di corte li quali sono per la frabicha di pientia dati a stefano ghinucci loro. [ASR, *Tesoreria segreta*, 1288, c. 121 (Tyszkiewicz, p. 127; cited in Müntz, p. 301 n. 4)]

Doc. 48. 28 September 1462. A detta Santita . . . ducati 100 dati di comandamento di Sua Santita a Salamone Piccogliuomini li quali li da Sua Santita perche rifaccia la facciata della sua casa di pientia. . . . [ASR, *Tesoreria segreta*, 1288, c. 122 (Müntz, p. 303)]

Doc. 49. 28 September 1462. A detta Santita . . . ducati 50 dati di comandamento di Sua Santita a vescovo di pientia et per lui al porina porini lo quale conprase masarite per lo vescovado. [ASR, *Tesoreria segreta*, 1288, c. 122ᵛ]

Doc. 50. 4 October 1462. A detta Santita di N.S. . . . ducati 200 dati di comandamento di Sua Santita a M° puccio di pauolo da fiorenze li quali sonno per parte duna paga la quale dia avere M° bernardo e compagni li quali hanno presi a fare a rischio el campanile della chiesa di pientia el palazo del comune di pientia per ducati 2700 di camera li quali denari dieno avere in quatro paghe. [ASR, *Tesoreria segreta*, 1288, c. 124 (Tyszkiewicz, p. 127)]

Doc. 51. 5 October 1462. A detta Santita . . . ducati 17 dati di comandamento di Sua Santita a frate giovanni piovarno da pientia li quali Sua Santita . . . per uno paio di Buoi che lui lassa . . . li quali denari data a M° puccio di pauolo da fiorenze che limporta. [ASR, *Tesoreria segreta*, 1288, c. 124]

Doc. 52. 22 October 1462. A detta Santita . . . ducati 800 dati di comandamento di Sua Santita al bancho danbuogio Spanocchi e conpagni li quale di per la frabicha di Pientia. . . . [ASR, *Tesoreria segreta*, 1288, c. 126 (cited in Müntz, p. 301 n. 4)]

Doc. 53. 31 October 1462. A detta Santita . . . ducati 11 e grossi 6 e bologni 5-1/2 mandati di comandamento di Sua Santita al porina porini per misser niccolo M° di capella li quali sono per due cantine che lui conpro a pientia per li nipoti di Sua Santita. [ASR, *Tesoreria segreta*, 1288, c. 127]

Doc. 54. 1 December 1462. Alla Santita di N.S. papa pio secundo . . . dati di comandamento di Sua Santita al bancho danbruogio spanocchi e conpagni ducati 600 di camera li quali sonno per la fabricha di pientia. . . . [ASR, *Tesoreria segreta*, 1289, c. 51 (Tyszkiewicz, p. 127; cited in Müntz, p. 301 n. 4)]

Doc. 55. 24 December 1462. A detta Sua Santita . . . ducati 475 dati di comandamento di Sua Santita al bancho danbruogio spanocchi, porto Stefano Ghinucchi, li quali sonno lo resto della prima paga che dieno avere M° Bernardo da fiorenza e conpagni, che fanno lo campanile, palazo del comuno di pientia, e detto pagamento per quarto del tutto del pagamento ducati 675, li quali 475 ducati ebbe dal bancho M° puccio nipote e conpagnio di M° Bernardo. . . . [ASR, *Tesoreria segreta*, 1289, c. 55ᵛ (Tyszkiewicz, p. 128; Müntz, pp. 303–4)]

Doc. 56. 31 December 1462. A detta Santita . . . ducati 400 dati di comandamento di sua Santita al bancho danbruogio Spanocchi e conpagni li quali sonno per la frabicha di pientia ebbe agostantino loro. [ASR, *Tesoreria segreta*, 1289, c. 57ᵛ (Tyszkiewicz, p. 127; cited in Müntz, p. 301 n. 4)]

Doc. 57. 6 March 1463. A detta Santita . . . ducati 100 dati di comandamento di Sua Santita al bancho danbruogio spanocchi e conpagni li quali faciesero pagare in Siena a Pietro turamini e fratelli li quali pagassero ad agniolo del biondo e lorenzo di marzo da Pientia li quali vogliano fare due case e rispondare al capitolo de' canonici di pientia ducati 2 per uno secondo ordinara Misser giovanni Saraceni li quali denari ebbe agostantino loro. . . . [ASR, *Tesoreria segreta*, 1289, c. 69ᵛ]

Doc. 58. 30 March 1463. A detta Santita . . . ducati 200 dati di comandamento di Sua Santita al bancho danbruogio spanocchi e conpagni li quali pagasero alli maestri di pientia che fanno lo campanile e lo palazo del comune, et detti denari sonno per parte della siconda paga, la quale e ducati 675. [ASR, *Tesoreria segreta*, 1289, c. 72ᵛ (Müntz, p. 304)]

Doc. 59. 10 April 1463. A detta Santita . . . ducati 475 dati di comandamento di Sua Santita al bancho danbruogio Spanocchi e conpagni li quali pagasero a M° Bernardo e M° Puccio e conpagni da Fiorenza, li quali lavorano lo canpanile e lo palazo del comune di pientia, e questi ducati 475 sonno il resto della siconda paga che monta in tutto ducati 2700, che nanno auti ducati 1350 ebbe Girolamo loro del fondaco. [ASR, *Tesoreria segreta*, 1289, c. 74ᵛ (Tyszkiewicz, p. 128; Müntz, p. 304)]

Doc. 60. 14 April 1463. A detta Santita . . . ducati 150 dati di comandamento di Sua Santita ad alisandro mirabelli piccogliuomini li quali sonno per parte della sua casa che a venduta a Mª Caterina sorella di Sua Santita per pregio di ducati 620 di quali in altra per tota niauta ducati 250. [ASR, *Tesoreria segreta*, 1289, c. 76]

Doc. 61. 21 April 1463. A detta Santita . . . ducati 52 dati di comandamento di Sua Santita al porina porini per finire cierte case che lui restava a fare a pientia. [ASR, *Tesoreria segreta*, 1289, c. 78]

Doc. 62. 26 April 1463. A detta Santita . . . ducati 220 dati di comandamento di Sua Santita ad alisandro mirabelli per lo resto della sua casa che a venduta a madonna Caterina sorella di sua Santita la quale vende ducati 620. . . . [ASR, *Tesoreria segreta*, 1289, c. 78ᵛ]

Doc. 63. 28 April 1463. A detta Santita . . . ducati 100 dati di comandamento a domenico dantonio detto riccio da pientia per fare uno abergo li quali denari debba dare l'anno ducati 4 alla chiesa di pientia. [ASR, *Tesoreria segreta*, 1289, c. 79]

Doc. 64. 21 May 1463. A detta Santita . . . ducati 25 dati di comandamento di Sua Santita a Misser giovanni dalla roccha canonico di pientia li quale desse a matteo barbiere da pientia per limosina per che far una casa a pientia. [ASR, *Tesoreria segreta*, 1289, c. 82]

Doc. 65. 27 May 1463. A detta Santita . . . ducati 1600 dati di comandamento di Sua Santita al bancho danbruogio Spanocchi e conpagni li quali faciesero pagare in Siena al bancho di lorenzo Buoninsegne e gano manni e conpagni li quali pagasero a goro Massaini e Meo Massaini li quali anno venduto a misser Jacomo e Misser andrea piccogliuomini nipoti di N.S. le loro pocisioni che anno a frabica in Pientia per fiorini 4585 di lire 4 il fiorinio a muneta senese. [ASR, *Tesoreria segreta*, 1289, c. 82^v]

Doc. 66. 29 May 1463. A detta Santita . . . ducati 200 dati di comandamento di Sua Santita al bancho danbuogio Spanocchi e conpagni li quali faciesero pagare in Siena a turamini li quali pagasero al porina porini per case quindici fa fare Sua Santita a Pientia ebbe Ventura loro. . . . [ASR, *Tesoreria segreta*, 1289, c. 83 (Müntz, p. 304)]

Doc. 67. 29 May 1463. A detta Santita . . . ducati 55 dati di comandamento di Sua Santita al detto bancho li quali faciesero pagare in Siena al detto che pagase a porina per piaze e case conprate per fare dette case per lire 278 di lire a muneta senese e detti denaro ebbe el detto Ventura. [ASR, *Tesoreria segreta*, 1289, c. 83]

Doc. 68. 29 May 1463. A detta Santita . . . ducati 25 dati di comandamento di Sua Santita al detto bancho li quali faciese pagare al detto che pagase a porina per fare in biancare la chiesa di Santo Franciescho di Pientia ebbe el detto Ventura. . . . [ASR, *Tesoreria segreta*, 1289, c. 83 (Müntz, p. 304)]

Doc. 69. 9 June 1463. A detta Santita . . . ducati 50 dati di comandamento di Sua Santita a frate giovanni di M^o martino frate dello spedale di Siena li quali denari li o dati per lo spedale che si fa in pientia. [ASR, *Tesoreria segreta*, 1289, c. 86]

Doc. 70. 20 June 1463. A detta Santita . . . ducati 300 dati di comandamento di Sua Santita al bancho danbruogio Spanocchi e conpagni li quali pagasero in Siena al bancho di gano di manno e conpagni li quali pagasero a goro e meo Massaini per li fatti di frabica. . . . [ASR, *Tesoreria segreta*, 1289, c. 87^v]

Doc. 71. 25 June 1463. A detta Santita . . . ducati 300 dati di comandamento di Sua [Santita] al bancho danbruogio Spanocchi e conpagni li quali faciesero pagare in Siena al bancho di gano e conpagni li quali pagasero a goro e meo Massaini per li fatti di frabica. . . . [ASR, *Tesoreria segreta*, 1289, c. 89]

Doc. 72. 7 July 1463. A detta Santita . . . ducati 675 dati di comandamento di Sua Santita al bancho danbruogio Spanocchi e conpagni li quali sonno per la terza paga che a avere M^o Bernardo e conpagni da Fiorenza per lo canpanile e lo palazo del comuno che fanno et li detti denari Duccio loro casiere. [ASR, *Tesoreria segreta*, 1289, c. 92^v (Tyszkiewicz, p. 128; Müntz, p. 304)]

Doc. 73. 20 July 1463. A detta Santita . . . ducati 255 e grossi 2 e bologni 1 dati di comandamento di Sua Santita al bancho danbruogio Spanocchi li quali faciesero pagare in Siena a turamini li quali pagasero al pornia per le case xii si fanno a pientia per comesione di N.S. . . . [ASR, *Tesoreria segreta*, 1289, c. 93 (Müntz, p. 304)]

Doc. 74. 25 July 1463. A detta Santita . . . ducati 300 dati di comandamento di Sua Santita al bancho danbruogio Spanocchi li quali faciesero pagare in Siena a misser giovanni Saracini per piu case a fatte fare per pientia. [ASR, *Tesoreria segreta*, 1289, c. 93^v]

Doc. 75. 1 August 1463. A detta Santita . . . ducati 300 dati di comandamento di Sua Santita al bancho danbruogio Spanocchi li quali faciesero pagare in Siena per ordine di madonna Laudomia sorella di Sua Santita li quali fanno a pagare a goro e meo Massaini per la vendita di frabica. . . . [ASR, *Tesoreria segreta*, 1289, c. 94]

Doc. 76. 4 August 1463. A detta Santita . . . ducati 600 dati di comandamento di Sua Santita al bancho danbruogio Spanocchi e conpagni li quali faciesero pagare in Siena a turamini li quali pagasero al porina per le xii case fa per N.S. a pientia. [ASR, *Tesoreria segreta*, 1289, c. 95^v]

Doc. 77. 17 August 1463. A detta Santita . . . ducati 675 dati di comandamento di Sua Santita al bancho danbruogio Spanocchi e conpagni li quali pagasero a M° bernardo e M° puccio e conpagni da fiorenza li quali fanno lo canpanile e lo palazo del comuno di pientia e quali denari sonno per la quarta et ultima paga, e detti denari pagati a Duccio loro casiere. . . . [ASR, *Tesoreria segreta*, 1289, c. 96 (Müntz, p. 304)]

Doc. 78. 23 August 1463. A detta Santita . . . ducati 600 dati di comandamento di Sua Santita al detto bancho al detto Duccio li quali faciesero pagare alla magnifica madonna Laudomia per la compra di frabica cioe di goro e meo Massaini et questi sonno per la paga di settembre e ottobre. [ASR, *Tesoreria segreta*, 1289, c. 97]

Doc. 79. 5 September 1463. Alla Santita di N.S. . . . ducati 50 dati di comandamento di Sua Santita per le mani di misser Tome nostro ad antonio dagniolo da pientia per una sua casa fa la a Pientia. [ASR, *Tesoreria segreta*, 1289, c. 98]

Doc. 80. 11 November 1463. A detta Santita . . . ducati 400 dati di comandamento di Sua Santita al detto bancho e al detto li quali faciesero pagare in Siena a turamini liquali pagasero al porina per le dodici case fa fare Sua Santita. . . . [ASR, *Tesoreria segreta*, 1289, c. 103 (cited in Müntz, p. 304)]

Doc. 81. 11 November 1463. A detta Santita . . . ducati 100 dati di comandamento di Sua Santita al detto bancho et al detto li quali faciesero pagare in Siena a turamini li quali pagasero al porina per piu case [cose?] resta a fare a Pientia oltre le xii case. [ASR, *Tesoreria segreta*, 1289, c. 103 (cited in Müntz, p. 304)]

Doc. 82. 18 November 1463. A detta Santita . . . ducati 422 e grossi 9 e bologni 4-1/2 dati di comandamento di Sua Santita al bancho danbruogio Spanocchi ebbe agostantino loro li quali faciesero pagare in Siena al bancho di lorenzo buoninsegni e conpagni li quali pagasero sicondo ordinava la magnificha madonna laudomia per resto della compra di frabicha . . . goro e meo Massaini e goro vende piu una casa e una vignia posta a pientia che di tutto questo e lo resto a ragione di lire 5 cinque lo ducato di camera. [ASR, *Tesoreria segreta*, 1289, c. 103^v]

Doc. 83. 5 February 1464. A detta Santita . . . ducati 15 dati di comandamento di Sua Santita a M° giachetto del papagallo li quali desse a uno M° lo quale a venduto uno oriolo per mandare a pientia, li quali denari sono per parte. [ASR, *Tesoreria segreta*, 1289, c. 122^v (Müntz, p. 305)]

Doc. 84. 19 February 1464. A detta Santita . . . ducati 12 dati di comandamento ad arigo de Anfordia per resto dello oriolo di pientia a venduto a N.S. et a concio e per le spese venuto da Roma a Pientia e ritornato. . . . [ASR, *Tesoreria segreta*, 1289, c. 122^v]

Doc. 85. 19 February 1464. A detta Santita . . . ducati 43 e grossi 6 e bologni 5 dati di comandamento di Sua Santita al porina porini per case [cose?] fatte a Pientia e suo salario. [ASR, *Tesoreria segreta*, 1289, c. 122^v]

Doc. 86. 20 February 1464. A detta Santita . . . ducati 300 pagai per comandamento di sua Santita al bancho di lorenzo buoninsegni e gano manni e compagni di Siena li quali pagasero alla comunita di pientia per comprare cose inmobili. . . . [ASR, *Tesoreria segreta*, 1289, c. 123]

Doc. 87. 20 February 1464. A detta Santita . . . ducati 10 dati di comandamento di Sua Santita a Benedetto da Bologna lo quali dono per stanze fatte in commandatione di Sua Santita. [ASR, *Tesoreria segreta*, 1289, c. 123]

Doc. 88. 3 March 1464. A detta Santita . . . ducati 248 e grossi 2 e bologni 4 pagai per comandamento di Sua Santita a detto misser giovanni Saracini in lire mille trecieto per una casa non finita conprata da riccio da pientia e comprata per lopera della chiesa di pientia. [ASR, *Tesoreria segreta*, 1289, c. 125]

Doc. 89. 4 March 1464. A detta Santita . . . ducati 2 dati di comandamento di Sua Santita al porina li quali desse a M° Pietro del albacho per misurare la casa di riccio a Pientia. [ASR, *Tesoreria segreta*, 1289, c. 125^v (Müntz, p. 305)]

Doc. 90. 29 March 1464. A detta Santita . . . ducati 333 dati di comandamento di Sua Santita al bancho danbruogio Spanocchi contatore agostantino loro li quali pagasero a M° antonio lonbardo lo quale a preso fare la casa fu di riccio a pientia della quale Sua Santita fa fare una hostaria per la frabicha della chiesa. [ASR, *Tesoreria segreta*, 1289, c. 128 (Müntz, p. 305)]

NOTES

Preface

1. Quoted in *A Documentary History of Art, I: The Middle Ages and the Renaissance,* ed. Elizabeth G. Holt (Garden City, N.Y.: Doubleday Anchor, 1957), p. 248. Almost identical sentiments were voiced by the future Pope Pius II in a letter written in 1449 from the Austrian city of Wiener Neustadt to Gregory Heimburg: "While I was in the town of St. Gallen in Swabia I came upon an ancient library in an old monastery which contained beautifully illuminated books by German authors. This made me wonder why in the present time the art of writing beautifully had disappeared in that region but I stopped wondering when I remembered that there was a period when eloquence in Italy was dead and barbarian ignorance prevailed. From the tenth or eleventh to about the fourteenth century there was no one who could speak correctly and clearly in Italy. The art of this period illustrated the drop in culture because if you inspected the tombs and paintings which are about two or three hundred years old you would find only the shapes of beasts and monsters and not of men. Yet we know that in antiquity Apelles, Zeuxis, Polycletus, Phidias, and Praxiteles were all famous. We derive the image of ourselves from statuary which lends all the more force to Vergil's statement, 'I admit they will fashion living

faces from marble.' Painting in antiquity has also received great praise from celebrated authors who thought ancient painting as beautiful or more so than statuary. In our age painting and sculpting have revived! Eloquence too has been restored and is especially strong in Italy." Aeneas Silvius Piccolomini (Pius II), *Selected Letters of Aeneas Silvius Piccolomini,* trans. and ed. Albert R. Baca, San Fernando Valley State College Renaissance Editions 2 (Northridge, Calif.: San Fernando Valley State College, 1969), pp. 42–43.

2. For a Latin text, see *Commentarii* (1584; rpt. Frankfurt/Main: Minerva, 1974). A critical Latin edition was recently published by the Vatican as *Commentari rerum memorabilium que temporibus suis contigerunt,* ed. Adriano van Heck, 2 vols., Studi e Testi 312–13 (Vatican City: Tip. Poliglota Vaticana, 1984). The standard Italian translation is *I Commentari,* trans. Giuseppe Bernetti (Siena: Cantagalli, 1972). A complete translation into English is found in *The Commentaries of Pius II,* trans. Florence Alden Gragg, ed. Leona C. Gabel (Northampton, Mass.: Smith College Studies in History, 1936–37, 1940, 1947, 1951). An abridgment of the latter was published as *Memoirs of a Renaissance Pope: The Commentaries of Pius II,* trans. Florence Alden Gragg, ed. Leona C. Gabel (New York: Capricorn Books, 1959). A discussion of the *Commentaries* and its various editions and translations

is given in Ivo Petri, *Attualità dei Commentari di Pio II (Enea Silvio Piccolomini): Introduzione e saggi di lettura* (Siena: Cantagalli, 1984).

3. Pius, *Memoirs*, p. 374.

4. Though Pienza was never large, I call it a city, not only because Pope Pius and his contemporaries referred to it as *urbs* or *civitas* but because of the intent of what was undertaken there. Conceptually, if not in actual size, this Tuscan community was transformed into a city. As the pope's court poet Giovanni Antonio Campano wrote: "Me Pius ornatam templo, murisque refertam / Esse urbem voluit, quae fueram oppidulum." See Appendix I, Doc. I.

5. For a chronologically organized bibliography relevant to the architecture of Corsignano/Pienza, consult Nicholas Adams and Charles Mack, "Pienza: An Architectural Bibliography," *Studi e Documenti di Architettura* (in press).

6. Leonardo Benevolo, *The Architecture of the Renaissance*, trans. Judith Landry (London: Routledge and Kegan Paul, 1978), 1:163.

1. *From Corsignano to Pienza:
The Project Begins*

1. Information on the papal party's arrival in Pienza is found in a letter written by the Sienese official Niccolò Severini, 21 February 1459. "Hieri da sera giunse a Sartiano et in quello luogo habergò con sei cardinali, nel quale luogo fu ricevuto honoratamente. E questo dì xxi del presente mese a mezzo dì è entrata le sua Beatitudine coi Cardinali in Corsignano dove è stato ricevuto con singularissima letitia et festa et annoli questi huomini facto uno magno et relevato onore con grande spesa et apparato honoratissimo in tutti i modi et rivevutane grande commendatione. Gli ambasciatori fecero di tutto per quanto fu loro possibile. La sua Santità starà qui domane et già à dato ordine che domatina si celebri solenne messa in Sancto Francesco, da poi venerdì favente deo verrà a Chuna. E

de lo honore facto qui al beatissimo Padre Antonio Massaino de la S.V. Commissario è stato potissima cagione con grande diligentia." This text is given in Mannucci, *Pienza*, pp. 25–26. See also Pius, *Memoirs*, p. 102. Further discussions of the pope's Mantuan journey can be found in F. Cerasoli, "Il viaggio di Pio II da Roma a Mantova, 22 gennaio–27 maggio 1459: ricerche, rettifiche, dettagli," *Buonarotti*, 4, ser. 3, no. 6 (1891), 213–18; in Francesco Naldi Bandini Piccolomini, "La prima visita di Pio II a Corsignano," *Arte e Storia*, Supplement: Pienza e Pio II pubblicato in occasione del V centenario della nascita di Enea Silvio Piccolomini, 24, ser. 3, no. 8 (1905), 3–4; and in C. Ugurgieri della Berardenga, *Pio II Piccolomini con notizie su Pio III e altri membri della famiglia* (Florence: Leo S. Olschki, 1973), p. 240 n. 215.

2. Much of my information concerning the nature of the pre-Renaissance hamlet, including this estimate, is based upon Nicholas Adams' "Humanist Glory and Feudal Power (1459–1464): The Construction of Pienza," *Acts of the Conference on Urban Life, March 1983* (Newark, Del., 1986). I am grateful to Professor Adams for providing me with a copy of his paper and for kindly sharing with me other materials and observations.

3. Pius, *Memoirs*, p. 97.

4. Ibid., p. 102.

5. Ibid.

6. Reconstructions of the history of the ancient and medieval community are to be found most completely and conveniently presented in Ivo Petri, *Pienza: Storia breve di una simbolica città* (Genoa: Edigraphica, 1972), pp. 28–78, and by Sara Rossi in Luciana Finelli and Sara Rossi, *Pienza, tra ideologia e realtà* (Bari: Dedalo Libri, 1979), pp. 101–10, as well as in Carli, *Pienza*, pp. 15–24. Some differing interpretations of the growth and physical characteristics of the town are given in Giancarlo Cataldi, "Pienza e la sua piazza: Nuova ipotesi tipologica di lettura," *Studi e Documenti di Architettura*, 7 (1978), 90–97. The state of late medieval Corsignano is consid-

ered in Adams, "Humanist Glory." Plans of the town and its principal buildings, along with cross sections and elevations are to be found in a number of publications, including Heinrich Holtzinger, *Pienza: Aufgenommen und gezeichnet von den Architekten K. Mayreder und C. Bender* (Vienna, 1882); Carl von Stegmann and Heinrich von Geymüller, *The Architecture of the Renaissance in Tuscany Illustrating the most Important Churches, Palaces, Villas, and Monuments* (1885–1906; rpt., in English, New York: Architectural Book Publishing, 1924), 1:72–82. The most thorough and accurate series of architectural drawings are those presented in Giancarlo Cataldi et al., *Rilievi di Pienza* (Florence: Uniedit, 1977).

7. Discussions of the excavations and earlier church are found in Alfredo Barbacci, "Il duomo di Pienza e i suoi restauri," *La Diana,* 9 (1934), 1–134, and "Ruderi di una chiesa Romanica rinvenuti sotto il duomo di Pienza," *Bollettino d'Arte,* 26, ser. 3 (1933), 352–58; in Mannucci, *Pienza,* p. 317; and in Carli, *Pienza,* pp. 16, 21–22. Some have questioned the precise location of Corsignano's church of Santa Maria. See Carli, *Pienza,* pp. 52–53 n. 11; Cataldi, "Pienza e la sua piazza," 94; Mannucci, *Pienza,* p. 42; and E. Repetti, *Dizionario geografico fisico storico della Toscana* (1833–35; rpt. Florence: Cassa di Risparmio, 1972), 4:190–202.

8. These fragments have been installed in the north wall of the lower church. See Alfredo Barbacci, "Il ritrovamento e il ripristino dell'antica decorazione del Duomo di Pienza," *Bollettino d'Arte,* 25 (1931–32), 282–88.

9. On the church of San Francesco and its cloister, see particularly Mannucci, *Pienza,* pp. 200–201, which also gives the text of Cardinal Francesco's will in which provision is made for the restoration of the cloister. See, in addition, Mannucci's "Il convento di San Francesco in Pienza: Documenti e notizie," *Bullettino Senese di Storia Patria,* 26 (1919), 266–74, and his "La Chiesa di S. Francesco in Pienza," *La Diana,* 1 (1926), 275; Alfred A.

Strnad, "Francesco Todeschini-Piccolomini: Politik und Mäzenatentum im Quattrocento," *Römische Historische Mitteilungen,* 8–9 (1964–65), 324.

10. Only once does Corsignano figure in the literature of the Middle Ages, in Giovanni Boccaccio's *Decameron,* where it is mentioned in the tale of Cecco Fortarrigo and Cecco Anguilieri (fourth story, day nine).

11. Don Aldo Franci has informed me that the Piazza Galletti is a post–World War II creation, resulting from the removal of the debris of the bomb-damaged houses that once occupied that area. The dimensions of the present-day Piazza Martiri della Libertà also were altered in the same way. The modern plan of Pienza might be compared with that given in Alfredo Barbacci, "L'edificazione e il decadimento del duomo di Pienza," *Bollettino d'Arte,* 10, ser. 2 (1931), 324. Aside from the few medieval remnants, the extensive housing areas of the Renaissance, and the recent construction, most building seems to have been done in the nineteenth century. See Adams, "Acquisition," p. 99, n.2.

12. Many of Adams' findings are summarized in "Acquisition," pp. 104–5.

13. A communal well once occupied the center of this piazza (also known as the Piazza di Spagna). It was removed when the area was paved some years ago but was revealed again in excavations undertaken in 1984. It is a point of interest that commercial activity was centered here while the later Renaissance piazza of Pope Pius was reserved for affairs of state and church and maintained a more formal atmosphere. This piazza receives attention in Fanelli and Rossi, *Pienza,* pp. 114–15, where, however, it is treated as a product of the Renaissance intervention. In this regard, the comments of Paul Zucker, *Town and Square from the Agora to the Village Green* (New York: Columbia University Press, 1959), p. 69 are worth noting: "In towns which had developed with a previously existing, more or less isolated cathedral, the market square generally extended laterally to the

cathedral, or was even isolated from it; but at any rate was outside the so-called local community area. . . . In this way one of the most typical features of medieval cities originated, a feature which became of the greatest aesthetic importance for the town as a whole: the parallel existence of two separate squares. One of them was located before the church as a parvis or was otherwise adjacent to it, the other a certain distance away, as market square."

14. Among those works treating the life of Pope Pius are: Cecilia M. Ady, *Pius II: The Humanist Pope* (London: Methuen, 1913); Felice Battaglia, *Enea Silvio Piccolomini e Francesco Patrizi: Due politici senesi del quattrocento* (Siena: Istituto Comunale d'Arte e Storia, 1936); William Boulting, *Aeneas Sylvius: Orator, Man of Letters, Statesman, and Pope* (London: Archibald Constable, 1908); N. Casella, "Recenti studi su Enea Silvio Piccolomini," *Rivista di Storia della Chiesa in Italia*, 26 (1972), 473–88; Mandell Creighton, *A History of the Papacy from the Great Schism to the Sack of Rome* (London: Longmans, Green, 1911), 3:202–358; Domenico Maffei, ed., *Enea Silvio Piccolomini, Papa Pio II: Atti del convegno per il quinto centenario della morte e latri scritti* (Siena: Accademia Senese degli Intronati, 1968); C. Falconi, *Storia dei papi e del papato* (Rome: CEI, 1972), 4:33–55; Johannes Haller, "Pius II: Ein Papst der Renaissance," in his *Reden und Aufsätze zur Geschichte und Politik* (Berlin: Cotta, 1934), 67–100; R. J. Mitchell, *The Laurels and the Tiara: Pope Pius II, 1458–1464* (London: Harvill, 1962); Gioacchino Paparelli, *Enea Silvio Piccolomini (Pio II)* (Bari: Giuseppe Laterza, 1950), and *Enea Silvio Piccolomini: L' umanesimo sul soglio di Pietro* (Ravenna: Longo, 1978); Ludwig Pastor, *The History of the Popes*, 4th ed. (London: Kegan Paul, Trench, Trubner, 1923), vol. 3; T. G. Rowe, "The Tragedy of E. S. Piccolomini, Pope Pius II," *Church History*, 30 (1961), 288–313; *Selected Letters of Aeneas Silvius Piccolomini*, trans. and ed. Albert R. Baca, San Fernando Valley State College Renaissance Editions 2 (Northridge,

Calif.: San Fernando Valley State College, 1969); Alfred A. Strnad, "Pio II e suo nipote Francesco Todeschini-Piccolomini," in *Atti e Memorie della Deputazione di Storia Patria per le Marche*, 5, ser. 8 (1967), 35–84; L. Totaro, *Pio II nei suoi "Commentari"* (Bologna: Pàtron, 1978); C. Ugurgieri della Berardenga, *Pio II Piccolomini*; Georg Voigt, *Enea Silvio de' Piccolomini, als Papst Pius der Zweite, und sein Zeitalter* (1856–63; rpt. Berlin: Walter de Gruyter, 1967); A. Weiss, *Aeneas Sylvius Piccolomini als Papst Pius II: Sein Leben und Einfluss auf die literarische Kultur Deutschlands* (Graz: U. Moser, 1897); T. H. Whitfield, "Aeneas Sylvius Piccolomini," *Life of Spirit*, 15 (1961), 459–71; Berthe Widmer, *Enea Silvio Piccolomini, Papst Pius II: Biographie und ausgewählte Texte aus seinen Schriften* (Basel: Benno Schwabe, 1960), and *Enea Silvio Piccolomini in der sittlichen und politischen Entscheidung* (Basel: Helbing and Lichtenhahn, 1963); Rudolf Wolkan, *Der Briefwechsel des Eneas Sylvius Piccolomini* Fontes Rerum Austriacarum (Vienna: Hölder, 1909, 1912, 1918); and Giulio C. Zimolo, *Le vite di Pio II di Giovanni Antonio Campano e Bartolomeo Platina* (Bologna: Zanchelli, 1964). The last-mentioned volume contains a convenient chronology of the pope's life on pp. 175–83. All of these discussions of Pius II are, of course, supplemental to the pope's own *Commentarii*.

15. On the history of the Piccolomini family, see especially Alessandro Lisini and Alfredo Liberati, *Genealogia dei Piccolomini di Siena* (Siena: Enrico Torrini, 1900).

16. On Fra Pietro, see Voigt, *Enea Silvio de' Piccolomini*, 1:7.

17. For a consideration of the impact of San Bernardino on the future pope, consult Francesco Naldi Bandini Piccolomini, "San Bernardino da Siena e Papa Pio II: Cenni ed accenni di loro vite," *Bullettino di Studi Bernardiniani*, 3, 4 (1937) and 4, 3/4 (1938). Pius described the preaching of Bernardino in his *Historia Frederici*, vol. 3, col. 175, which is given in Widmer, *Enea Silvio Piccolomini*, pp. 422–23.

18. See, esp., Voigt, *Aenea Silvio de' Piccolomini,* 2:248–320, 342–58.

19. Beginning with this event, the major episodes of Pope Pius' life are beautifully captured in the frescoes executed between 1497 and 1503 by Pinturicchio in the Piccolomini Library of the Cathedral of Siena.

20. The great architectural programs undertaken and planned during the reign of Pope Nicholas have been considered in a number of publications, including Kunibert Bering, *Baupropaganda und Bildprogrammatik der Frührenaissance in Florenz-Rom-Pienza* (Frankfurt: Peter Lang, 1984), pp. 43–72; Charles Burroughs, "A Planned Myth and a Myth of Planning: Nicholas V and Rome," in *Rome in the Renaissance: The City and the Myth,* ed. P. A. Ramsey, Medieval and Renaissance Texts and Studies 18 (Binghamton: State University of New York, 1982), pp. 197–207; G. Dehio, "Die Bauprojecte Nicolaus des Fünften und L. B. Alberti," *Repertorium für Kunstwissenschaft,* 3 (1880), 241–57; Charles Mack, "Bernardo Rossellino, L. B. Alberti, and the Rome of Pope Nicholas V," *Southeastern College Art Conference Review,* 10 (1982), 60–69, and "Nicholas the Fifth and the Rebuilding of Rome: Reality and Legacy," in *Light on the Eternal City: Recent Observations and Discoveries in Roman Art and Architecture,* Papers in Art History from the Pennsylvania State University 2, ed. Hellmut Hager and Susan B. Munshower (University Park, Pa.: Pennsylvania State University, 1987); Torgil Magnuson, "Studies in Roman Quattrocento Architecture," *Figura* 9 (1958); Pastor, *History of the Popes,* 2:166–82; S. Tadolini, "Il piano per i Borghi di Nicolò V e L. B. Alberti," in *Strenna dei Romanisti* (Rome: Staderni, 1971), pp. 357–64; Carroll William Westfall, *In This Most Perfect Paradise: Alberti, Nicholas V, and the Invention of Conscious Urban Planning in Rome, 1447–55* (University Park, Pa.: Pennsylvania State University Press, 1974).

21. Giannozzo Manetti, *Vita Nicolai V summi pontificis nunc primum prodit ex manuscripta codice Florentino.* Manetti's biography of Pope Nicholas was included in *Rerum italicarum scriptores,* ed. Ludovico A. Muratori (Milan: Società Palatina, 1734), 3:2, 907–60. Those portions of this text dealing with the architectural programs are most easily accessible in an appendix to Magnuson, "Studies," pp. 351–62, and in Eugene Müntz, *Les Arts à la cours des papes pendent le XVe et le XVIe siècle* (1878; rpt. Hildesheim: Georg Olms, 1983), 1:339–51. In addition to Manetti's text, other fifteenth-century descriptions of Nicholas' intentions are to be found in Vespasiano da Bisticci, *Vite di uomini illustrati del secolo XV,* ed. Angelo Mai and Adolfo Bartoli (Florence: Barbara Bianchi, 1859), pp. 40–41; Stefano Infessura, *Diario della città di Roma di Stefano Infessura scribasenato,* ed. Oreste Tommasini, Fonte per la storia d'Italia (Rome: Forzani, 1890), p. 49; Mattia Palmieri, "De temporibus suis ab anno MCCCXLIX," in *Rerum italicarum scriptores,* ed. Giuseppe Maria Tartini (Florence: Viviani, 1748–70), p. 241; Bartolommeo Platina, *Le vite de' pontifici di Bartolommeo Platina dal Salvator fino Benedetto XlII da Onofrio Panrenio* (Venice: Savioni, 1730); and Niccola Della Tuccia in *Cronache e statuti della città di Viterbo,* ed. Ignazio Ciampi, Documenti di Storia Italiana 5 (Florence: Cellini, 1872), p. 215. Michele Canensi's biography of Pope Nicholas written ca. 1451–52 discussed the architectural programs as symbolic of the renewed authority of the papacy. See Massimo Miglio, "Una vocazione in progresso: Michele Canensi, biografo papale," *Studi Medievali,* ser. 3, 12 (1971), 463–524, with Canensi's text on 501–24 (esp. 516–17) and the discussion in Westfall, *In This Most Perfect Paradise,* pp. 33, 172.

22. Pius, *Memoirs,* p. 68.

23. See Widmer, *Enea Silvio Piccolomini,* p. 398.

24. Publius Maro Virgilis, *The Aeneid,* Bk. 1, line 349, in *Opera,* ed. Frederick A. Hirtzel (Oxford: Clarendon, 1900). It has recently been noted that the pope's subsequent choice of Mantua for his pan-European congress may have stemmed not only from the hoped-for support of Marquis Ludovico Gonzaga,

the city's ruler, but from the iconographic "charm" that city presented as the birthplace of Virgil. See Joseph Rykwert and Robert Tavernor, "The Church of S. Sebastiano in Mantua," *Architectural Design (Profile 21)*, 49, 5–6 (1979), 86.

25. Discussions of the architectural projects Pius sponsored in Rome can be found in Bering, *Baupropaganda*, pp. 73–77; Luciana Finelli and Sara Rossi, "San Pietro come team-work," *L'architettura, Croniche e Storia*, 22 (1977), 721–27; Christoph Luitpold Frommel, "Francesco del Borgo, Architekt Pius' II. und Pauls II.; I. Der Petersplatz und weitere römische Bauten Pius' II. Piccolomini," *Römisches Jahrbuch für Kunstgeschichte*, 20 (1983), 107–54; Müntz, *Les Arts*, 1:221–300; and Ruth Olitsky Rubinstein, "Pius II's Piazza S. Pietro and St. Andrew's Head," in *Essays in the History of Architecture Presented to Rudolf Wittkower*, ed. A. Fraser, Howard Hibbard, M. J. Lewine (London: Phaidon, 1967), pp. 22–33, and in *Enea Silvio Piccolomini*, ed. Maffei, pp. 221–44. For Giannantonio Campano's contemporary description of Pius' architectural accomplishments, see Appendix 1, Doc. 6.

26. See Müntz, *Les Arts*, 1:266–300.

27. Frommel, "Francesco del Borgo, I," p. 127.

28. On Francesco del Borgo, see ibid., p. 126, and Christoph Frommel, *Der Palazzo Venezia in Rom*, Gerda Henkel Vorlesung (Opladen: Westdeutschen Verlag, 1982), pp. 26–27. Rossellino's possible connection with this project is discussed in Mack, "Studies," pp. 315–16 n. 10.

29. The text is given in Müntz, *Les Arts*, 1:352–53.

30. On this visit, see Mitchell, *The Laurels and the Tiara*, p. 117.

31. Creighton, *History of the Papacy*, pp. 354–55.

32. Boulting, *Aeneas Silvius*, p. 4.

33. See Pius, *Memoirs*, pp. 277–82, 315–23.

34. Ibid., p. 102. Flavio Biondo's report would have us believe that the notion of rebuilding Corsignano did not originate until the pope's return trip from Mantua in 1460

(see Appendix 1, Doc. 2, for the text of Biondo's passage). The word of the *Commentarii* is supported by the documentary evidence, but Biondo's version may be evidence of an expanded concept for the architectural program which was not announced until the second visit. For a discussion of this conflicting testimony, see Mitchell, *The Laurels and the Tiara*, p. 288.

35. See Flavio Biondo's mention of the antique parallels to Pius' desires for his birthplace in Appendix 1, Doc. 2. On the medieval rebuilding of Agnani, see Marie Geneviève de la Costa-Messelière, "Deux cités pontificales," *L'Oeil*, 73 (1961), 45–53.

36. Pius, *Memoirs*, p. 288.

37. See Appendix 2, Docs. 25, 50, 55, 59, 72, and 77. Giorgio Vasari mistakenly attributed the work at Pienza to the Sienese Francesco di Giorgio Martini (*Lives*, 2:27). Francesco would have been only twenty when the work at Pienza was begun. Although he most certainly was not the pope's architect, he may very well have worked there; what seem to be quotations from Pienza appear in his own projects at Urbino and Jesi several years later. Architectural responsibility for Pienza was pretty well determined long ago. See, for example, Giovanni Battista Mannucci, "Il Rossellino architetto di Pienza?" *Rassegna d'Arte Senese*, 3 (1907), 15–18; C. F. von Rumohr, "Bernardo Rossellino und Francesco di Giorgio: Bauwerke Pius II zu Pienza und Siena," in his *Italienische Forschungen* (Berlin: Nicolai'schen Buchhandlung, 1827), 2:177–201. Yet even as late as the 1940s, Francesco di Giorgio was being assigned a part in designing the papal renovations. See Roberto Papini, *Francesco di Giorgio, architetto* (Florence: Electa Editrice, 1946), 1:237.

38. See Mack, "Studies," p. 424.

39. Archivio dell'Opera, Santa Maria del Fiore, Florence, *Stanziamenti* (1455–62), c. 98, published in Maryla Tyszkiewicz, *Bernardo Rossellino* (Florence: Stamperia Polacca, 1929), p. 132; Mannucci, *Pienza*, p. 68; Howard Saalman, *Filippo Brunelleschi: The Cupola of Santa Maria del Fiore*, Studies in Architecture

20 (London: A. Zwemmer, 1980), p. 291, Doc. 359.2. "Bernardo Mattei lastraiuolo qui ad presens est caput magister cupole et lanterne, antequam electus fuisset, fuit missus pro eo qui erat Corsignanum comitatus Senarum pro habendo ab eo consilium certorum lapidum."

40. On the life of Bernardo Rossellino, see Luciana Finelli, *L'umanesimo giovane: Bernardo Rossellino a Roma e a Pienza* (Rome: Veutro Editore, 1985); Mack, "Studies," and "Bernardo Rossellino," in the *Macmillan Encyclopedia of Architects* (1982), 3:611–12; Leo Planiscig, *Bernardo und Antonio Rossellino* (Vienna: Anton Schroll, 1942); Anne Markham Schulz, *The Sculpture of Bernardo Rossellino and His Workshop* (Princeton: Princeton University Press, 1976); and Tyskiewicz, *Bernardo Rossellino.*

41. See Mario Salmi, "Bernardo Rossellino ad Arezzo" in *Scritti di storia dell'arte in onore di Ugo Procacci,* ed. Maria Grazia Ciardi Dupré Dal Poggetto and Paolo Poggetto (Milan: Electa Editrice, 1977), 1:254–61.

42. On the Badia Fiorentina, see Charles R. Mack, "Notes Concerning an Unpublished Window by Bernardo Rossellino at the Badia Fiorentina," *Southeastern College Art Conference Review,* 5 (Dec. 1970), 2–5; Piero Sanpaolesi, "Costruzioni del primo quattrocento nella Badia Fiorentina," *Rivista d'Arte,* ser. 2, 24 (1942), 143–79.

43. On the Spinelli Cloister, see especially Howard Saalman, "Tommaso Spinelli, Michelozzo, Manetti, and Rossellino," *Journal of the Society of Architectural Historians,* 25 (1966), 151–64.

44. See especially Mack, "Rossellino, Alberti, and the Rome of Nicholas V," which presents an appendix (pp. 64–65) on the projects outside of Rome, and Mack, "Nicholas the Fifth and the Rebuilding of Rome," in which all the Rossellino-related documents are published.

45. Rossellino's involvement with San Stefano Rotondo has been explored most recently in Mack, "Nicholas the Fifth and the Rebuilding of Rome," and in Erminia Gentile Ortona, "Santo Stefano Rotondo e il restauro

del Rossellino," *Bollettino d'Arte,* 67 (1982), 99–106.

46. Rossellino's contribution to the Hospital of the Innocents received separate consideration in Charles R. Mack, "Brunelleschi's Spedale degli Innocenti Rearticulated," *Architectura,* 11 (1981), 135–36 n. 45.

47. Rossellino's involvement with the San Miniato Chapel was treated in Frederick Hartt, Gino Corti, Clarence Kennedy, *The Chapel of the Cardinal of Portugal, 1434–1459, at San Miniato in Florence* (Philadelphia: University of Pennsylvania Press, 1964).

48. Charles R. Mack, "Building a Florentine Palace: The Palazzo Spinelli," *Mitteilungen des Kunsthistorischen Institutes in Florenz,* 27 (1983), 261–84; Saalman, "Tommaso Spinelli, Michelozzo, Manetti, and Rossellino," pp. 160–63.

49. On Rossellino's possible connections with the Badia Fiesolana, see Mack, "Studies," pp. 369–70 n. 33; Amedeo Belluzzi, "La Badia Fiesolana," in Giulio Carlo Argan, et al., *Filippo Brunelleschi: La sua opera e il suo tempo* (Florence: Centro Di, 1980), 2:499–500. For the San Martino project, see Marco Spallanzani, "L'abside dell' Alberti a San Martino a Gangalandi," *Mitteilungen des Kunsthistorischen Institutes in Florenz,* 19 (1975), 241–50. It might be noted that one of the *scarpellatore* (stone carvers) on that project, Francesco d'Antonio di Vanni, was employed by the Rossellino shop in its work at the Chapel of the Cardinal of Portugal at San Miniato ai Monte in 1461 (Mack, "Studies," p. 426).

50. It should, however, be pointed out that the position of *capomaestro* of the Florence Cathedral was not all that time consuming by this time. Richard Goldthwaite, *The Building of Renaissance Florence: An Economic and Social History* (Baltimore: Johns Hopkins University Press, 1980), pp. 386–87.

51. The dates of Pope Pius' stay in Florence are given in ASR, *Spese minuti di palazzo,* 1473, c. 48–53^v.

52. For a discussion of Alberti's Florentine projects, consult Franco Borsi, *Leon Battista Alberti* (Milan: Electa Editrice, 1975).

53. Pius, *Memoirs,* p. 316. The extent of Alberti's possible participation in the project at Pienza is discussed in Rossi and Finelli, *Pienza,* pp. 124–27; Schiavo, *Pienza,* pp. 14–15. On the injection of Albertian concepts into the project, consult Vincenzo Fontana, *Artisti e committenti nella Roma del quattrocento: Leon Battista Alberti e la sua opera mediatrice,* Quaderni di Studi Romani 1, 37 (Rome: Istituto di Studi Romani, 1973), p. 49.

54. Adams, "Acquisition," pp. 99–110, 106–9.

55. See Appendix 2, Docs. 1, 2.

56. Giovanni Mannucci, "Notizie sul castello di Corsignano," *Rassegna d'Arte Senese,* 2 (1905), 63–68. The *castello* has recently been restored and part of it is in use as the medical clinic of Pienza. In addition to these towers, Pius supported the general reconditioning of the town's defenses. A 1466 letter from the Sienese representative in Pienza noted that some 300 *canne* of walling had been worked on. See Adams, "Acquisition," p. 100 n. 10.

57. On the Vatican towers of Nicholas V, see Mack, "Nicholas the Fifth and the Rebuilding of Rome"; on those in the papal states, see Mack, "Rossellino, Alberti, and the Rome of Nicholas V," pp. 64–65. Circular towers with battered bases were a feature of mid-fifteenth-century fortifications in Italy. In Tuscany, they survive at a number of locations including the towns of San Gimignano, Sarteano, Castiglione Garfagnana, and Staggia. See Eduardo Detti, Gian Franco Di Pietro and Giovanni Fanelli, *Città murate e sviluppo contemporaneo: 42 centri della Toscana* (Lucca: Centro Internazionale per lo Studio della Cerchia Urbane, 1968); Marcello Salvatori, "Considerazioni sulle fortificazioni del Brunelleschi," in Argan, et al., *Filippo Brunelleschi,* 2:685–701, esp. 691–92. The round towers of Monticchiello, only six kilometers distant from Pienza, appear to be the same type and date as those erected at the *castelnuovo* and may represent an unrecorded papal project in that town. An earlier version of this type of tower is to be recognized within the late fifteenth-century walls of the castle at Ostia. In his *Commentarii,* Pope Pius described that structure as "a high, round tower built by Martin V to guard the place" (*Memoirs,* p. 306). On such towers, in general, see Stanislaus von Moos, *Turm und Bollwerk: Beiträge zu einer politischen Ikonographie der Italienischen Renaissance-Architektur* (Zurich: Atlantis, 1974). The buttressed tower is also discussed in Mario Salmi, "San Agostino di Anghiari," in the *Atti del XII congresso di storia dell'architettura: L'architettura nell' Aretino* (Rome: Centro di Studi per la Storia dell'Architettura, 1969), 200–206.

58. Pius, *Memoirs,* pp. 100, 191–92.

59. Adams, "Humanist Glory."

60. See Chapter 3.

61. ASS, *Consiglio campanae,* 233, c. 109, published previously in S. Borghesi and L. Banchi, *Nuovi documenti per la storia dell'arte senese* (Siena: Enrico Torrini, 1898), p. 217; Mack, "Studies," p. 397; and Tyskiewicz, *Bernardo Rossellino,* p. 118: "Consilio populi et popularium magnifice civitatis Senarum solemniter et in numero sufficienti, consuetio loco convocato, servatis opportunis solemnitatibus, secundum formam statutorum. Facta proposita super petitione summi Pontificis, pro edifcatione templi et Domus apud oppidum Corsiniani, fuit obtentum quod auctoritate praesentis Consilii, intelligatur esse et sit remissum in Magnificos D. Capitaneum Populi et Vexilliferos Magistros, qui possint dare licentiam Architecto et Ordinatori misso per suam Sanctitatem, capiendi lapides, faciendi fornaces, incidendi abietes et ligna et alias res, ad dicta edifitia necessarias, et cedendi eas gratis pro ut eis videbitur et placebitur, et ut in Brevi suae sanctitatis continetur."

62. Pius, *Memoirs,* p. 277.

63. Adams, "Acquisition," p. 106.

64. Pius, *Memoirs,* p. 161. The dates of the pope's stay in the town are provided in ASR Camerale I, *Spese minute di palazzo* (1459–60), 1475, c. 113. His visit also is recorded in Niccola Della Tuccia, *Cronache e statuti della città di Viterbo,* pp. 80–81. "Nel detto anno [1460] a 10 di settembre, in mercordì, papa

Pio II partì da Siena per venire a Roma, e andò a un castello chiamato Corsignano, dove s'era allevato in sua puerizia. Li cortigiani e loro robe s'avviorno verso Viterbo, e assai some andorno a Roma: assai si scorcorno in Viterbo. E tuttavia la corte veniva. . . . Martedì a dì 30 di detto mese, a ore venti, papa Pio sopradetto venne a Viterbo partendosi da Montefiascone. . . ."

65. ASS, *Archivio del concistoro,* 564, c. 18ᵛ–19, previously published in Mack, "Studies," p. 397: "Simili modo e forma per eodem consilio facta per posita super infra septis. Et redditis consilii . . . misso dato e facto partito ad lupinos albos e Nigros fuit tandem victu obtatum e solepnet Reformatum per cxxxii lupinos albos redditos per sic xviii nigru radditis per non . . . obstantibus. Quod reliquus ex cortesianis d. N. papa pii ii senasis Vellet emere aliquas domus e plateas pro edificando juxta stratum principale castri corsignani . . . qui habent ibi domus e plateas debeant e teneant eas vendere dui cortegianis per conuenienti pretio declarando per domus albit . . . aligandos unum per qua libet parte e si non essent in concordia potestas corsignani qui per tempore fuerit si t'zius ad-declarandum detta prae. . . . Et qui ipsi Cortisiam emptore non teneant sovere aliquam cabellam dictamine Emtionii per eorum dictate rata tantum."

66. Rykwert and Tavernor, "S. Sebastiano," p. 86.

67. Müntz, *Les Arts,* 1:232 n. 4.

68. The records show that cannonballs were being supplied by a number of other stonemasons among them a *magistro Augustino da Placencia palatti apostolici architecto,* who was paid for these items on 15 October 1461 and 2 April 1462. This master is otherwise identified as the Augustinus Nicolai de Placentia, who was building a bridge across the Arbia River not far from Pienza in May 1458. See ibid., pp. 235 n. 2, 236.

69. Adams, "Acquisition," pp. 106–7. On Salomone and Buonconti, see Chapter 3.

70. See Chapter 3 and Appendix 1, Doc. 2.

71. See Appendix 2, Docs. 3–26.

72. Appendix 2, Doc. 25.

73. Appendix 2, Docs. 21–22.

74. Pius, *Memoirs,* p. 259. Niccola Della Tuccia, *Cronache e statuti della città di Viterbo,* p. 267, also alluded to this event. "Venuto maggio [1462], il papa partì da Roma, e con tutta la corte entrò in Viterbo e stetteci circa un mese e mezzo: poi partì perchè cominciò la morìa, e andò a Corsignano in quello di Siena, e bella città nominandola Pienza per essere stata sua patria."

2. The First Phase: The Monumental Area

1. Pope Pius elevated Pienza to bishopric status on 13 August and it has generally been supposed that he arrived in town about the same time. Letters written by Cardinal Francesco Gonzaga's tutor, Bartolommeo Marasca, show, however, that Pius was in Pienza by 27 July and that he had possibly arrived a month earlier. See D. S. Chambers, "The Housing Problems of Cardinal Francesco Gonzaga," *Journal of the Warburg and Courtauld Institutes,* 39 (1976), 27. Accompanying the pope on this trip were Cardinals Guillaume d'Estouteville (Rouen), Bernardo Eroli (Spoleto), Jean Jouffroy (Arras), Rodrigo Borgia (the papal vice-chancellor), Francesco Piccolomini (Pius' nephew), Jacopo Ammannati (Pavia), Niccolò Forteguerri (Tiano), and Francesco Gonzaga (Mantua). This entourage is reported in Marasca to Barbara von Brandenburg, 8 May 1462 (Chambers, "Housing Problems," p. 26 n. 38) and by Pius (*Memoirs,* p. 260), who added Cardinal Filippo Calandrini of Bologna to this list of escorts.

2. Quoted in Adams, "Acquisition," p. 102.

3. Pius, *Memoirs,* pp. 282–92.

4. See the transcription of this document in n. 87, below.

5. Adams, "Acquisition," p. 106, Docs. 1–7, p. 108, Doc. 37.

6. In addition to the overall treatments of

Pienza, see Gino Chierici, *Il palazzo italiano dal secolo XI al secolo XIX*, 2d ed. rev. (Milan: Antonio Vallardi, 1964), pp. 116–17; Giovanni Battista Mannucci, "Il Palazzo Piccolomini di Pienza," *Arte e Storia*, 27, 17–18 (1908), 133–35; Francesco Naldi Bandini Piccolomini, *Il palazzo pientino di Pio II* (Siena: Tip. Cooperativa, 1905).

7. Pius also underwrote a number of family-enhancing projects in Siena. See Mack, "Studies," pp. 332–45.

8. Not only did the pope suffer from gout and rheumatism but he also may have felt the lingering effects of frostbite incurred on his trip to Scotland years earlier (Pius, *Memoirs*, p. 33).

9. See Brenda Preyer, "The 'Chasa Overo Palagio' of Alberto di Zanobi: A Florentine Palace of About 1400 and Its Later Remodeling," *Art Bulletin*, 65 (1983), 393, for a discussion of the tendency away from the palace-with-shops beginning in the early fifteenth century.

10. Pius, *Memoirs*, p. 282. Architectural drawings and plans of the Palazzo Piccolomini can be found in a number of publications, including Cataldi, et al., *Rilievi di Pienza*, pls. 3, 4, 5; Holtzinger, *Pienza*, pls. 21–23; Stegmann and Geymüller, *The Architecture of the Renaissance in Tuscany*, 1:72, 74, 76.

11. The Palazzo Piccolomini is most often held to be imitative of the Palazzo Rucellai in Florence, but see my articles "The Rucellai Palace: Some New Proposals," *Art Bulletin*, 56 (1974), 517–29, and "The Palazzo Rucellai Reconsidered," in *Actas dell' XXIII congreso internacional de historia del arte (1973)* (Grenada: Universidad Grenada, 1977), 2:344–50, in which I propose that the Rucellai facade was erected ca. 1461 and was based upon that of the Piccolomini. This view has been favorably received by Giancarlo Cataldi, "Pienza e la sua piazza," p. 77 n. 8, and by Kurt W. Forster, "Discussion: The Palazzo Rucellai and Questions of Typology in the Development of Renaissance Buildings," *Art Bulletin*, 68 (1976), 109–13. For the traditional view

and counterarguments, see Paolo Sanpaolesi, "Precisazioni sul Palazzo Rucellai," *Palladio*, 13 (1963), 6–66, and Brenda Preyer, "The Rucellai Palace," in F. W. Kent, et al., *Giovanni Rucellai ed il suo zibaldone, II: A Florentine Patrician and His Palace* (London: Warburg Institute, 1981), pp. 155–225, esp. 189–97. Forster (p. 109) discusses precedents for the Piccolomini / Rucellai articulation system, which are to be noted on a number of frescoed facades in Florence. The descendents of this sort of articulated facade are diverse. Examples that might be cited would include the Palazzo Carminali (Bottigella) in Pavia and the Palazzi Marigliano and Corigliano in Naples (Chierici, *Il palazzo italiano*, pp. 163, 197–99). as well as Giuliano da Sangallo's Palazzo della Rovere in Savona and Luca Fancelli's Domus Nova in Mantua.

12. Pius, *Memoirs*, p. 283. The colorful nature of the original decorations of the palace are also noted in the contemporary poem of Porcellio Pandoni given in Appendix 1, Doc. 3.

13. Pius, *Memoirs*, p. 282.

14. For examples of such stonework, see Brenda Preyer, "The 'Chasa Overo Palagio' of Alberto di Zanobi," pp. 387–401.

15. Rossellino's use of such regular rustication might also have been inspired by the "mock" stonework executed in sgraffito on many Florentine palaces, which his own shop had used on the facade of the Palazzo Spinelli. This technique had been used throughout the century. See Forster, "The Palazzo Rucellai and Questions of Typology," pp. 109–10, and Günther Thiem and Christel Thiem, *Toskanische Fassaden-Dekoration in Sgraffito und Fresko* (Munich: F. Bruckmann, 1964), ad passim.

16. Mack, "New Proposals," p. 528; Finelli and Rossi, *Pienza*, p. 31. Also see Goldthwaite's *Building of Renaissance Florence*, p. 19.

17. Alberti, *Ten Books*, pp. 86, 193.

18. This has been suggested by Lise Bek, *Towards Paradise on Earth: Modern Space Conception in Architecture, a Creation of Renaissance*

Humanism, Analecta Romana Instituti Danici 9, Supplement (Odense, Denmark: Odense University Press, 1980), p. 124, and by Cecil Grayson, "Leon Battista Alberti, Architect," *Architectural Design (Profile 21),* 49, 5–6 (1979), 14.

19. Alberti, *Ten Books,* p. 193. The description may have been partly derived from a mosaic in San Apollinare Nuovo in Ravenna showing the palace of Theodoric. According to Joseph Rykwert, Alberti was a conceptual architect: "The essential building, the idea-building, could only be *thought.*" For Alberti the ideal building could be constructed only in the mind. The demands of necessity (location, financial considerations, desires of patrons, structural demands) would always prevent the full realization of perfection. See Joseph Rykwert, "Inheritance or Tradition," *Architectural Design (Profile 21),* 49, 5–6 (1979), 4.

20. For the Anfiteatro Castrense at the Castro Pretorio in Rome, see Carlo Roccatelli and Enrico Verdozzi, *Brickwork in Italy: A Brief Review from Ancient to Modern Times* (Chicago: American Face Brick Assoc., 1925), p. 30.

21. Pius, *Memoirs,* p. 316. Pirro Ligorio drew Le Mura in the late 1540s and Andrea Palladio drew it ca. 1554.

22. See T. F. C. Blagg, A. G. Luttrell, and Margaret B. Lyttelton, "Ligorio, Palladio, and the Decorated Roman Capital from Le Mura di Santo Stefano," *Papers of the British School at Rome,* 47 (1979), 102–16; Margaret Lyttelton and Frank Sear, "A Roman Villa near Anguillara Sabazia," *Papers of the British School at Rome,* 45 (1977), 227–51.

23. See Roccatelli and Verdozzi, *Brickwork in Italy,* pp. 27–28.

24. Antonio Manetti, *The Life of Brunelleschi,* trans. Catherine Enggass, ed. Howard Saalman (University Park: Pennsylvania State University Press, 1970), p. 96. For a discussion of Brunelleschi's intentions for the facade of the Hospital of the Innocents, see Mack, "Brunelleschi's Spedale degli Innocenti Rearticulated," pp. 137–45, with recon-struction drawing by Gloria Ward-Clemmensen, p. 145.

25. On the antiquity of the Piccolomini, see Pius, *Memoirs,* p. 29; Ugurgieri della Beradenga, *Pio II Piccolomini con notizie,* pp. 11–12. One of the pope's secretaries, Leonardo Dati, composed an "ancient" chronicle, ostensibly written by Gaius Vibenna, in which figures a Bacio Piccolomi. See Lisini and Liberati, *Genealogia dei Piccolomini di Siena,* pp. 3–4.

26. Forster, "The Palazzo Rucellai and Questions of Typology," p. 111.

27. Pius, *Memoirs,* p. 282. The pope went on to note: "Under each row of windows were two ornamental bands commonly called cornices, made of stone like the Tiburtine, splendidly wrought and encircling the palace like two garlands. . . . At the corners of the building and in many places between the windows he had hung stone shields on which by the art of the sculptor and the painter the arms of the Piccolomini shone in gold and silver and other colors. There were also many iron rings and here and there devices to hold torches by night and banners by day. There were also smaller square windows to light the lower apartments. These had metal gratings. Seats two and sometimes three steps high of the same stone as the cornices ran round the building" (*Memoirs,* pp. 282–83).

28. This treatment approaches that of the astylar base of the Palazzo della Cancelleria of some thirty or more years later, designed, perhaps, by Francesco di Giorgio Martini, who may have worked at Pienza.

29. On the iconography of the cross window, see Carroll William Westfall, "Alberti and the Vatican Palace Type," *Journal of the Society or Architectural Historians,* 33 (1974), 106. For the nature of the *bifore,* see Rab Hatfield, "Some Unknown Descriptions of the Medici Palace in 1459," *Art Bulletin,* 52 (1970), 244. The use of the *bifore*-cross windows gives to the Piccolomini Palace a character rather like the name of its patron. The *bifore* was most often associated with religious or official secular buildings, and the cross

window with the papacy itself. By using the combination window on his palace, Pope Pius would seem to have visually linked his old life as the humanist Aeneas Silvius with his new life as a religious and pointed to this palace as the source of authority in Pienza.

30. George L. Hersey, *Pythagorean Palaces: Magic and Architecture in the Italian Renaissance* (Ithaca: Cornell University Press, 1976), esp. pp. 175–80, quotations from pp. 170, 174, 175, 176.

31. See Appendix 1, Doc. 2.

32. Paul von Naredi-Rainer, "Musikalische Proportionen: Zahlenästhetik und Zahlensymbolik im architektonischen Werk L. B. Albertis," *Jahrbuch des Kunsthistorischen Institutes der Universität Graz,* 12 (1977), 117–20, 172–73.

33. Pius, *Memoirs,* p. 283.

34. Dante Biolchi, *La casina del Cardinale Bessarione, Roma* (Rome: Riporto Antichità e Belle Arti del Comune di Roma, 1954).

35. On the ubiquitousness of walled doorways in the Renaissance palace, see Preyer, "The 'Chasa Overo Palagio' of Alberto di Zanobi," p. 392.

36. Mack, "Rossellino, Alberti, and the Rome of Nicholas V," p. 61, and "Building a Florentine Palace," p. 279.

37. Pius, *Memoirs,* p. 283.

38. Eugenio Battisti, "Natura Artificiosa to Natura Artificialis," in *The Italian Garden,* ed. David R. Coffin, First Dumbarton Oaks Colloquium on the History of Landscape Architecture, 1971 (Washington, D.C.: Dumbarton Oaks, 1972), 26–27.

39. On Vitelleschi's Tarquinian palace, see Salvatore Aurigemma, "Restauri nel Palazzo Vitelleschi in Tarquinia," *Palladio,* 14 (1964), 179–92; Giuseppe Cultrera, "Il Palazzo Vitelleschi in Corneto Tarquinia," *Ausonia,* 10 (1921), 260–97; and Westfall, "Alberti and the Vatican Palace Type," pp. 107–8. Several contemporary appraisals of the cardinal's palace were made by the Viterbese chronicler Giovanni d'Iuzzo and are given in *Cronache e statuti della città di Viterbo,* ed. Ignazio Ciampi,

Documenti di Storia Italiana 5 (Florence: Cellini, 1872), pp. 55 n. 6, 168, 171 n. 3.

40. On these Vatican loggias, see Deoclecio Redig de Campos, *Di alcune tracce del palazzo di Niccolo III nuovamente tornate alle luce* (Rome: Tip. Poliglotta Vaticana, 1942); Westfall, *In This Most Perfect Paradise,* p. 149.

41. On such "paradise gardens," consult Westfall, *In This Most Perfect Paradise,* pp. 130–31, 154–56. Also see Battisti, "Natura Artificiosa to Natura Artificialis," pp. 3–36. A possible later derivative of the loggias of the Palazzo Piccolomini can be found in the villa of La Simonetta designed ca. 1547 by Domenico Giunti for Ferrante Gonzaga (Chierici, *Il palazzo italiano,* pp. 266–67).

42. Lyttelton and Sear, "A Roman Villa near Anguillara Sabazia," p. 112, pl. 38.

43. Pius, *Memoirs,* p. 285.

44. Ibid., pp. 285–86.

45. Ibid., p. 285.

46. D'Iuzzo's description appears in *Cronache e statuti della città di Viterbo,* p. 105 n. 2. For the Renaissance interpretation of the *paradiso terrestro* see Bek, *Towards Paradise on Earth,* pp. 23–129; Westfall, *In This Most Perfect Paradise,* esp. pp. 147–51, 161–63; Battisti, "Natura Artificiosa to Natura Artificialis," pp. 3–36. The mention of an aviary in Forteguerri's palace in Viterbo recalls Pulci's *novella* of Pius II, in which we are told of a former acquaintance of Aeneas Silvius who hoped to ingratiate himself with the new pope by presenting him with an appropriate gift. Advised in the matter by one of the papal officials, a certain Messer Goro, he decided to present the pontiff with a rare parrot but was tricked into purchasing a green woodpecker. This bird was installed in an elaborate cage beautifully painted with the papal coat of arms and was sent to the pope in Pienza (or Corsignano as it is called in Pulci's story), where it was recognized with amusement by Pius and his court for the mundane bird it really was. See William Boulting, *Aeneas Silvius,* pp. 323–24. That one could have expected Pius' *giardino pensile* to have

featured fauna as well as flora is suggested in the pope's description of his 1463 visit to the country villa of Lodovico Scarampo, the patriarch of Aquileia, in Albano. There he was delighted to find a well-planted garden filled with exotic pets. On this visit see Pius, *Memoirs*, p. 315; Mitchell, *The Laurels and the Tiara*, p. 223.

47. Hatfield, "Medici Palace," pp. 233–34. Pope Pius' appreciation of Cosimo de' Medici's achievements as a patron of architecture was recorded in several places. In addition to his statement in the *Commentarii* (*Memoirs*, p. 107) that Cosimo "built a palace fit for a king; he restored some churches and erected others," Pius praised the Florentine's architectural accomplishments in the *De Europa*, quoted in Müntz, *Les Arts*, 1:221 n. 2.

48. Hatfield, "Medici Palace," p. 234. Another contemporary, Alberto Avogadro, added, "And this is a partial list of masterpieces of *ars topiaria* in the Medici garden: elephants, a wild boar, a ship with sails, a ram, a hare with its ears up, a wolf fleeing from dogs, an antlered deer." See Iô Lamus, *Deliciae Eruditorum* (Florence, 1742), 12:117–49; Battisti, "Natura Artificiosa to Natura Artifcialis," p. 16 n. 28.

49. In Fra Francesco Colonna's *Hypnerotomachia Poliphili* of 1467, we hear of other lavishly designed gardens featuring floral designs of coats of arms, human figures, and the like. See F. R. Cowell, *The Garden as Fine Art from Antiquity to Modern Times* (London: Weidenfeld and Nicholson, 1978), p. 151. Battisti ("Natura Artificiosa to Natura Artificialis," pp. 15–16) calls attention to Giovanni Rucellai's description of his garden at Quaracchi with its topiary "spheres, porticoes, temples, vases, urns, apes, donkeys, oxen, a bear, giants, men, women, warriors, a harpy, philosophers, popes, cardinals" as given in his memoirs. For Rucellai's text see Battisti, p. 15 n. 27, or Giovanni Rucellai, *Il zibaldone quaresimile*, ed. A. Perosa (London: Warburg Institute, University of London, 1960), p. 22. Of the garden of the Pic-

colomini Palace, Georgina Masson, who believes the Pienza garden authentic, writes in *Italian Gardens* (New York: Harry N. Abrams, 1961), p. 76: "Here for once the original quattrocento garden design and furniture have survived almost untouched. The stone borders of the raised beds, which surround the garden on three sides, and of the four central parterres, are still there, also the octagonal well-head with its exquisitely sculptured reliefs of garlanded urns and shells and the Piccolomini arms surrounded by twining acanthus. In one respect, however, the original layout has been altered. It was first laid out before Laurana created his epoch-making design for the *giardino pensile* at Urbino and, instead of the present circular space in the middle of the crossing of the paths made by the actual owner, there were simply four rectangular beds like those of medieval times; the charming little fountain is also a recent addition." The originality of the layout seems dubious, however. For Sienese garden design, see Cesare Brandi, Rosario Assunto, Alessandro Tagliolini, *Introduzione ai giardini del senese* (San Quirico d'Orcia: Archivio Italiano dell'Arte dei Giardini, 1976). Also see the gardening suggestions in Alberti, *De re aedificatoria*, p. 193.

50. See Battisti ("Natura Artificiosa to Natura Artifcialis," p. 17 n. 31), who notes that "the gardens, walls and loggia were usually painted"; and Bek, *Towards Paradise on Earth*, pp. 108–9, pls. 33, 35. For evidence that decorations of some sort were applied to the walls of the loggia of the Palazzo Piccolomini, see Ludwig Heydenreich, "Pius II. als Bauherr von Pienza," *Zeitschrift für Kunstgeschichte*, 6 (1937), 108, rpt. in Ludwig Heydenreich, *Studien zur Architektur der Renaissance: Ausgewählte Aufsätze* (Munich: Fink, 1981), p. 58. One might suspect that appropriately vegetative decorations were intended for the walls of the adjoining kitchen wing.

51. The importance of axiality in the architectural aesthetic of the Renaissance is treated in Bek, *Towards Paradise on Earth*, esp. pp 90–

91 (where the axial orientation of Giovanni Rucellai's Villa Lo Specchio at Quaracchi is discussed), and pp. 96–103 (which deals specifically with Pienza). Eugenio Battista ("Natura Artificiosa to Natural Artificialis," p. 14) offers the following observation: "The Renaissance transformation occurs not in the garden, itself, but in the overall layout of the palace or villa, and in the relationship between garden and landscape. In Boccaccio, the garden remains totally separate as, for example, in some conservative Renaissance villas. One needs a special key to open the door and must walk through open or covered passages before arriving there. In the fifteenth century, especially in Florence, the garden is considered a second courtyard and is aligned axially with the palace. Both the central door of the palace and the garden gate were opened on special occasions to give visitors the view of a green, flowered background ending the axis which extended through the entire building."

52. Leon Pressouyre, "St. Bernard to St. Francis: Monastic Ideals and Iconographic Programs in the Cloister," *Gesta*, 12 (1973), 71–84.

53. See the diagram in Bek, *Towards Paradise on Earth*, p. 127, fig. 32. The purchases are also recorded in the Sienese *gabelle*, which have been published in Adams "Acquisition," pp. 107–8.

54. Pius, *Memoirs*, p. 285. Battisti, "Natura Artificiosa to Natura Artificialis," p. 26, relates Pius' description to the Petrarchian concept: "The earliest expression of this attitude (already peculiar to the Benedictine monks) is found in Petrarch, in his description of an ascension of Mont Ventoux."

55. See most especially Bek, *Towards Paradise on Earth*, pp. 64–78; Westfall, *In This Most Perfect Paradise*, pp. 143–54.

56. Pius, *Memoirs*, p. 285. Note the similarity to Leonardo's designs for a stable in Carlo Pedretti, *Leonardo, Architect*, trans. Sue Brill (New York: Rizzoli, 1985), pp. 258–63.

57. Ibid.

58. See Mack, "Rosellino, Alberti, and the Rome of Nicholas V," p. 61, and "Building a Florentine Palace," p. 279.

59. The testimony of Flavio Biondo also supports this conclusion. See Appendix 1, Doc. 2.

60. Pius, *Memoirs*, p. 283.

61. Ibid. Actually, the *cortile* presents an axial emphasis. The northern and southern loggias are deeper than the eastern and western. Indeed, the southern loggia is twice as deep as the adjacent loggias, partly to accommodate sufficient storage and partly—as at the Palazzo Medici—as a way of anticipating the open garden area beyond.

62. Ibid., p. 284.

63. For a discussion of the evolution of the cross window, consult Federico Hermann, *Il Palazzo di Venezia* (Rome: Libreria dello Stato, 1948), pp. 21–25; Vincenzo Golzio and Giuseppe Zander, *L'arte in Roma nel secolo* XV (Bologna: Cappelli, 1968), pp. 59–104; Charles R. Mack, "Notes Concerning an Unpublished Window by Bernardo Rossellino at the Badia Fiorentina," *Southeastern College Art Conference Review*, 5 (Dec. 1970), 2–5. Cross windows appear to have been introduced into the Roman region during the 1450s. They were used, for instance, in the palaces on the Capitoline Hill. See Carlo Pietrangeli, *Le prime fasi architettoniche del Palazzo Senatoria* (Rome: Edizioni di Capitolium, 1965), p. 25. Cross windows may be observed pictorially in frescoes Benozzo Gozzoli painted in the Church of San Francesco in Montefalcro, ca. 1450–52. They also are to be seen in a later (1463?) fresco, the *Burial of Saint Augustine*, which Benozzo painted in the Church of San Agostino in San Gimignano and, even later (1468), in one of his scenes inside Pisa's Camposanto. For these, see figs. 31, 32, 33, 76, and 89 in Elena Contaldi, *Benozzo Gozzoli* (Milan: Hoepli, 1928). The possibility of antique sources for the cross window form (e.g., the false door on the facade of the Etruscan Tomb of the Caryatids at Luni) is remote.

64. For some possible (but, in my opinion, dubious) early Tuscan examples of cross win-

dows, see Natale Rauty, "Le finestre a cro-
ciera del Palazzo Panciatichi a Pistoia," in *Atti
del 2° convegno internazionale di studi: Il gotico a
Pistoia nei suoi rapporti con l'arte gotica italiana*
(Pistoia: Centro Italiano di Studi e d'Arte
Pistoia, 1966), 93–101.

65. Giovanni Battista Mannucci, "Il palazzo di Pio II ed i suoi restauri," *Rassegna d'Arte
Senese*, 7 (1911), 22–30, and *Pienza*, pp. 93–
94. In support of the painted decorations, see
the poem of Porcellio Pandoni in Appendix 1,
Doc. 3.

66. Pius, *Memoirs*, p. 283.

67. This room was restored in the summer
of 1984 for use as an exhibition area by the
commune of Pienza.

68. Pius, *Memoirs*, p. 283.

69. Ibid., p. 284. The pope's legs were
frequently painful. See Mitchell, *The Laurels
and the Tiara*, pp. 67–68.

70. The *piano nobile* is now open to the
public. On the building's history, see Carli,
Pienza, pp. 84–85 n. 69. See also Mannucci,
"Il palazzo di Pio II ed i suoi restauri," pp.
22–30.

71. On such palaces, see Mack, "The
Rucellai Palace: Some New Proposals," and
"Building a Florentine Palace: The Palazzo
Spinelli"; Preyer, "The 'Chasa Overo Pa-
lagio' of Alberto di Zanobi."

72. Alberti, *Ten Books*, pp. 189, 109.

73. Ibid., pp. 17, 104, 110.

74. Howard Burns, "A Drawing by L. B.
Alberti," *Architectural Design (Profile 21)*, 79,
5–6 (1979), 45–56, and "Un disegno architettonico di Alberti e la questione del rapporto
fra Brunelleschi ed Alberti," in *Filippo Brunelleschi*, 1:105–23.

75. Burns, "A Drawing by L. B. Alberti,"
p. 46.

76. For Pliny's villa, consult especially
Bek, *Towards Paradise on Earth*, pp. 175–80.
For Vitruvius, see Marcus Vitruvius Pollio,
The Ten Books on Architecture, trans. Morris
Hicky Morgan (Cambridge: Harvard Univer-
sity Press, 1914), pp. 180–81.

77. Alberti, *Ten Books*, pp. 418–19.

78. Pius, *Memoirs*, pp. 284–85.

79. Ibid., p. 277.

80. Ibid., pp. 282, 283.

81. Alberti, *Ten Books*, p. 109.

82. Pius, *Memoirs*, p. 285.

83. Aeneas Silvius Piccolomini, *De gestis
concilii basiliensis commentariorum*, trans. and
ed. Denys Hay and W. K. Smith (Oxford:
Clarendon, 1967), pp. 231, 233.

84. Alberti, *Ten Books*, p. 109.

85. For two most interesting early Renaissance palaces, the designs of which could
have had some influence on the Palazzo Piccolomini and on that of Cardinal Vitelleschi
in Tarquinia, see Carol Pulin, "The Palaces of
an Early Renaissance Humanist, Cardinal
Branda Castiglione," *Arte Lombarda*, 41
(1982), 23–32.

86. Mannucci, *Pienza*, pp. 241–42.
Lodrisio Crivelli's poem describing Pienza
was written on 15 February 1464 on the
occasion of the pope's last visit to Pienza
(Appendix 1, Doc. 4). Leslie F. Smith,
"Lodrisio Crivelli of Milan and Aeneas Silvius, 1457–1464," *Studies in the Renaissance*, 9
(1962), 56.

87. Archivio Piccolomineo, *Pergamene ad
annum*, 130, 19 July 1463, published previously in Borghesi and Banchi, *Nuovi documenti per la storia dell' arte senese*, pp. 215–17;
Mack, "Studies," pp. 409–10; and Mannucci,
Pienza, pp. 90–92: "Pius episcopus, servus
servorum Dei, ad futuram rei memoriam.
Precellens Romani Pontificis prudentia, futuris eventibus prospicere, equa ratione affectans
personas generis nobilitate conspicuas, vir-
tutum quoque dignitatum et morum ingenui-
tate pollentes, que secundum humanam
propagationem naturali sibi federe con-
iunguntur, munificentie sue liberalitate at-
tollit, earumque statui ordinata caritate sic
studet providere utiliter, sicque dissidiis ob-
viare quod earum splendori et meritis opor-
tunum adiiciat sublevamen. Horum igitur
consideratione inducti, palatium nostrum,
quod nuper in civitate Pientina, agri senensis,
in fundo paterno destructa domo, quae ibi
prius erat iuxta illius Ecclesiam Cathedralem,
a solo ereximus cum horto seu viridario, nec

non stabulis et domo cum oleario atque aliis pertinentiis suis, atque jurisdictionibus quibuscumque, dilectis Filiis et secundum carnem Nepotibus nostris, nobilibus viris Antonio Duci Amalfitano, Jacobo et Andreae de Piccolominibus motu proprio, liberalitate spontanea, tenore praesentium et certa scientia, perpetuo concedimus et donamus irrevocabiliter ea donatione, quae dicitur inter vivos; quam donationem ex certa scientia facimus, et vim perpetue firmitatem habere volumus, cuiuscumque etiam maximi valori dictum palatium existeret, juribus in contrarium facientibus non obstantibus quibuscumque, quibus expresse et certa scientia derogamus. Volentes ac etiam statuentes et decernentes, quod primogeniti Antonii, Iacobi et Andree predictorum dictum palatium possideant, illiusque directum utileque ac plenum et omnimodum dominium habeant, et post eos secundigeniti descendendo, videlicet masculi legitimi et naturales iura primogeniture habentes: deficientibus vero masculis, ut prefertur qualificatis, eorum filie legitime similiter et naturales, si in domo Piccolomineae et Piccolominibus viris nupte fuerint, possint ad instar masculorum in palatio predicto succederes: quod si Antonius, Iacobus et Andreas, aut duo tantum vel unus eorum, filios masculos legitimos et naturales habuerint vel habuerit, illi vel ille qui filiis caruerint, vel caruerit usum dicti palatii, ac etiam jus in eo competens aliis fratribus vel altero fratri, eorumque vel eius filiis dare possit pro sue libito voluntatis. Et si, quod absit, tam masculi quam femine ex ipsis Antonio, Iacobo et Andrea descendentes defecerint, ut in domo proximior de Piccolomineo domo in eodem palatio succedat, et successive de uno in alium vel alios proximiores dominium transferatur et successio fiat, ita quod magis propinqui dicte domus in successione huiusmodi preferantur: districtius inhibentes tum Antonio, Iacobo et Andree predictis, quam aliis quibuscumque eorum heredibus et successoribus in futurum, ut dictum palatium, mutando formam edificii dividere, eiusve edificia mutare sive illud in toto vel in parte vendere, Ypothecare aut in dotem tradere, seu alio quovis quesito colore distruhere et alienare presumant: sed perpetuo futuris temporibus ipsorum Antonii, Iacobi et Andree natorumque et posterorum eorumdem per rectam lineam descendentium, ac postremo in eventum defectionis domus predicte propinquiorum de predicta domo de Piccolominibus usibus reservetur. Decernentes ex nunc omnes et singulas divisiones, mutationes, venditiones, ypothecas seu pignorationes traditiones, distractiones et alienationes de dicto palatio, aut quicquid in contrarium fieri vel attemptari contigerit, irritas atque inanes atque irrita et inania nulliusque roboris vel momenti. Nulli ergo omnino hominum liceat hanc paginam nostre concessionis, donationis voluntatis derogationis statuti, constitutionis, inhibitionis et decreti infringere, vel ei ausu temerario contraire. Siquis autem hoc attemptare presumpserit indignationem omnipotentis Dei ac Beatorum Petri et Pauli Apostolorum eius se noverit incursurum. Datum Tibure, Anno incarnationis Dominice millesimo quadringentesimo sexagesimo tertio. Quartodecimo Kal. Augusti, Pontificatus nostri anno quinto."

88. ASS, *Denunzie,* Lira 160, terza di San Martino, c. 113–113ᵛ, previously published in Mack, "Studies," p. 413: "Item. In nela citta di Pientia uno palazo con sue appartenentie. El quale come cia schuno puo sapere ci da spessa grandissima senza alcuna utilità che per la fama sua altetta forestieri da longa de quali ongni gron . . . tene sonno assai ale spese nostre crediamo che le V. Spᵗᵃ cenalegiranno per la graande spesa vi habiamo. . . ."

89. Pius, *Memoirs,* p. 286. Aside from discussions found in the general works on Pienza, the cathedral has been the subject of several separate articles and publications, including Alfredo Barbacci, "L'edificazione e il decadimento del duomo di Pienza," *Bollettino d'Arte,* Ser. 2, 10 (1931), 317–34; "Le cause de cedimento del duomo di Pienza," *Bollettino d'Arte,* Ser. 2, 10 (1931), 491–511; "Il ritrovamento e il ripristino dell'antica decorazione del duomo di Pienza," *Bollettino d'Arte,* Ser.

3, 25 (1931–32), 282–88; "Il duomo di Pienza e i suoi restauri," La *Diana*, 9 (1934), 1–134; Richard Kurt Donin, *Österreichische Baugedanken am Dom von Pienza*, Forschungen zur österreichischen Kunstgeschichte 5 (Vienna: Erwin Müller, 1946); Carla Faldi Guglielmi, *Duomo di Pienza* (Bologna: Officine Grafiche Poligrafici il Resto del Carlino, 1967); and A. Socini, "Un'antica questione relativa alle fondazioni del duomo di Pienza," *Rivista d'Arte*, 6 (1909), 85–94. Architectural plans and elevations can be found in Cataldi, et al., *Rilievi*, pls. 3, 4, and 5; Holtzinger, *Pienza: Aufgenommen und gezeichnet*, pl. 17; Stegmann and Geymüller, *The Architecture of the Renaissance in Tuscany*, 1:79–80; and Barbacci, "Il duomo di Pienza e i suoi restauri," fig. 26.

90. The sequence of dates in the establishment of the bishopric of Pienza and the consecration of its cathedral are found conveniently discussed in Finelli and Rossi, *Pienza*, p. 29 n. 25, p. 113; Schiavo, *Monumenti*, p. 69; and Mannucci, pp. 26–36 (together with transcriptions of the pertinent papal bulls). Pius included the text of his bull banning additions to the cathedral in his *Commentarii* (*Memoirs*, p. 289).

91. Pius, *Memoirs*, p. 291. Flavio Biondo, however (it would seem mistakenly), says that the cathedral was consecrated on the feast day of Saint Matthew (See Appendix 1, Doc. 2).

92. Pius, *Memoirs*, p. 286. Pope Pius (*Memoirs*, p. 288) alluded to charges that were made against Rossellino "that he had blundered in the construction." Such complaints may well have been justified. As a Florentine, Rossellino did not possess the experience of building on a hilly terrain that his Sienese detractors did. Francesco di Giorgio Martini also noted the unsound foundations of Rossellino's cathedral: "As it happened in Pienza, the Tuscan town, where because of a similar imprudence in building: the most beautiful church has cracked open." See Maryla Tyskiewicz, *Bernardo Rossellino*, trans. Rosa Rosmaryn, ed. Anne Markham Schultz

(Florence: TS Kunsthistorisches Institut), p. 40. The structural problem has been considered by Barbacci, "L'edificazioni e il decadimento," pp. 317–34; "Le cause de cedimento," pp. 494–511; "Il duomo di Pienza," pp. 85–94; and by Socini, "Un antica questione," pp. 85–94. The Cathedral has suffered damage both from nature (an earthquake in 1545, which collapsed sections of vaulting) and man (bombardment in World War II) and has been repaired upon several occasions. See Mannucci, *Pienza*, p. 34, and Finelli and Rossi, *Pienza*, pp. 28–29 n. 24, for good synopses of the various programs of reconstruction.

93. Pius, *Memoirs*, p. 286. The marble baptismal font is the most notable piece of liturgical furniture in the lower church. This elaborate example of architectural sculpture stands upon a round two-stepped podium. An ornately carved basin decorated with fluting, egg-and-dart moldings, and acanthus leaves terminates in a capitallike support bearing a four-sided tabernacle. Columns define each corner of the tabernacle and frame the shell niches that decorate the sides. A high entablature rests upon the columns and forms the base for a pyramidal roof. This type of font may be connected with the font in the Siena Baptistery (by Jacopo della Quercia and others, 1416–34) and with a ciborium in the National Gallery, Washington, D.C., which has often been associated with Desiderio da Settignano. On the latter, see Ida Cardellini, *Desiderio da Settignano* (Milan: Edizioni di Comunità, 1962), pp. 252–56. Also see Schulz, *The Sculpture of Rossellino and His Workshop*, pl. 135, for another font closely related to the one in Pienza.

94. Howard Saalman, "Michelozzo Studies," *Burlington Magazine*, 108 (1966), 242; Deoclecio Redig de Campos, *Il restauro della aule di Niccolo V e di Sisto IV nel Palazzo Apostolico Vaticana* (Rome: Tipografia Poliglotta Vaticana, 1967). One is reminded also of the split-level design of the Cathedral of Siena with its lower baptistery.

95. Abbot Suger, *Abbot Suger on the Abbey*

Church of St. Denis and Its Art Treasures, trans. Erwin Panofsky (Princeton: Princeton University Press, 1957), p. 101; Hatfield, "Some Unknown Descriptions," pp. 238–39. Carli (Pienza, pp. 37–44) believes that the cathedral was given an orientation which allowed for the maximum admittance of light and that light played a role of substantial religious significance in the building. The use of such large glass windows in a church dedicated to the Virgin would seem to have been particularly appropriate. See Millard Meiss, "Light as Form and Symbol in Some Fifteenth-Century Paintings," Art Bulletin, 27 (1945), 43–68, rpt. in Millard Meiss, The Painter's Choice: Problems in the Interpretation of Renaissance Art (New York: Harper and Row, 1976), pp. 3–18.

96. Pius, Memoirs, p. 287. For a discussion of Italian hall churches, see W. Krönig, "Hallenkirchen in Mittelitalien," Kunstgeschichtliches Jahrbuch der Bibliotheca Hertziana, 2 (1938), 1–142; Golzio and Zander, L'arte in Roma, pp. 158–62.

97. Heydenreich, "Pius II. als Bauherr von Pienza" (1981), pp. 65–68; Donin, Österreichische Baugedanken. On Pius' interest in Germanic church architecture, see Müntz, Les Arts, 1:221. On Hans Stetheimer, see Peter Baldass, "Hans Stetheimers wahrer Name," Wiener Jahrbuch für Kunstgeschichte, 14 (1950), 47–64; Eberhard Hanfstaengel, Hans Stetheimer: Eine Studie zur spätgotischen Architektur Altbayerns (Leipzig: Hermann, 1911). One also might think of the Sankt Georgkirche (1453) in Wiener Neustadt, Austria, the imperial residence of Frederick III. Pope Pius probably would have been familiar with the church's appearance. The Klosterneuburg near Vienna also has been suggested as a possible model. See Fontana, Artisti e committenti nella Roma del quattrocento, p. 50. Piero Torriti, Pienza: Città del Rinascimento (Genoa: Edigraphica, 1965), p. 76 n. 10, cites the Cathedral of Graz, Austria, as yet another possible prototype.

98. Heydenreich, "Pius II. als Bauherr von Pienza" (1937), p. 116.

99. Mitchell, The Laurels and the Tiara, p. 202.

100. Pius, Memoirs, p. 287. The pope's rather eclectic artistic tastes are clear in his appraisal of the medieval Cathedral of Orvieto, which he described as "inferior to no church in Italy" with a facade "filled with statues by the best sculptors, chiefly Sienese, who are not inferior to Phidias and Praxiteles." He went on to praise these works whose "faces stand out from the white marble as if alive and the bodies of men and beasts are so well rendered that art seems to have equaled nature" (Memoirs, p. 163). On the variety in Pius' architectural appreciation, see Müntz, Les Arts, 1:223.

101. That Pius had his own ideas about architecture is clear from his writings but he also had respect for the professional. This is indicated by his tale of the Milanese lawyer, Polino, who stupidly decided to cut the beams for his house himself, measured wrongly, and thereby "ruined the beams and the building too." This story appears in a letter from the future pope to Wilhelm von Stein, 1 June 1444, published in Piccolomini Selected Letters, p. 35. It is tempting, however, to attribute a determining influence to a forceful patron. Ugo Procacci has done this in regard to Cosimo de' Medici's role at the Badia Fiesolana in "Cosimo de Medici e la costruzione della Badia Fiesolana," Commentari, 19 (1968), 80–97. David Coffin suggested the same for Lorenzo de' Medici at the Poggioreale of Alfonso of Aragon. See his Review of George Hersey, Alfonso II and the Artistic Renewal of Naples, 1485–1495 (New Haven: Yale University Press, 1969), Journal of the Society of Architectural Historians, 31 (1972), 66. Lorenzo's possible role as designer as well as patron has recently been emphasized in Piero Morselli and Gino Corti, La chiesa di Santa Maria delle Carceri in Prato (Florence: Società Pratese di Storia Patria, 1982). But see the review of this volume by Linda Pellecchia in the Journal of the Society of Architectural Historians, 44 (1985), 185–86.

102. For a discussion of San Lorenzo in Perugia, see Ottorino Gurrieri, *La cattedrale di S. Lorenzo in Perugia* (Perugia: Azienda Autonoma di Turismo, 1961).

103. Tsyzkiewicz, *Bernardo Rossellino* (trans.), p. 39, notes: "The plan of the Cathedral of Pienza is the tribune of St. Peter's turned into a church by the addition of a little transept." For the relationship of the Renaissance to Lombardy, see Agnoldomenico Pica, "Il Brunellesco e le origini del rinascimento lombardo," in *Atti del 1° congresso nazionale di storia dell'architettura, Firenze, 1936* (Florence: Sansoni, 1938), 165–71.

104. Pius, *Memoirs*, p. 36.

105. Ady, *Pius II*, p. 161. The pope stated in the *Commentarii* (*Memoirs*, p. 100) that he dedicated the Cathedral of San Domenico in Perugia; he meant, of course, the Cathedral of San Lorenzo.

106. Pius, *Memoirs*, pp. 287–88. Drawings of these window traceries are given in Barbacci, *Il Duomo di Pienza*, figs. 28, 29.

107. On such capitals, see Howard Burns, "Un disegno architettonico di Alberti e la questione del rapporto fra Brunelleschi ed Alberti," in Argan et al., *Filippo Brunelleschi*, 1:115–16.

108. For such antique capitals, see Nancy L. Hirshland, "The Head-Capitals of Sardis," *Papers of the British School at Rome*, 35 (1967), 12–22; Eugen von Mercklin, *Antike Figural Kapitelle* (Berlin: Walter de Gruyter, 1962).

109. Pius, *Memoirs*, p. 287.

110. Heydenreich, "Pius II. als Bauherr von Pienza" (1937), p. 133. Also see Howard Saalman, "Early Renaissance Architectural Theory and Practice in Antonio Filarete's 'Trattato di Architettura,'" *Art Bulletin*, 41 (1959), 96.

111. Pius, *Memoirs*, p. 287. For a discussion of these decorations and their several renewals, consult Barbacci, "Decorazione."

112. Pius, *Memoirs*, p. 287. The artists chosen by Pius to provide altarpieces for his cathedral were Matteo di Giovanni, Giovanni di Paolo, Sano di Pietro, and Lorenzo di Pietro, called Il Vecchietta. A discussion of their contributions to the artistic program of the cathedral is found most conveniently in Carli, *Pienza*, pp. 93–124.

113. See Thiem, *Toskanische Fassaden-Dekoration*, pp. 67–68, 73–74.

114. Pius, *Memoirs*, p. 288.

115. See Schiavo, *Monumenti*, pp. 62, 106 n. 28; Mannucci, *Pienza*, p. 58.

116. Pius, *Memoirs*, pp. 286–87. If statues were, indeed, to adorn the facade, they were never executed.

117. On the reconciliation of internal and external heights, see Schiavo, *Monumenti*, p. 31.

118. Pius, *Memoirs*, pp. 286–87.

119. Richard Goldthwaite, *The Building of Renaissance Florence: An Economic and Social History* (Baltimore: Johns Hopkins University Press, 1980), p. 19.

120. On the missing pediment of the Pazzi Chapel, see Mario Salmi, "Sant'Andrea a Camoggiano e la cappella de'Pazzi," in *Festschrift Ulrich Middeldorf*, ed. Antje Kosegarten and Peter Tigler (Berlin: Walter de Gruyter, 1968), 136–42. For comments on Brunelleschi's intentions, see Mack, "Brunelleschi's Spedale degli Innocenti Rearticulated," pp. 138–39 n. 54.

121. Walter Paatz and Elizabeth Paatz, *Die Kirchen von Florenz* (Frankfurt: Klostermann, 1940–54), 2:41–42.

122. Miranda Ferrara, "Santa Maria delle Grazie a Pistoia: Alcuni aspetti del rapporto Michelozzo-Brunelleschi," in Argan et al., *Filippo Brunelleschi*, 2:571–75.

123. For San Agostino, see Howard Saalman, "The Palazzo Comunale in Montepulciano: An Unknown Work by Michelozzo," *Zeitschrift für Kunstgeschichte*, 28 (1965), 4, 31.

124. Schiavo, *Monumenti*, p. 29 suggests the three-arched facade of the late Romanesque church of Santa Caterina in Pisa as a prototype for that of the Pienza cathedral.

125. Alberti, *Ten Books*, p. 140; Pius, *Memoirs*, p. 286.

126. Cecil Grayson, *An Autograph Letter from Leon Battista Alberti to Matteo de' Pasti*,

November 18, 1454 (New York: Pierpont Morgan Library, 1957), p. 19.

127. On the *ombrellone* of San Andrea, see Eugene J. Johnson, *S. Andrea in Mantua: The Building History* (University Park: Pennsylvania State University Press, 1975), pp. 21–22.

128. Rudolf Wittkower, *Architectural Principles in the Age of Humanism,* Columbia University Studies in Art History and Archaeology 1 (New York: Random House, 1965), pp. 46–47.

129. Alberti, *Ten Books,* p. 113.

130. One is reminded of the distinction Alberti drew (*Ten Books,* p. 188) between the ornament of religious and secular buildings: "I think that a sacred edifice should be adorned in such a manner that it should be impossible to add anything that can conduce either to majesty, beauty or wonder: whereas a private structure should be so contrived that it shall be impossible to take anything from it without lessening its dignity. Other buildings, that is to say, the profane of a public nature, should observe the medium between these two extremes."

131. Pius, *Memoirs,* p. 287.

132. Heydenreich, "Pius II. als Bauherr von Pienza" (1937), pp. 118–22; Mack, "Nicholas the Fifth and the Rebuilding of Rome."

133. Pius, *Memoirs,* p. 288. Although the tower today probably stands as intended and as built, it has undergone restoration, as is shown by the coat of arms it bears—that of a later Piccolomini bishop who was responsible for rebuilding the campanile after it was damaged in the earthquake of 1545. See Mannucci, *Pienza,* p. 34; Schiavo, *Monumenti,* pp. 47–48, 106 n. 25.

134. The form of the Pienza campanile is not at all like that which Alberti recommended (*Ten Books,* p. 171) or which he built in Ferrara in the 1440s.

135. Donin, *Österreichische Baugedanken,* p. 68; Schiavo, *Monumenti,* p. 47.

136. Paatz, *Die Kirchen von Florenz,* 1:279.

137. Mack, "Studies," pp. 62, 79 n. 6.

138. Ibid., pp. 329–33; Mario Montanari,

Mille anni della chiesa di S. Pietro in Perugia e del suo patrimonio (Foligno: Poligrafica F. Salvati, 1966), pp. 216–22.

139. Many of the architectural motifs of Pienza seem to have been echoed in the sixteenth-century structures of nearby Montepulciano. In fact, the two towns together offer an interesting study of the relationships between Early and High/Late Renaissance approaches to architectural situations.

140. Pius, *Memoirs,* p. 288, 286.

141. A number of aesthetic implications in the layout of this piazza are considered in Chapter 4.

142. Lando Bartoli, "Un restauro e un problema di prospettiva: Il Palazzo Rasponi-Spinelli in Firenze" (Florence: Cooperativa Libraria Universitatis Studi Florentini, 1967). This significant typescript is not widely accessible. A copy is in the Bibliothek des Kunsthistorischen Instituts in Florence. See also Mack, "Building a Florentine Palace," pp. 265–66.

143. Pius, *Memoirs,* p. 286.

144. Nicolai Rubenstein, "The Piazza della Signoria in Florence," in *Festschrift Herbert Siebenhüner,* ed. Erich Hubala and Gunter Schweikhart (Würzburg: Ferdinand Schöningh, 1978), 22, 24, 26, 29. Rubenstein notes that in 1319 the Florentine square was paved in stone and brick (p. 22) and that in 1390 "the shape of the Piazza was further emphasized by its paving being divided into rectangular sections of bricks" (p. 26). Also see Wolfgang Braunfels, *Mittelalterliche Stadtbaukunst in der Toskana* (1953; rpt. Berlin: Gebr. Mann, 1966), p. 104.

145. Creighton Gilbert, in *Change in Piero della Francesca* (Locust Valley, N.Y.: J. J. Augustin, 1968), pp. 48–49, has perceptively associated the later work of Piero with the new architecture of Rome and Pienza. A family (Albertian?) resemblance has been noted between the Piazza Pio II and the piazzas represented in the three cityscape panels variously attributed to Piero della Francesca, Francesco di Giorgio Martini, Luciano Laurana, Baccio Pontelli, and others

and now in museums in Baltimore, Berlin, and Urbino.

146. Pius, *Memoirs,* p. 286.

147. As, for example, in "Pienza," *Le cento città d'Italia,* Supplement 12044 (Milan: Sonzogno, 31 Oct. 1899), 73, 76, 77.

148. Pius, *Memoirs,* p. 292. The streets of larger communities were paved, however, by the fourteenth century. See Braunfels, *Mittelalterliche Stadtbaukunst,* pp. 104–5.

149. On similar concepts, see Braunfels, *Mittelalterliche Stadtbaukunst,* pp. 116–30.

150. Pius, *Memoirs,* p. 288.

151. The well in Pienza, in turn, was the obvious source for Sangallo when he designed the Pozzo de'Grifi in neighboring Montepulciano.

152. Mario Salmi, *Civiltà artistica della terra aretina* (Novara: Istituto Geografico de Agostini, 1971), p. 112. Salmi notes that the well in San Giovanni Valdarno was demolished in 1856. Its original position is shown on a 1553 plan of the town. ASF, *Cinque del contado,* no. 258, c. 602, published in Italo Moretti, *Le "terre nuove" del contado fiorentino* (Florence: Salimbeni, 1979), p. 38.

153. ASF, *Catasto 829,* c. 671–75, published in Hartt, Corti, and Kennedy, *The Chapel of the Cardinal of Portugal,* pp. 178–80. Also see Mack, "Studies," p. 189.

154. Pius, *Memoirs,* p. 289. Plans and elevations of the Canons' House may be found in Cataldi et al., *Rilievi,* pls. 3, 6.

155. Adams, "Acquisition," p. 107. Adams also concludes that Giliforte's purchases may have involved the site of the Canon's House ("Acquisition," p. 102).

156. Mannucci, *Pienza,* p. 63. The museum was established in 1901 by the 25th bishop of Pienza, Giacomo Maria Bellucci.

3. The Second Phase: Other Public and Private Buildings

1. Pius, *Memoirs,* p. 282. Recorded transactions in the Vatican account books and in the Sienese *gabelle* indicate the expenditure of some 27,000 ducats. See Appendix 2, Docs. 1–26, and Adams, "Acquisition," pp. 106–7, Docs. 1–7, 13, 15, 20–21. A passage in a letter from the Sienese ambassador in Rome, Giovanni Battista Piccolomini, written in 1462 confirms the expense: "Between building and other necessary possessions, he has spent many thousands of ducats." This document in the State Archives of Siena is quoted in Adams, "Acquisition," p. 105.

2. Pius, *Memoirs,* pp. 288–89. Compared to the reputed construction cost of the Palazzo Medici (60,000 to 100,000 florins), Pius seems to have gotten off cheaply. Hatfield, "Some Unknown Descriptions," p. 235. On the extraordinary nature of the gifts awarded Rossellino, see Goldthwaite, *The Building of Renaissance Florence,* pp. 347–50, 388–91.

3. Pius, *Memoirs,* pp. 233–34. Pius' contemporaries, Niccola Della Tuccia and Giovanni d'Iuzzo, also recorded the discovery of these deposits and the effect upon the papal treasury. The former noted that the annual income to the papacy from these mines exceeded a million ducats. See *Cronache e statuti della città di Viterbo,* pp. 87–88, 268. Giovanni d'Iuzzo served as superintendent of the alum mines. The impact is considered in G. Barbieri, *Industria e politica mineraria nello stato pontificio dal '400 al '600* (Rome: Cremonese, 1940); and Lazio G. Zippel, "L'allume di Tolfa e il suo commercio," *Archivio di Società Romana di Storia Patria,* 30 (1907), 1–5, 387–462. The huge sums the papal treasury expected to realize from the operation of the alum mines were noted in a poem by Lodrisio Crivelli written in the summer of 1462 and published in Leslie F. Smith, "Lodrisio Crivelli of Milan and Aeneas Silvius, 1457–1464," *Studies in the Renaissance,* 9 (1962), 48. Smith contradicts Della Tuccia, claiming (p. 48) that the annual profit from the operation was approximately 100,000 ducats.

4. Pius, *Memoirs,* p. 289.

5. Adams, "Acquisition," p. 107, Doc. 21.

6. A Piccolomini relative, Niccolò d'Andrea (1396–1476) was married to Battista di Pietro Porrini in 1450. See Lisini and Liberati,

Genealogia dei Piccolomini di Siena, p. 59, table 5. The Sienese palace of the Piccolomini is discussed in Mack, "Studies," pp. 332–41. Porrina's name, included in a variety of Pientine building records, is also mentioned in a memorandum dated 13 February 1464 by the Sienese commissioner in Pienza, Niccolò di Mariano, published in Mannucci, *Pienza,* pp. 243–44.

7. Aside from general works on Pienza, see the discussion of the Palazzo Vescovile in Roberto Papini, *Francesco di Giorgio architetto* (Florence: Electa Editrice, 1946), 1:237 n. 146 (where the building is erroneously attributed to Francesco di Giorgio Martini); and Francesco Naldi Bandini Piccolomini, "Le case Borgia e Gonzaga in Pienza," *Arte e storia*, Supplement "Pienza e Pio II pubblicato in occasione del V centenario della nascita di Enea Silvio Piccolomini," 24, ser. 3, 8 (1905), 5–6. Also see Papini's monograph, p. 239, for architectural drawings and a plan of the palace. Additional plans are to be found in Cataldi et al., *Rilievi di Pienza,* pls. 3, 4, and 6; Holtzinger, *Pienza,* pl. 20; and Schiavo, *Monumenti,* p. 77. One cannot help but be reminded of the Palazzo Venezia in Rome. For an up-to-date review of the evolution of that palace, consult Frommel, *Der Palazzo Venezia in Rom,* and "Francesco del Borgo, Architekt Pius' II. und Pauls II.; II.: Palazzo Venezia, Palazzetto Venezia und San Marco," *Römisches Jahrbuch für Kunstgeschichte,* 21 (1984), 71–164. A building of similar design can be noted in the background of Pinturicchio's fresco (late 1480s) *Death of San Bernardino da Siena* in the Bufalini Chapel of Santa Maria in Aracoeli in Rome; it may relate, however, more to the nearby Palazzo Venezia.

8. Among them, Nicholas Adams and Howard Saalman (verbal).

9. This interesting 'phenomenon' was first discussed in Bek, *Towards Paradise on Earth,* p. 100. Bek (pp. 103–4) sees the arrangement of the windows at the Palazzo Venezia as a possible source for this scheme.

10. See Bartoli, "Un restauro e un problema di prospettiva"; Mack, "Building a Florentine Palace," pp. 265–66.

11. Pius, *Memoirs,* p. 289. In addition to those surveys of Pienza cited earlier, the Communal Palace has received attention in Chierici, *Il palazzo italiano dal secolo XI al secolo XIX,* p. 121; Giuseppe Marchini and Niccolò Rodolico, *I palazzi del popolo nei comune toscani del Medio Evo* (Milan: Electa Editrice, 1962), pp. 59–60; and in Thiem, *Toskanische Fassaden,* pp. 67–68. An article devoted to the Palazzo Comunale which was published in the 1986 issue of *Studi e Documenti di Architettura* appeared too late for utilization in the present consideration. Architectural renderings are given in Cataldi et al., *Rilievi,* pls. 3, 6; Holtzinger, *Pienza,* p. 20; and in Stegmann and Geymüller, *The Architecture of the Renaissance in Tuscany,* 1:82. One can only speculate as to why Pius chose to relocate his city hall. Perhaps the decision involved the definition he wished to establish between clerical and secular activities with the Corso il Rossellino forming an implied "town-and-cassock" boundary. Then, too, it would have been only logical to have kept the accommodations for Pienza's new bishop as close to the cathedral as possible.

12. Appendix 2, Doc. 24 (apparently repeated in Doc. 43), Doc. 28 (also is recorded in the *gabella* documents given in Adams, "Acquisition," p. 107), Doc. 46.

13. Appendix 2, Docs. 50, 55, 58, 59, 72, 77, 83, 84.

14. The organization of the Palazzo Comunale in Pienza, in which a corner loggia and a tower are combined within the same structure, recalls a similar arrangement at the medieval Palazzo dei Vicari in Certaldo. See Franco Cardini and Sergio Rareggi, *Palazzi pubblici di Toscana: I centri minori* (Florence: Sansoni, 1983), pp. 59, 195, 220. At Pienza, a third story articulated by pilasters was superimposed on the Palazzo Comunale at some point in its history. This addition is shown in an engraving in "Pienza," *Le cento città d'Italia 126,* Supplement 12044 (Milan: Sonzogno, 31 Oct. 1899), 73, and in an old photograph

reproduced in Adolfo Venturi, *Storia dell'arte italiana: L'architettura del quattrocento* (1923; rpt. Vaduz: Nendeln, 1967), 8:1, 503. This story apparently was removed in the restoration of 1900. For other photographs of the palace, see Thiem and Thiem, *Toskanische Fassaden,* p. 68.

15. A consideration of these decorations is given in Thiem and Thiem, *Toskanische Fassaden,* pp. 67–68.

16. Brunelleschi's intentions for the hospital are discussed in Charles Mack, "Brunelleschi's Spedale degli Innocenti Rearticulated," pp. 129–46.

17. Thiem, *Toskanische Fassaden,* p. 67.

18. Ibid.

19. On Buonconvento, see Detti, Di Pietro, and Fanelli, *Città murate e sviluppo contemporaneo,* p. 76. The Montepulciano tower is discussed in Saalman, "The Palazzo Comunale in Montepulciano," p. 27. For a general survey of regional town halls and their towers, consult Marchini and Rodolico, *I palazzi del popolo nei comune toscani del Medio Evo.*

20. Alberti (*Ten Books,* p. 173) noted that "it is certain that one of the greatest ornaments . . . of a square . . . is a handsome portico, under which the old men may spend the heat of the day, or be mutually serviceable to each other." Other quattrocento loggia/town hall combinations are to be found in Radda in Chianti (early fifteenth century) and Fiesole (ca. 1463). Giorgio da Sabenico's Palazzo Comunale at Pesaro of ca. 1450 shows the influence of Brunelleschi's Spedale degli Innocenti in its use of the open and inviting loggia, and such civic porticoes may have their origin in the hospital format. Rossellino's palace in Pienza is of this new type but retains the old fortresslike tower. The Palazzo del Comune at Jesi, which was begun in 1487 by Francesco di Giorgio Martini, is clearly derived from that in Pienza but lacks the portico. See Chierici, *Il palazzo italiano,* 1:120. It should be pointed out, perhaps, that blind arches run across the facade of the medieval town hall in Buonconvento;

they once may have formed an open portico. An open loggia was installed in the town hall of Viterbo in the early 1460s under the probable sponsorship of Pope Pius. See the description of Niccola Della Tuccia in *Cronache e statuti della città di Viterbo,* p. 82, with additional description of the construction of this building on p. 80.

21. Pius, *Memoirs,* p. 289. On Pius' cardinals and other members of the official Vatican family, see A. V. Antonovics, "A Late Fifteenth-Century Division Register of the College of Cardinals," *Papers of the British School at Rome,* 35 (1967), 87–101; Adolf Gottlob, *Aus der Camera Apostolica des 15. Jahrhunderts: Ein Beitrag zur Geschichte des päpstlichen Finanzwesens und des endenden Mittelalters* (Innsbruck: Verlag der Wagner'schen Universitäts-Buchhandlung, 1889); Walther von Hofmann, *Forschungen zur Geschichte der Kurialen Behörden vom Schisma bis zur Reformation,* Bibliothek des Königlichen Preussischen Historischen Instituts in Rom 12–13 (Rome: Loescher, 1914); Andreas Kraus, "Die Sekretäre Pius II: Ein Beitrag zur Entwicklungs-geschichte des päpstlichen Sekretariats," *Römische Quartalschrift für christliche Altertumskunde und Kirchengeschichte,* 53 (1958), 25–80; and Walter Schurmeyer, *Das Kardinalskollegium und Pius II* (1914; rpt. Vaduz: Kraus Reprint, 1965). To Pius, the cooperative construction of palaces seemed to symbolize the collegiality he wished to achieve within his curia, the same sort of commitment apparently expected by Pope Nicholas V. See Carroll William Westfall, "Alberti and the Vatican Palace Type," *Journal of the Society of Architectural Historians,* 33 (1974), 101–21; Pius, *Memoirs,* pp. 252–54.

22. Pius, *Memoirs,* p. 230. For Ammannati's life, see Giuseppe Calamari, "Il Cardinale di Pavia, Jacopo Ammannati-Piccolomini," *Bollettino di ricerche e di studi per la storia di Pescia e di Valdinievole,* 3 (1929), 3ff., and *Il confidente di Pio II: Cardinale Jacopo Ammannati-Piccolomini (1422–1479)* (Rome: Augustea, 1932); Isidoro Del Lungo, "Un creato di papa Pio II," *Miscellanea di studi in*

onore Attilio Hortis (Trieste: G. Caprin, 1910), 1:225–28; F. R. Hausmann, "Die Benefizien des Kardinals Jacopo Ammannati-Piccolomini: Ein Beitrag zur Ökonomischen Situation des Kardinals im Quattrocento," *Römische Historische Mitteilungen*, 13 (1971), 27–80; Sebastiano Pauli, *Disquisizione istorica della patria e compendio della vita di Giacomo Ammannati Piccolomini, Cardinale di S. Chiesa, detta il Papiense vescovo di Lucca e Pavia* (Lucca: Pellegrino Frediani, 1712); and Zimolo, *Le vite di Pio II*, p. 63 n. 5.

23. In addition to Calamari's *Confidente*, 1:20–41, consult Schürmeyer, *Kardinalskollegium*, p. 112; and Zimolo, *Le vite di Pio II*, p. 65 n. 5.

24. Calamari, *Confidente*, 2:358–60; Schürmeyer, *Kardinalskollegium*, pp. 115–16.

25. This letter is published in its original Latin in Mannucci, *Pienza*, pp. 376–79; "Sunt mihi in ca aediculae duae sane bene aedificatae: altera in meum paucorumque, qui mihi sunt necessarii: altera in familiae usum. Ambae prospectus latissimos habent, suntque ad voluptatem aestivi temporis pulchre excogitatae." An Italian translation appears in Calamari, *Confidente*, 2:170–71. Mannucci (p. 102) notes that Ammannati continued to pass the summer months of July and August in Pienza for a number of years following the death of Pope Pius.

26. See Adams, "Acquisition," pp. 106–7, Docs. 8, 10, 11, and 12. For discussions and plans of the Palazzo Ammannati, see in particular Cataldi et al., *Rilievi*, pls. 3, 5, 6; Thiem and Thiem, *Toskanische Fassaden*, pp. 66–67. A rather curious transaction was recorded on 5 February 1463 which may (or may not) relate to the properties occupied by the Palazzo Ammannati. On that day the pope purchased a house for 29 ducats from a Sienese merchant named Sano di Marco. The building acquired by the pope was described as the "house of the lady," located across from the papal palace. The site would fit the Ammannati Palace but could refer to other properties in the immediate vicinity on the north side of the Corso il Rossellino. Why the

pope was involved in the transaction is unclear. The document from the Sienese *gabelle* is published in Adams, "Pienza," p. 108, Doc. 37, and discussed on p. 103.

27. Pius, *Memoirs*, p. 289. For Gonzaga's letter, see n. 67, below.

28. Similar corbels also can be found at the Palazzo Bruni in Arezzo (sometimes mistakenly attributed to Bernardo Rossellino because he had worked in that city and had designed the funerary monument for Leonardo Bruni). Although I question the attribution of that palace to Rossellino, a number of its architectural features (window cornices, layout of *cortile*, another variety of corbel used in some of the rooms which resembles that employed in Rossellino's Spinelli Cloister) do strongly indicate that the Palazzo Bruni was designed ca. 1460–70 by an architect working in the Rossellino orbit.

29. Palaces with attached belvedere towers are discussed in von Moos, *Turm and Bollwerk*, pp. 68–78.

30. For examples, consult Christian Elling, *Function and Form of the Roman Belvedere* (Copenhagen: I Kommission Has Ejnar Munkgaard, 1950).

31. On these Roman palaces and others of the type, see Westfall, "Alberti and the Vatican Palace Type," pp. 102–5, 111–14. The palace of Ammannati's old employer, Cardinal Domenico Capranica, offers a particularly attractive prototype. See Elling, *Belvedere*, p. 24, and Prospero Simonelli and Giuseppe Fratadocchi, *Almo Collegio Capranica: Lavori di restauro anno mariano* (Rome: Angelo Belardetti, 1955), pp. 35–36, and the reconstruction drawing on p. 42. It also should be noted that Filarete represented palaces with belvederes in his *Treatise;* he may well have picked up the element during his long stay in Rome. See Antonio Filarete, *Treatise on Architecture*, trans. John Spencer (New Haven: Yale University Press, 1965).

32. The Latin text of this letter appears in Jacopo Ammannati, *Epistolae et commentarii* (Milan: Alessandro Minuziano, 1506), p. 669, letter 283. "Veni Pientiam et sum in aediculis

meis; quae olim in gratiam Pii aedificatae: gratissimum nunc praebent secessum. . . . Si quaeris quod agae, brevi accipe. Innoluor libris, lego et scribo et uagor. Contemplor quoque sancta illa vestigia prisnri: quae toto hoc col le sunt saepe impressa." An Italian translation is given in Calamari, *Confidente*, 1:170.

33. On Cardinal Jouffroy, see Charles Fierville, *Le Cardinal Jouffroy et son temps (1412–1473): Étude historique* (Coutances: Salettes, 1874); Schiavo, *Monumenti*, p. 106 n. 39; Zimolo, *Le vite di Pio II*, pp. 114–15 n. 11. A negative view of Jouffroy's character was given in Pius, *Memoirs*, pp. 225–27, 364–68. That the coat of arms, which appears on one of the window frames, is that of Jouffroy was verified recently through the diligent researches of Nicholas Adams.

34. Vespasiano da Bisticci, *Renaissance Princes, Popes, and Prelates. The Vespasiano Memoirs: Lives of Illustrious Men of the XVth Century*, trans. William George and Emily Waters, intro. Myron P. Gilmore (New York: Harper and Row, 1963), p. 56; Pius, *Memoirs*, pp. 364, 230–31.

35. Pius, *Memoirs*, p. 289. In addition to brief mention in the general works on Pienza, see Giovanni Battista Mannucci, "I quattro cardinali fedeli a Pio II nelle costruzioni pientine," *Bullettino Senese di Storia Patria*, 62–63 (1955–56), 95–99. The manuscript of Nicholas Adams and Fausto Formichi, "The Identification of the Palazzo Jouffroy, Pienza," forthcoming in an issue of *Studi e Documenti di Architettura* reached me too late to incorporate the authors' interesting findings into the body of my text. Their study does much to clarify the many problems presented by the Palazzo Jouffroy and demonstrates the need for undertaking similar examinations of each of the buildings in this phase of the renewal; only when this is done will we be able to construct a truly accurate picture of Pienza's Renaissance urbanscape (social as well as physical). My own observations on the Palazzo Jouffroy have been considerably refined, especially during an inspection of the

building made in the summer of 1984 in the company of Nicholas Adams, Giancarlo Cataldi, Lero Di Cristina, Fausto Formichi, David Friedman, and Henry Millon. I have benefited greatly from a number of the perceptive observations they made on that occasion.

36. Archivio dello Spedale di S. Maria della Scala, Siena, *Deliberazione*, no. 128, 5, c. 132, published in Mannucci, *Pienza*, pp. 104–5; Borghesi and Banchi, *Nuove documenti*, pp. 212–13; Mack, "Studies," pp. 400–401: "In prima inteso et avuta piena informatione come il Reverendissimo Cardinale Atrebatense avendo nella città Pia, olim Corsignano, nel contado di Siena, principiato uno bello et nobile casamento, el quale volendo fornire gli bisogna la casa et sito de lo Spedale d'esso luogo, subbito ad lo Spedale di Siena, posto ne la detta città Pia, del quale vole dare florenos cento sanesi d'oro larghi, et tassare ad lo Spedale nostro tutto el cuprime et legname che è in esso spedale et casa; et così per parte de la sua Reverendissima Signoria Frate Giovanni di Martino ha riferito al detto messer lo Rettore: unde per onore de la detta città, et fare cosa che piaccia ad la Santità di nostro Signore Papa Pio, el quale à carissimo che la detta città si nobiliti di belli et honorevoli casamenti, et anco per compiacere al detto Reverend. Cardinale, el quale è uno nobile et da bene signore et affetionato ad la nostra città di Siena et al detto Ospedale; et anco avuto buona informatione come el detto spedale et casa di Corsignano è molto occupato per gli hedificii nuovamente fatti in esso luogo da l'una parte et l'altra, in modo che malagevolmente si può riparare: unde per le cagioni predette deliberarono di concordia che esso spedale si conceda et venda al detto Reverendissimo Cardinale per florenos cento d'oro sanesi et quello più che si potrà; con questo che tutto el coprime et legname d'esso spedale rimanghi ad esso spedale di Siena per adoperarlo per un nuovo Spedale da farsi in essa città Pia: et con questo ancora ch'esso Reverendissimo Cardinale sia tenuto et debbi ad tutte sue spese, et senza nissun costo d'esso

spedale di Siena, dare et concedere uno luogo o vero piaza, che piaccia ad esso Rectore in essa città Pia, per fare uno nuovo Spedale conveniente ad la detta città et ad la casa nostra. Item che el prezo predetto d'essi fiorini cento larghi non si possi spendere nè convertire in altra cosa, se non in hedificio del detto nuovo Spedale. Item, se ad lo Spedale di Siena ne venisse alcuno preiudicio, o vero alcuna prohibitione avesse esso Spedale per vendarsi, esso Reverendissimo Cardinale ce ne debbi fare absolvere et liberare solennemente dalla Santità di Nostro Signore lo Papa, dando el privilegio de l'absolutione al detto messer lo Rectore senza alcuna spesa d'esso Spedale. Et se esso Spedale da vendarsi avesse alcuna gravezza, rimanga al detto Spedale da farsi di nuovo."

37. This was the view of Mannucci, *Pienza*, pp. 103–5.

38. Schiavo, *Monumenti*, p. 93.

39. Carli, *Pienza*, p. 30.

40. Schiavo, *Monumenti*, p. 6.

41. See, for instance, the map in Carli, *Pienza*, p. 28.

42. This view, presented in Mack, "Studies," pp. 297–300, was accepted and refined in Cataldi, "Piazza," pp. 110–12. For elevations and plans of the Palazzo Jouffroy, see especially Cataldi et al., *Rilievi*, pls. 3, 4. Flavio Biondo, who died in 1463, indicated that work on the palace was finished by the time of the summer visit of 1462: "Of those [houses] already completed, I have seen one, that of Jean Jouffroy of Burgundy, Cardinal of Arras." Appendix 1, Doc. 2.

43. In addition to the plan in Cataldi et al., *Rilievi*, pl. 3, the layout of the courtyard was presented in Holtzinger, *Pienza*, p. 20; and in Papini, *Francesco di Giorgio*, p. 239. Both Holtzinger and Papini treated the *cortile* as if it were part of the adjoining Palazzo Vescovile.

44. Papini (*Francesco di Giorgio*, p. 239) presented a drawing of this capital.

45. In Mack, "Studies," p. 300, I distinguished this building from its neighbors and tentatively associated it with the official whom Pius called simply "Tommaso" in his *Commentarii* (*Memoirs*, p. 289). Cataldi

("*Piazza*," pp. 102–3) acknowledged the separate character of the structure but correctly followed the papal text and assigned the building to "the treasurer." Elevations and plans are to be found in Cataldi et al., *Rilievi*, pls. 1, 2.

46. Cataldi, "Piazza," p. 102, has opted for Spannocchi; Don Aldo Franci (orally) and Torriti, *Pienza*, p. 35, prefer Forteguerri.

47. In the *Commentarii*, Pope Pius identified (*Memoirs*, p. 267) Spannocchi as "Ambrogio of Siena, an official of the papal court." Spannocchi, of the Sienese banking family, held the position of *depositarius* in the Vatican, 1455–57 and again under Pius, 1459–64. Gottlob, *Camera apostolica*, p. 111. The Spannocchi were connected by marriage with the Piccolomini. Lisini and Liberati, *Genealogia dei Piccolomini*, p. 11. See also Antonovics, "Division Register," p. 93.

48. On Forteguerri, see Gaetano Beani, *Niccolò Fortiguerri cardinale di Teano* (Pistoia, 1891); Sebastiano Ciampi, *Memorie di Niccolò Forteguerri istitutore del liceo e del collegio Forteguerri di Pistoia nel secolo XV* (Pisa: Ranieri Prosperi, 1813); L. Gai, "Niccolò Forteguerri nei suoi rapporti con l'ambiente culturale pistoiese del quattrocento," in *Studi Storici Pistoiesi* (1976), 62ff.; Gottlob, *Camera apostolica*, p. 272; Quinto Santoli, *Il Cardinale Forteguerri* (Pistoia, 1926); Smith, "Lodrisio Crivelli," p. 60; Strnad, "Francesco Todeschini-Piccolomini," p. 175; Ugurgieri della Beradenga, *Pio II Piccolomini*, p. 222; and Zimolo, *Vite di Pio II*, p. 113 n. 4. Forteguerri's building activities in Viterbo, Siena, and elsewhere are recounted by the chroniclers Giovanni d'Iuzzo and Niccola Della Tuccia in *Cronache e statuti*, pp. 98–99, 103, 105. Della Tuccia called Forteguerri the pope's *tesoriero maggiore* (p. 257) in 1458 but, in 1460, after his elevation to the cardinalate, described him as *stato segretario e auditore* (p. 79). Titles in the papal finance office seem to have been somewhat loosely applied and understood. In 1459 Della Tuccia described a Pietro (Niccolò ?) di Forteguerra da Pistoia as being *tesoriere del patrimonio* (p. 72).

49. On Niccolò Picoluomo, see Carli,

Pienza, p. 68 n. 38; Müntz, *Les Arts,* 1:299–300; Paparelli, *Enea Silvio Piccolomini,* p. 340; Paster, *History of the Popes,* 3:336; Ugurgieri della Berardenga, *Pio II Piccolomini,* p. 405; and Giulio C. Zimolo, "La 'Vita Pii II P.M.' del Platina nel cod. Vat. Ottob. lat. 2056," in *Studi in onore di mons. C. Castiglioni prefetto dell'Ambrosiana* (Milan: Guiffrè, 1957), 901, and *Le vite di Pio II,* pp. 54 n. 1, 113 n. 3, 117 n. 2, 160. Mirabelli, who had been associated in business with Spannocchi, is discussed in Müntz, *Les Arts,* 1:322; Smith, "Lodrisio Crivelli," p. 60; and Zimolo, *Le vite di Pio II,* pp. 66–67 n. 6.

50. Buonconti is noted in Flavio Di Bernardo, *Un vescovo umanista alla corte pontificia Gianantonio Campano (1429–1473),* Miscellanea Historiae Pontificiae 39 (Rome: Università Gregoriana Editrice, 1975), p. 132 n. 52; Gottlob, *Camera Apostolica,* p. 272; Müntz, *Les Arts,* p. 322; Smith, "Lodrisio Crivelli," p. 60; Georg Voigt, *Enea Silvio de' Piccolomini,* 3:165, 544; and Zimolo, *Le vite di Pio II,* pp. 54–55.

51. Even more obscure than Buonconti, Laziosi does receive mention in Di Bernardo, *Un vescovo umanista,* p. 132 n. 52; Hofmann, *Kurialen Behörden,* p. 92; and Gottlob, *Camera Apostolica,* p. 272.

52. Adams, "Acquisition," p. 107, Docs. 15, 16.

53. Ibid.

54. Note, however, Lodrisio Crivelli's tribute to Pienza (Appendix 1, Doc. 4) seems to suggest that Mirabelli "instead of Giliforte is considered a fellow citizen of Pius." Did Buonconti begin the palace which, then, was taken over by Mirabelli?

55. This building has been discussed briefly in all the general works on Pienza and the association with Gonzaga accepted as fact without any actual documentary foundation. Plans and elevations can be found in Cataldi et al., *Rilievi,* pls. 1, 2.

56. Cataldi's interpretation ("Piazza," p. 103) was repeated in Torriti, *Pienza,* p. 35.

57. Adams, "Acquisition," p. 107, Docs. 18, 19, p. 109, Doc. 48.

58. On Lolli, see Hofmann, *Kurialen Be-* *hörden,* 2:115, 123; Lisini and Liberati, *Genealogia dei Piccolomini,* pl. 1; Giovanni Battista Mannucci, "La famiglia Lolli-Piccolomini," *Arte e Storia* 29 (1910), 27–29; and Zimolo, "La 'Vita Pii II P.M.' del Platina," p. 895 n. 36, and *Le vite di Pio II,* pp. 26–27 n. 4.

59. Nicholas Adams has suggested to me that this may be but a literary artifice. In any case, Lolli would have done well to have spent more time in the healthful climate of Pienza; he died of the plague in Siena in 1478.

60. The stone molding line along the walls reminds one of a similar element in the lower church of the cathedral of Pienza.

61. This critique appears in the letter written from Wiener Neustadt in 1449 to Gregory Heimburg, published in Pius II, *Selected Letters,* p. 43.

62. Lodrisio Crivelli (Appendix 1, Doc. 4, below) also indicated Gonzaga's participation in the Pientine program. Those other materials will be cited in the notes which follow. The primary source for this documentation and its explanation is found in D. S. Chambers, "The Housing Problems of Cardinal Francesco Gonzaga," *Journal of the Warburg and Courtauld Institutes,* 39 (1976), 21–58.

63. Adams, "Acquisition," p. 107, Docs. 23–25.

64. The elevation of these clerics is described in Pius, *Memoirs,* pp. 225–31. For the best study of Cardinal Francesco, together with a bibliography (p. 21 n. 4), see Chambers, "Housing Problems."

65. Pius, *Memoirs,* p. 230.

66. Chambers, "Housing Problems," pp. 23–25.

67. Gonzaga's letter is published in Mack, "Studies," pp. 401–2; Bandini-Piccolomini, "Le case Borgia e Gonzaga," pp. 5–6; Mannucci, *Pienza,* pp. 100–101; and is discussed in Chambers, "Housing Problems," pp. 28–29. " . . . essendo ieri dalla Santità di Nostro Signore quella me comincioe fare istantia de dovere edificare una casa in Corsignano e rispondendo io ad essa che non me ritrovava el modo, et che m'era forza de farne una a Roma. Sopraggionse in questo ragionamento el Reverendissimo Vice-Cancelliere al quale

già altre volte n'e stata data battaglia e lui sempre haveva cercato di subterfugere più che era possibile. Qui Nostro Signore continuò a parlare verso di lui e di me, che foe necessario a ciascuno di nui de promettergli. El Rever. mo Monsignor de Pavia che già li ha fatto la casa lo aiutava alla gagliarda, et scusandomi io d'esser povero, allegorono che se non era ricco di benefitii, haveva ben lo illustre Signor mio patre che era potente e che m'aiuteria. Disse Nostro Signore: non sarà questa spesa più che 1000 ducati e che me daria puoi il primo buon Vescovato che vacasse. Vuole sua Beatudine che ad ogni modo si cominci quest'anno il lavorero acciocchè ritornandosi l'anno seguente come mostra avere intentione, possi vedere l'edificio. . . . satisfare a questo desiderio del Nostro Signore che non dubiti Vostra Signoria essendo sua Beatitudine intento ad ornare questa sua patria, come è, non li porria esser fatta cosa più accepta. Pareriami gran male, essendo io promoto per sua Santità, a non condiscendere a questo suo appetito."

68. Published in Chambers, "Housing Problems," p. 29 nn. 52, 53.

69. Bandini-Piccolomini, "Le case Borgia e Gongaga," p. 6.

70. Chambers, "Housing Problems," pp. 29 and 48–49, Docs. 11–12.

71. Adams, "Acquisition," p. 107, Docs. 23–25.

72. Ibid., p. 106, Doc. 9. Chambers, "Housing Problems," p. 48.

73. Chambers, "Housing Problems," pp. 29 n. 55, 30 nn. 57, 58. One can only wonder if Cardinal Francesco might have hoped for the services of his father's house architect, Luca Fancelli. On Fancelli, see especially Charlotte M. Brown, "Luca Fancelli in Mantua," Mitteilungen des Kunsthistorischen Institutes in Florenz, 16 (1972), 153–66; Paolo Carpeggiani, "La fortuna di un mito: Artisti e` modelli fiorentini nell' architettura mantovana dell'umanismo (e nuovi documenti per la Tribuna dell' Annunziata)," in Argan et al., Filippo Brunelleschi, 2:817–37. Could Fancelli's use of articulation on his Mantuan projects have been influenced by exposure to

that employed by Rossellino on the Palazzo Piccolomini? Of course, Fancelli's association with Alberti could account for his use of the scheme. Fancelli's Nova Domus of the Palazzo Ducale in Mantua ca. 1480 bears a relationship to the Palazzo Ammannati in Pienza.

74. Chambers, "Housing Problems," p. 30 n. 61, pp. 50–51, Doc. 15, p. 3 n. 63, p. 51, Doc. 17.

75. Ibid., p. 30 n. 65, pp. 51–52, Doc. 18.

76. Ibid., p. 31 nn. 66, 67, 68. Lodrisio Crivelli's poem (Appendix 1, Doc. 4) suggests that the Palazzo Gonzaga existed as something more than intention in February 1464.

77. Cataldi, "Piazza," p. 103. Plans and elevations are to be found in Cataldi, et al., Rilievi, pls. 1 and 2.

78. Plans and elevations can be found in Cataldi, et al., Rilievi, pls. 1, 2.

79. Schiavo, Monumenti, p. 94.

80. Ibid., pp. 93–94 n. 55; Lisini and Liberati, Genealogia dei Piccolomini, p. 49, and table 3.

81. Schiavo's reattribution was accepted by Carli, Pienza, p. 30 (with some hesitation); Cataldi, "Piazza," pp. 103, 106; Mack, "Studies," p. 303; and Torriti, Pienza, p. 35.

82. Adams, "Acquisition," pp. 106–8, Docs. 8, 17, 41. For the 1459 transaction, see Doc. 3.

83. Pius, Memoirs, p. 289. Tommaso del Testa Piccolomini is discussed in Carli, Pienza, p. 68 n. 38; Hofmann, Kurialen Behörden, 2:92, 187; Mannucci, Pienza, p. 48; and Strnad, "Francesco Todeschini-Piccolomini," pp. 166 n. 61, 157 n. 24.

84. Zimolo, "La 'Vita di Pii II P.M.' del Platina," p. 901 n. 43, and Le vite di Pio II, p. 117. He probably is also the same as the T. Urbani mentioned in Di Bernardo, Un vescovo umanista, p. 131 n. 52. Also see Gaetano Luigi Marini, Degli archiatri pontifice (Rome: Stamperia Pagliarini, 1784), 2:160.

85. Adams, "Acquisition," p. 108, Doc. 31.

86. Chambers, "Housing Problems," p. 29 n. 53.

87. Cataldi, "Piazza," p. 103. The building

is shown in plan and elevation in Cataldi et al., *Rilievi,* pls. 3, 5, 6.

88. A number of scholars currently are suspicious of the antiquity of the facade of this building. See Adams, "Acquisition," p. 102 n. 21.

89. Ibid., p. 110, App. 3a, pp. 106–7, Doc. 11.

90. This certainly is the impression one may draw not only from the *Commentarii* but also from the comments of a number of the pope's contemporaries. See Appendix 1, Doc. 2 for confirmation by Flavio Biondo.

91. The proposal concerning the palace of Giacomo and Andrea Piccolomini presented here has a certain logic. Flavio Biondo (Appendix 1, Doc. 2) wrote, "I heard that two palaces were planned by your [Pius'] distinguished sisters and two others likewise by your distinguished nephews." What I suggest would tie the intended palaces of Laudomia Todeschini Piccolomini and her sons together, and the documentary evidence, as I have reconstructed it, seems to support this conclusion. Yet I do offer my suggestion with considerable hesitation and a necessary word of caution, for the evidence may not be really as firm as I might wish. Much of my argument rests upon the wording of my Doc. 65 of 27 May 1463. I have transcribed a crucial portion of it as reading "a frabica in [or a] Pientia" and have related the series of payments to it. The same Massaini brothers received the payments as installments on the amount specified in the May entry for what is described as being "li fatti di frabica," "la vendita di frabica," or "la compra di frabicha." Nicholas Adams has questioned my reading, believing the passage in the May 1463 document to read "a frabica e Pientia." For him, this would indicate purchases not only in Pienza but also in the village of Fabrica di Roma (near Viterbo). If this reading is accepted, the other entries in the series would also refer to this town and not to Pienza. Unfortunately, the name of the town and the word for "building" are the same (allowing for spelling errors) and the capitalization of proper names was erratically

observed in quattrocento documents. Considering the testimony of Flavio Biondo and the Massaini's Sienese and Pientine connections (See Appendix 2, Doc. 82), I prefer tentatively to retain my reconstruction. I might also point out that in their tax statement of 1465 (ASS, *Denunzie,* Lire 160, c. 113–173ᵛ) the brothers list properties in Pienza, Bibbiena, Montechiello, and Petroio, but not in Fabrica di Roma.

92. Adams, "Acquisition," p. 106 n. 9.

93. This information is contained in an entry from ASR, *Tesoreria segreta,* 1289, published in E. Casanova, "Un anno della vita privata di Pio II," *Bullettino Senese di Storia Patria,* 38, Ser. 2 (1931), 33: "1463 (?). Ducati 200 . . . a misser Andrea nipote di Sua Santità, li quali dette a madonna Laudomia, sorella della Santità Sua, la quale faciesse aconciare case che anno alle loro pocisioni fuori della cipta di Pientia." No trace of this undated document appears in the account book today, but it may have been inserted in the book on a slip of paper (not unusual) which subsequently has disappeared.

94. Appendix 2, Docs. 60, 62. The third payment was published by Casanova, "Anno privata," p. 32, and has the same history as that in the previous note: "1463 (?). Ducati 250 . . . ad Alisandro Mirabelli maestro di Casa di S. Santità li quali sono per parte di ducati 620 della sua casa di Pientia, che lui a venduta a Sua Santità, la quale a comprata da lui per donare a madonna Caterina, sorella di Sua Santità." Pius also helped Caterina to build the Palazzo della Papesse in Siena. Mack, "Studies," pp. 341–45.

95. Thiem, *Fassaden-Dekoration,* p. 68.

96. On Estouteville, see Xavier Barbier de Montault, *Le Cardinal Estouteville bienfacteur des églises* (Anjou, 1859); Zimolo, *Le vite di Pio II,* p. 114 n. 6. His palace in Rome is discussed in Westfall, "Vatican Palace Type," pp. 102–3. On the work at Ostia, consult Benevolo, *The Architecture of the Renaissance,* 1:144; Gustavo Giovannoni, "L'urbanistica del rinascimento" in *L'urbanistica dal antichità ad oggi,* ed. Giovanni Giovannoni et al. (Florence: Sansoni, 1943), p. 100. For work in

France, see Reginald Blomfield, *A History of French Architecture from the Reign of Charles VIII till the Death of Mazarin, 1494–1661* (1921; rpt. New York: Hacker, 1973), 1:41.

97. For the cardinals, see n. 21. Lodrisio Crivelli mentions the French Cardinal Louis d'Albret as a potential builder in Pienza (Appendix 1, Doc. 4). On d'Albret, see Zimolo, *Le vite di Pio II*, p. 115 n. 1.

98. The connection with Barbo is raised in Smith, "Crivelli," p. 58. On various aspects of the life and activities of the famous Bessarion of Trebisond, cardinal of Nicea, see Biolchi, *La casina del Cardinale Bessarione;* Bistici, *Princes, Popes and Prelates*, pp. 137–42; Ludwig Mohler, *Kardinal Bessarion als Theologe, Humanist, und Staatsmann*, 3 vols. (Paderborn: Ferdinand Schöningh, 1923–42); Rudolf Rocholl, *Bessarion: Studie zur Geschichte der Renaissance* (Leipzig: A. Deichert'sche Verlags-G. Böhme, 1904); Henri Vast, *Le Cardinal Bessarion (1403–1472): Étude sur la Chrétienté et la Renaissance vers le milieu du XVᵉ siècle* (1878; rpt. Geneva: Slatkine-Megariotis Reprints, 1977); Zimolo, *Le vite di Pio II*, p. 65 n. 1. Crivelli's *Barbate* could be a mistranscription of Giuliano Baratto, a friend of Pope Pius, in whose house in Rome the future pope convalesced in 1445. On Baratto, see Paparelli, *Enea Silvio Piccolomini*, p. 112; Zimolo, *Le vite di Pio II*, p. 125. For portraits of Bessarion, all with flowing beard, see Vespasiano da Bisticci, *Vite di uomini illustri del secolo XV*, eds. Paolo d'Ancona and Erhard Aeschlemann (Milan: Hoepli, 1951), pls. facing pp. 92, 94, 96. On a relief of the reception of the relic of Saint Andrew at the Ponte Molle on 12 April 1462, sculpted by Paolo Romano (1464–65) for the tomb of Pius II and now in the church of San Andrea della Valle, Rome, only one of the represented prelates is shown bearded. This cleric is positioned across the altar from the pope and, together with Pius, is the principal participant. As we learn from Pius (*Memoirs*, pp. 245–46), this must be Bessarion: "He [Bessarion] carried the reliquary containing the sacred head, which he deposited on the center of the altar while a chorus intoned hymns. . . . Bessarion in tears, taking the sacred head of the Apostle, offered it to the weeping Pope."

99. Piccolomini, *Commentarii*, p. 433. The phrase is omitted in Gragg and Gabel's translation (Pius, *Memoirs*, p. 289) and translated as "molti suoi ministri" in the recent Italian edition of Bernetti (*I commentari*, 3:229). Although a quantity is, perhaps, intended the word *plumbi* would seem to refer to ministerial rank (those who have the authority to affix lead seals to official documents).

100. The document will be published in Adams, "Humanist Glory."

101. Adams, "Acquisition," p. 108, Doc. 30.

102. Ibid., p. 106, Doc. 7.

103. This project, described in the documents as involving *una hostaria* or *uno abergo*, might not be for an inn or hotel as we understand it. Since the cathedral seems to have been involved in the transactions, one might suppose that all these arrangements concerned the Canons' House (see suggestion in Mack, "Studies," p. 328, n. 184). Yet that facility had been completed by the time of the pope's visit in 1462. Another possibility is suggested in Crivelli's description of Pienza (Appendix 1, Doc. 4). Crivelli mentions the *proseucha* built by Pius to provide "a refuge, the consolation of the needy wretch" in which "the tired man receives rest, and the poor man receives nourishment." The best translation of *proseucha*, in this context, would be "almshouse" or "hospice" and it is more than likely that it was for this end that the *abergo* or *hostaria* was intended—not a commercial venture at all but an act of charity which demonstrated the pope's commitment to the betterment of his new Pienza. Another example of his benevolence can be found in his will in which Pius included provision for the construction of a communal mill on the Orcia River (see Adams, "Acquisition," p. 103). If the *abergo* is the *proseucha* mentioned by Crivelli, then the question arises whether this building was a separate operation from the new hospital (see Appendix 2, Doc. 45).

104. Chambers, "Housing Problems," pp.

26–27. The difficulties in finding accomoda-
tions will be considered in Adams, "Humanist Glory."

105. Adams, "Acquisition," p. 110, App.
3c.

106. Adams, "Acquisition," p. 108, Doc.
42. Adams notes (p. 109) that the notorial
records located the property in the *castelnuovo*
quarter and that the house was rented back
from the bishopric to Domenico di Antonio.

107. Mannucci, *Pienza*, p. 249, but here
the purchase price was given as 200 rather
than 100 ducats. 5 May 1463. "Da Menico di
Antonio per il Capitolo dei canonici di S.
Maria di Pienza una casa posta nella città di
Pienza in quartiero Castrinovi pel prezzo di
200 ducati pagati come sopra [i.e., per mezzo
di Niccolò di Piccolomini cubiculario di S.
Santità]." This document comes from the
Archivio Capitolare di Pienza.

108. It should be noted that throughout
this period the new bishopric was actively
acquiring income-yielding properties. See the
documents from the Archivio Capitolare di
Pienza reproduced in Mannucci, *Pienza*, pp.
248–50; Adams, "Acquisition," p. 103.

109. Adams, "Acquisition," p. 109, Doc.
50. In a commentary on this entry, Adams
notes that more information on this transaction was given in the notorial records in
which the acquired property was described as
having been located in the *castelnuovo* quarter
across from the Church of San Francesco.

110. Finelli and Rossi, *Pienza, tra idealogia e
realtà*, p. 115.

111. Pius, *Memoirs*, p. 289.

112. The block also is shown in plan and
elevation in Cataldi et al., *Rilievi*, pls. 1, 2.

113. Pius, *Memoirs*, pp. 264–68. The procession in Viterbo is also described by Niccola Della Tuccia in *Cronache e statuti della città
di Viterbo*, pp. 84–87. The projections of
which Pius spoke were the *sporti* or *mignoni*
(enclosed balconies) added to many a medieval or Renaissance house. On such structures, see P. Moschella, "Le case a sporti in
Firenze," *Palladio*, 6 (1942), 107. The so-
called house of Gregorio Lolli (here tentatively identified as that of Tommaso Pic-

colomini or the carpenter Magio), preserves
such an example. A particularly good impression of the effect of *sporti* can be gained by a
walk along the Via Jannelli in Cortona. A few
years after Pius had campaigned against projections and balconies that encroached upon
the public way, King Ferrante of Naples
complained to Pope Sixtus IV about those he
saw in Rome. See Stefano Infessura, *Diario
della città di Roma di Stefano Infessura
scribasenato*, ed. Oreste Tommasini, Fonti per
la storia d'Italia (Rome: Forzani, 1890), pp.
79–80.

114. Pius, *Memoirs*, p. 264.

115. Fausto Formichi, "Le dodici 'case
nuove' di Pienza," *Studi e Documenti di Architettura*, 7 (1978), 117–28. A brief discussion,
together with plans and elevations is also
provided in Cataldi et al., *Rilievi*, pp. 22–23.

116. Appendix 2, Doc. 41. This transaction apparently was recorded in the Sienese
gabelle ten days later when the location was
given. Adams, "Acquisition," p. 108, Doc.
33.

117. Adams, "Acquisition," p. 108, Doc.
40.

118. Chambers, "Housing Problems," p.
49, Doc. 12. The problem of the displace-
ment of the citizens of old Corsignano by the
residents of the new Pienza is considered in
more detail by Nicholas Adams in his forthcoming "Humanist Glory."

119. See Axel Boëthius, *The Golden House
of Nero: Some Aspects of Roman Architecture*
(Ann Arbor: University of Michigan Press,
1960), esp. pp. 129–88; Walter Paatz, "Ein
antikischer Stadthaustypus im mittelalterlichen Italien," *Römisches Jahrbuch für
Kunstgeschichte*, 3 (1939), 127–30.

120. On this sort of row housing, see
Gianfranco Caniggia, *Strutture dello spazio
antropico: Studi e note*, Biblioteca di Architettura: Saggi e Documenti 3 (Florence: Uniedit,
1976). The Pienza houses were discussed at
the 1981 annual meeting of the College Art
Association in San Francisco in a paper presented by Henry A. Millon. The fact that this
row of houses either replaced or nearly abut-
ted the town walls is interesting, for it resem-

bles that of comparable "housing developments" along the Via Jannelli and Via Rinfrena in Cortona. The problem of the position of the Pientine project is considered in Finelli and Rossi, *Pienza*, p. 115.

121. For another mention of the proposed lake, consult Arnoldo Verdiani-Bandi, "I castelli di Val d'Orcia e la repubblica di Siena," *Bullettino Senese di Storia Patria*, 8 (1901), 410. Also see Smith, "Crivelli," p. 62 n. 148.

122. Pius, *Memoirs*, p. 281.

123. Nicholas Adams, "Architecture for Fish: The Sienese Dam on the Bruna River—Structures and Designs, 1468–ca. 1530," *Technology and Culture*, 25 (1984), 768–97.

4. *Pienza as an Urban Statement*

1. Leonardo Bruni, *Laudatio Florentinae urbis* (1404), quoted in Hans Baron, *The Crisis of the Early Renaissance,* 2d ed. rev. (Princeton: Princeton University Press, 1966), p. 207; and Samuel Y. Edgerton, Jr., *The Renaissance Rediscovery of Linear Perspective* (1975; rpt. New York: Harper and Row Icon Editions, 1976), p. 36. Richard Goldthwaite, in his *Building of Renaissance Florence,* p. 19, has noted an anomaly in the urban planning of Early Renaissance Florence: private palaces "did not so much organize space as make an appearance in it, and with all the elaboration of facade types . . . if they did anything, jolted the tradition of uniformity and order of earlier town planning. More than one writer has commented on the apparent contradiction between, on the one hand, civic ideals and an aesthetic sense of geometric order and, on the other, lack of urban planning and the individuality of private architecture. In the history of urban planning with respect to what actually got built in Florence (as opposed to what the theorists talked about), the Renaissance [in Florence] lies dormant between the age of the earlier commune and the age of the Medici princes." We should also note the Aristotelian organization of Pius' new city,

which proceeds from the general to the particular. For a brief consideration of Aristotelian architecture in the Renaissance, see Lawrence Lowic, "Francesco di Giorgio on the Design of Churches: The Use and Significance of Mathematics in the *Trattato*," *Architectura*, 12 (1982), 153–54.

2. Alberti, *Ten Books*, p. 113.

3. Heydenreich, "Pius II. als Bauherr von Pienza." (1981), pp. 75–78. See the comments on Heydenreich's discussion in Braunfels, *Mittelalterliche Stadtbaukunst in der Toskana*, p. 126. Paul Zucker, in *Town and Square from the Agora to the Village Green*, p. 89, notes that medieval squares, such as those in Padua (Piazze dei Frutti and delle Erbe), Vicenza (Piazza dei Signori), Modena, and Bologna, are simply amalgamations of spaces surrounding major public buildings; they have "no intrinsic spatial meaning of their own."

4. Raymond Curran, *Architecture and the Urban Experience* (New York: Van Nostrand Reinhold, 1983), pp. 6–7.

5. Zucker, *Town and Square.*

6. General studies on medieval town planning in Italy include Braunfels, *Mittelalterliche Stadtbaukunst;* Detti, Di Pietro, and Fanelli, *Città murate;* Luigi Piccinato, "Urbanistica medioevale," in *L'urbanistica dall' antichità ad oggi,* ed. G. Giovannoni et al. (Florence: Sansoni, 1943), pp. 63–89. For specialized studies of the new towns, see David Friedman, "Le terre nuove fiorentine," *Archeologia medievale,* 1 (1974), 231–47; Charles Higounet, "Les "Terre nuove" florentines du XIVe siècle," in *Studi in onore di Amintore Fanfani, III: Medioevo* (Milan: A. Giuffre, 1962), 3–17; Moretti, *Le 'terre nuove' del contado fiorentino;* Maina Richter, "Die 'Terra murata' im florentinischen Gebiet," *Mitteilungen des Kunsthistorischen Institutes in Florenz,* 5 (1940), 351–86. A book dealing with the topic, *Florentine Towns: Urban Planning in the Late Middle Ages,* by David Friedman, is forthcoming.

7. Braunfels, *Mittelalterliche Stadtbaukunst,* pp. 78, 103–5; Gino Chierici, "Paganico,"

Rassegna d'Arte Senese, 15 (1922), 22–33. Another possible, as yet unexplored source for what occurred in Pienza is the Adriatic town of Senigallia, colonized by Rome in the third century B.C. and rebuilt by Sigismondo Malatesta, who renewed the old *cardo* and *decumanus* and actually conducted certain excavations at the site. See Boëthius, *The Golden House of Nero*, p. 166. Senigallia formed part of the territory wrested from Malatesta by Pope Pius and given to his favorite nephew, Antonio Todeschini-Piccolomini.

8. Ludwig Dörner, *Wiener Neustadt: Ein praktisches Taschenbuch für Wiener Neustadt und Umgebung* (Bad Fischau N.O.: Wienerwald Verlag, 1962).

9. Detti, Di Pietro, and Fanelli, *Città murate*, p. 312.

10. Ibid., p. 76.

11. The literature on these topics is extensive, but see, in general, Benevolo, *The Architecture of the Renaissance*, vol. 1; Giovannoni, "L'urbanistica del Rinascimento," pp. 93–115; and Zucker, *Town and Square*.

12. Generally on this, see Goldthwaite, *Renaissance Florence*, pp. 2–7.

13. For Brunelleschi, see Battisti, *Filippo Brunelleschi*, and the forthcoming study of Brunelleschi by Howard Saalman. The comments of Zucker, *Town and Square*, p. 111, are also of interest.

14. Isabelle Hyman, "Notes and Speculations on S. Lorenzo, Palazzo Medici and an Urban Project by Brunelleschi," *Journal of the Society of Architectural Historians*, 34 (1975), 105–6.

15. Alberti, *Ten Books*, p. 137.

16. Ibid., p. 92.

17. Ibid., p. 173.

18. Heydenreich, "Pius II. als Bauherr" (1937), p. 142; James S. Ackerman, *The Architecture of Michelangelo* (1961; rpt. Harmondsworth: Penguin Pelican Books, 1971), pp. 140–41.

19. Finelli and Rossi, *Pienza*, pp. 15–17; and Ludwig Heinrich Heydenreich and Wolfgang Lotz, *Architecture in Italy, 1400–1600*,

trans. Mary Hottinger (Harmondsworth: Penguin Pelican Books, 1974), p. 338 n. 21. On the work done in Fabriano under Nicholas V (for which there is no evidence of Rossellino's involvement), see Mack, "Rossellino, Alberti, and the Rome of Nicholas V," pp. 64–65.

20. Saint Augustine, *On Christian Doctrine*, trans. D. W. Robertson, Jr. (Indianapolis: Bobbs-Merrill, 1958), 1:2.

21. Aeneas Silvius Piccolomini, *De ritu, situ, moribus et conditione germaniae*, quoted in Ady, *Pius II*, p. 255.

22. On the explosive energy of spaces, see Rudolf Arnheim, *The Dynamics of Architectural Form* (Berkeley: University of California Press, 1977), pp. 86–87. Here he is discussing this effect in the Vicolo della Pace before Santa Maria della Pace in Rome.

23. Detti, Di Pietro, and Fanelli, *Città murate*, p. 76.

24. Alberti, *Ten Books*, p. 75.

25. See Braunfels, *Mittelalterliche Stadtbaukunst*, pp. 101, 103–4, 110–13. Goldthwaite, *Renaissance Florence*, p. 7, notes that the plans formulated in 1388–89 for the widening of Florence's Via Calzaiuoli called for the rebuilding of facades of all the private dwellings along it in accordance with a uniform standard. Nicholas V also had regularized the most important streets of Rome as part of his program of urban renewal. "Nicholas gave proof of his feeling for town planning by ordering special attention to be given to the three main thoroughfares of Rome . . . where traffic-obstructing buildings were to be removed." Heydenreich and Lotz, *Architecture in Italy*, p. 51. On the Roman streets, also consult Torgil Magnuson, "Studies in Roman Quattrocento Architecture," *Figura*, 9 (1958), 36 and Charles Burroughs, "A planned Myth and a Myth of Planning," pp. 197–207.

26. Ivor De Wolfe, *The Italian Townscape* (London: Architectural Press, 1963), p. 80.

27. On Alberti's relationship to the radically planned city type of Filarete, see Hermann Bauer, *Kunst und Utopie: Studien über*

das *Stadtsdenken in der Renaissance* (Berlin: Walter de Gruyter, 1965), p. 98.

28. Raymond Curran, *Architecture and the Urban Experience,* p. 24, notes: "At root, the urban experience is, and has always been, the collective experience of places and spaces conceived for linkage between people and for social interaction. It is the experience of places where movement can be an end in itself and in which you are always 'where it's at.' A spontaneous living theater, it's the experience of places where people come to see and to be seen, places to be a showman and for 'doing your thing.'" Arnheim writes: "If human beings are to interact with a building functionally, they must be united with it by visual continuity. Huge though a building may be as a whole, it can make contact with the visitor by providing a range of sizes, some small enough to be directly relatable to the human body. These human-sized architectural elements serve as connecting links between the organic inhabitants and the inorganic habitation" (*Dynamics,* p. 133).

29. Berchorius quoted in William S. Heckscher, *Sixtus IIII Aeneas insignes statuos romano popolo restituendas censuit* (The Hague: M. Nijhoff, 1955), p. 67; and in Westfall, *In This Most Perfect Paradise,* p. 98; and in Arnheim, *Dynamics,* p. 208.

30. Curran, *Architecture and the Urban Experience,* p. v.

Appendix 1

1. Giannantonio Campano (Giovanni Antonio De Teolis), 1429–77, had a distinguished career as humanist poet and cleric. He accompanied Pope Pius on the trip to Mantua and was with him on that inspirational visit to Corsignano/Pienza in February 1459. From 1460 to 1463, he served as secretary to Cardinal Alessandro Oliva, the prior general of the Augustinian Order. Campano also acted as Pius' court poet from 1460 to 1462 and, in that capacity, composed the verse on Pienza included by the pope in his memoirs. In October 1462, Pius conferred upon Campano the bishopric of Crotone. In addition to his poetical praise of Pope Pius, Campano wrote (before 1474) a *vita* of his great patron. On Campano, see Flavio Di Bernardo, *Un vescovo umanista alla corte pontificia Gianantonio Campano, 1429–1477* (Rome: Università Gregoriana Editrice, 1975); Frank R. Hausmann, "Campano, Giovanni Antonio," *Dizionario biografico degli italiani* (1974) 17:424–29; and Voigt, *Enea Silvio de Piccolomini,* 3:621–26.

2. Lodrisio Crivelli of Milan (1412–88) was a humanist scholar and professor of law who served as secretary to several princely and clerical patrons in Milan. He also held a position on the faculty of the Milan College of Jurisconsults from 1445 until 1463, at which point he entered the service of Francesco Sforza. Crivelli probably first encountered the future Pius II at the Council of Basel, to which he accompanied one of his patrons. Crivelli met him again when Piccolomini was negotiating in Milan on behalf of Emperor Frederick III. Thenceforth, the two maintained an intermittent correspondence, while Aeneas Silvius advanced through the clerical ranks. Shortly after his election to the papacy, Pius made Crivelli one of his apostolic secretaries, although the Milanese humanist continued in Sforza's service. Crivelli was dismissed from the duke's employ in 1463, at which time he took up an active position in the papal secretariate alongside Gregorio Lolli and Flavio Biondo. On Crivelli's life, consult, in particular, F. Gabotto, "Ricerche intorno allo storiografo quattrocentista Lodrisio Crivelli," *Archivio Storico Italiano,* ser. 5, 7 (1891), 266–98; Smith, "Lodrisio Crivelli of Milan and Aeneas Silvius," pp. 31–63.

3. Porcellio Pandoni (ca. 1405–after 1485) is the least well documented of the authors in this appendix. As had the others, Pandoni sought employment with a variety of princely patrons. He began his career at the Council of Basel in 1434, where he may have met Aeneas Silvius. Later, he was jailed by Pope Eugenius

IV for his role in the antipapal faction. The rest of his life was spent traveling about from one Italian court to the other. Recognized for his poetical accomplishments, he was crowned poet laureate by Frederick III in Naples. This, and his earlier association with the Council of Basel, probably drew him into the Piccolomini circle. See U. Fritelli, *Giannantonio de' Pandoni detto il Porcellio* (Florence, 1900).

4. Flavio Biondo da Forli (1392–1463) was one of the most celebrated humanists and historians of his day, the author of many scholarly treatises and secretary-diplomat to a variety of church and lay princes. The three volumes of his *Roma instauratae* were completed while he was in the service of Pope Eugenius IV. He was forced out of Rome during the reign of Nicholas V, the victim of court calumny, and he used the occasion to travel extensively throughout Italy to prepare his *Italia illustrata,* which was published in 1453. Between 1457 and 1459, he wrote a history of ancient Rome (*Roma triumphans*), which he presented to Pope Pius II at the Congress of Mantua. Restored to papal favor, Flavio enjoyed employment as an apostolic secretary. In 1462 he dedicated the supplemental volume of the *Italia illustrata* to Pope Pius. Flavio Biondo's reputation assured him a chapter in Vespasiano da Bisticci's *Vite di uomini illustri* and his life was summarized in Chapter 23 of Book 11 of the *Commentarii* of Pope Pius. An outline of his life is found in Riccardo Fubini, "Biondo, Flavio," *Dizionario biografico degli italiani* (1968), 10:536–59.

5. Campano's poem (Doc. 1) has appeared several times in Italian.

6. This poem (C. P., IV, 19, p. 132) was included in the *Commentarii* of Pope Pius II. It also is reproduced and discussed in Di Bernardo, *Un Vescovo umanista,* pp. 131–32. Campano composed the verse upon the occasion of Corsignano's change of name to Pienza.

7. The Latin text appears in Flavio Biondo, *Scritti inediti e rari di Biondo Flavio,* ed. Bartolomeo Nogara, Studie Testi 48 (Rome: Tipografia Poliglotta Vaticana, 1927), pp. 236–38.

8. Biondo differs with the *Commentarii* here.

9. The feast day of Saint Lawrence is 10 August. Biondo is in error for the Pope did not arrive in Pienza until 11 September 1460. He could have had in mind the feast of Saint Matthew (21 September).

10. Actually the summer of 1462.

11. Flavio Biondo's recollection is at odds with that the pope's here. Biondo also is wrong about the name of Pienza's cathedral, which was dedicated to the Virgin Mary, and on the date of the town's change in name (early June 1462).

12. Biblioteca Civica, Trieste, II, 25 (T), c. 106^v–107. The pertinent passage was given in Müntz, *Les Arts,* pp. 229–300; and in Smith, "Lodrisio Crivelli," pp. 62–63.

13. Apparently this is a reference to Cardinal Giacomo Ammannati and his palace.

14. Here Pandoni apparently refers, with considerable exaggeration, to the cathedral of Pienza.

15. The painted fictive decorations on the walls of the palace are indicated here.

16. The lake, of course, was never built.

17. The Latin text of this poem (Ms. Biblioteca Vallicelliana, Rome, codex F 93, c. 289–93) is given in Smith, "Lodrisio Crivelli," pp. 56–62.

18. Crivelli's description guides us up the Corso from the Porto al Prato (Morello).

19. This is a reference to the lower church, dedicated to Saint John the Bapist.

20. The allusion is to the Piccolomini coat of arms.

21. The Palazzo Comunale is meant.

22. See Smith, "Lodrisio Crivelli," p. 60 n. 95. Ammannati, as bishop of Pavia, had been a "subject" of the Duke of Milan.

23. Cardinal Francesco Todeschini-Piccolomini, the future Pope Pius III.

24. The soldier to whom Crivelli refers may be another of Laudomia's sons, Antonio, the duke of Amalfi and Sessa. Antonio led the

papal forces in the army of his father-in-law, King Ferrante of Naples.

25. These men may be Laudomia's other sons Giacomo and Andrea.

26. This may be a reference to Cardinal Niccolò Forteguerri, who commanded the armies of the papal states.

27. This poem (C. P. VIII, 6, p. 188) has been published and discussed in Di Bernardo, *Un vescovo umanista*, p. 132.

28. The Latin text of this passage in Campano's *Pii II vita* has been published in Zimolo, *Le vite di Pio,* pp. 67–70.

29. The references are to Pius' Roman projects.

30. The footraces of 21 September 1462 seem to have made a lasting impression. Or is Campano's description of Pienza taken directly from the pope's autobiography?

Appendix 2

1. Two additional entries are given in notes 93 and 94 to Chapter 3. The Roman documents should be compared and integrated with those from the Archivio di Stato in Siena published in Nicholas Adams, "Ac-quisition," pp. 106–10. It should be noted that several of the entries from Rome match those from Siena: Doc. 27 (Adams, 31), Doc. 31 (Adams, Appendix 3c), Doc. 32 (Adams, Appendix 3b), Doc. 33 (Adams, Appendix 3a), Doc. 36 (Adams, 32), Doc. 37 (Adams, 27), Doc. 38 (Adams 26), Doc. 39 (Adams, 29), Doc. 40 (Adams, 28). Doc. 28 may relate to Adams, 22, Doc. 41 to Adams, 33 and 40, Doc. 79 to Adams, 20 and Docs. 88–90 to Adams, 50.

2. The pagination of ASR, *Tesoreria segreta,* 1288, has recently been revised; in general, each old page number has now been increased by two (e.g., old c. 71 is now c. 73). This new numbering system has been used for the documents presented here.

3. Most of the documents presented here were included, however, in my unpublished doctoral thesis (Mack, "Studies," pp. 396–414).

4. On wage rates and purchasing power, see Florence Edler, *Glossary of Medieval Terms of Business: Italian Series, 1200–1600* (Cambridge, Mass.: Medieval Academy of America, 1934), p. 317; Goldthwaite, *The Building of Renaissance Florence,* pp. 301–50.

5. Mack, "Rossellino, Alberti, and the Rome of Nicholas V," p. 66.

BIBLIOGRAPHY

Ackerman, James S. *The Architecture of Michelangelo*. 1961; rpt. Harmondsworth: Penguin Pelican Books, 1971.

Adams, Nicholas. "The Acquisition of Pienza, 1459–1464." *Journal of the Society of Architectural Historians*, 44 (1985), 99–110.

——. "Architecture for Fish: The Sienese Dam on the Bruna River—Structures and Designs, 1468–ca. 1530." *Technology and Culture*, 25 (1984), 768–97.

——. "Humanist Glory and Feudal Power (1459–1464): The Construction of Pienza," *Acts of the Conference on Urban Life, March 1983*. Newark, Delaware, 1986.

Adams, Nicholas, and Fausto Formichi. "The Identification of the Palazzo Jouffroy, Pienza." *Studi e Documenti di Architettura*, in press.

Adams, Nicholas, and Charles R. Mack. "Pienza: An Architectural Bibliography." *Studi e Documenti di Architettura*, in press.

Ady, Cecilia M. *Pius II: The Humanist Pope*. London: Methuen, 1913.

Alberti, Leon Battista. *L'architettura (De re aedificatoria)*. Latin text with Italian trans. by Giovanni Orlandi and notes by Paolo Portoghesi. 2 vols. Milan: Il Porfilo, 1966.

——. *Ten Books on Architecture*. Trans. James Leone. 1726; rpt. New York: Transatlantic Arts, 1966.

——. *Zehn Bücher über die Baukunst*. Trans. and ed. Max Theuer. Darmstadt: Wissenschaftliche Buchgesellschaft, 1975.

Ammannati-Piccolomini, Jacopo (Giacomo). *Epistolae et commentarii Jacobi Piccolomini cardinalis papiensis*. Milan: Alessandro Minuziano, 1506.

Antonovics, A. V. "A Late Fifteenth-Century Division Register of the College of Cardinals." *Papers of the British School at Rome*, 35 (1967), 87–101.

Apollonj, Bruno Maria. "Fabbriche civile nel quartiere del Rinascimento in Roma." In *I Monumenti Italiani, Rilievi Raccolti, 12*. Rome: Reale Accademia d'Italia, 1937(9).

Argan, Giulio Carlo. *The Renaissance City*. Trans. Susan E. Bassnett. New York: G. Braziller, 1969.

Arnheim, Rudolf. *The Dynamics of Architectural Form*. Berkeley: University of California Press, 1977.

Augustine, Saint. *On Christian Doctrine*. Trans. D. W. Robertson, Jr. Indianapolis: Bobbs-Merrill, 1958.

Aurigemma, Salvatore. "Restauri nel Palazzo Vitelleschi in Tarquinia." *Palladio*, 14 (1964), 179–92.

Baldass, Peter. "Hans Stetheimers wahrer Name." *Wiener Jahrbuch für Kunstgeschichte*, 14 (1950), 47–64.

Bandini-Piccolomini, Francesco Naldi. "Le case Borgia e Gonzaga in Pienza." *Arte e Storia* (Supplement "Pienza e Pio II pubblicato in occasione del V centenario della nascita di Enea Silvio Piccolomini"), 24, Ser. 3, 8 (1905), 5–6.

_____. *Il palazzo pientino di Pio II*. Siena: Tip. Cooperativa, 1905.

_____. "La prima visita di Pio II a Corsignano." *Arte e Storia* (Supplement "Pienza e Pio II pubblicato in occasione del V centenario della nascita di Enea Silvio Piccolomini"), 24, Ser. 3, 8 (1905), 3–4.

_____. "San Bernardino da Siena e papa Pio II: Cenni ed accenni di loro vite." *Bullettino di Studi Bernardiniani*, 3, 4 (1937), and 4, 3/4 (1938).

Barbacci, Alfredo. "Le cause del cedimento del duomo di Pienza." *Bollettino d'Arte*, 9, Ser. 2 (1931), 494–512.

_____. "Il duomo di Pienza e i suoi restauri." *La Diana*, 9 (1934), 1–134.

_____. "L'edificazione e il decadimento del duomo di Pienza." *Bollettino d'Arte*, 10, Ser. 2 (1931), 317–34.

_____. "Il ritrovamento e il ripristino dell'antica decorazione del duomo di Pienza." *Bollettino d'Arte*, 25, Ser. 3 (1931–32), 282–88.

_____. "Ruderi di una chiesa romanica rinvenuti sotto il duomo di Pienza." *Bollettino d'Arte*, 26, Ser. 3 (1933), 352–58.

Barbier de Montault, Xavier. *Le Cardinal Estouteville bienfaiteur des églises*. Anjou, 1859.

Barbieri, Gino. *Industria e politica mineraria nello stato pontificio dal '400 al '600*. Rome: Cremonese, 1940.

Bargagli-Petrucci, Fabio. *Pienza, Montalcino e la Val d'Orcia Senese*. 1911; rpt. Bergamo: Italia Artistica, 1933.

Baron, Hans. *The Crisis of the Early Renaissance*. 2d ed. rev. Princeton: Princeton University Press, 1966.

Bartoli, Lando. *Un restauro e un problema di prospettiva: Il Palazzo Rasponi-Spinelli a Firenze*. Florence: Cooperativa Libraria Universitatis Studi Florentini, 1967.

Battaglia, Felice. *Enea Silvio Piccolomini e Francesco Patrizi: Due politici senesi del quattrocento*. Siena: Istituto Comunale d'Arte e di Storia, 1936.

Battisti, Eugenio. *Filippo Brunelleschi*. Milan: Electra Editrice, 1976.

_____. "Natura Artificiosa to Natura Artificialis." In *The Italian Garden*. Ed. David R. Coffin. First Dumbarton Oaks Colloquium on the History of Landscape Architecture, 1971. Washington D.C.: Dumbarton Oaks, 1972, pp. 3–36.

Bauer, Harmann. *Kunst und Utopie: Studien über das Kunst- und Staatsdenken in der Renaissance*. Berlin: Walter De Gruyter, 1965.

Baum, Julius. *Baukunst und dekorative Plastik der Frührenaissance in Italien*. 3d ed. Stuttgart: I. Hoffmann, 1936.

Baumgarten, Paul Maria. *Aus Kanzlei und Kammer, Erörterungen zur Kurialien Hof-und Verwaltungsgeschichte im XIII., XIV., und XV. Jahrhundert*. Freiburg im Breisgau: Herder, 1907.

Beani, Gaetano. *Niccolò Fortiguerri cardinale di Teano*. Pistoia, 1891.

Bek, Lise. *Towards Paradise on Earth. Modern Space Conception in Architecture: A Creation of Renaissance Humanism*. Analecta Romana Instituti Danici 9, Supplement. Odense, Denmark: Odense University Press, 1980.

Belluzzi, Amedeo. "La Badia Fiesolana." In Giulio Carlo Argan et al., *Filippo Brunelleschi: La sua opera e il suo tempo*. Florence: Centro Di, 1980, 2:495–502.

Benevolo, Leonardo. *The Architecture of the Renaissance*. Trans. Judith Landry. Vol. 1. London: Routledge and Kegan Paul, 1978.

Bering, Kunibert. *Baupropaganda und Bildprogrammatik der Frührenaissance in Florenz-Rom-Pienza*. Bochumer Schriften zur Kunstgeschichte 4. Frankfurt: Peter Lang, 1984.

Bernetti, Giuseppe. "Ricerche e problemi nei *Commentarii* di E. S. Piccolomini." *La Rinascita*, 2 (1939), 449–75.

Berrer, J. W. *Leone Battista Albertis Bauten und ihr Einfluss auf die Architektur*. Kassel: Schönhoven, 1911.

Berti, Luciano. *Il museo di Arezzo*. Rome: Libreria dello Stato, 1960.

Biographical and Bibliographical Dictionary of the Italian Humanists and of the World of Classical Scholarship in Italy, 1300–1800. Ed. M. E. Cosenza. 4 vols. Boston: G. K. Hall, 1962.

Biolchi, Dante. *La casina del Cardinale Bes-sarione, Roma*. Rome: Riporto Antichità e Belle Arti del Comune di Roma, 1954.

Biondo, Flavio. "Roma instaurata." In *Codice topografico della città di Roma*. Ed. R. Valentini and G. Zucchetti. Rome: Tipografica del Senato, 1940–53, 4:256–323.

———. *Scritti inediti e rari di Biondo Flavio*. Ed. Bartolomeo Nogara. Studi e testi 48. Rome: Tipografia Poliglotta Vaticana, 1927.

Bisticci, Vespasiano da. *Renaissance Princes, Popes, and Prelates. The Vespasiano Memoirs: Lives of Illustrious Men of the XVth Century*. Trans. William George and Emily Waters, intro. Myron P. Gilmore. New York: Harper and Row, 1963.

———. *Vite di uomini illustri del secolo XV*. Ed. Paolo d'Ancona and Erhard Aeschlemann. Milan: Ulrico Hoepli, 1951.

———. *Vite di uomini illustri del secolo XV*. Ed. Angelo Mai and Adolfo Bartoli. Florence: Barbara Bianchi, 1859.

Blagg, T. F. C., A. G. Luttrell, and A. G. Lyttelton. "Ligorio, Palladio, and the Decorated Roman Capital from Le Mura di Santo Stefano." *Papers of the British School at Rome*, 47 (1979), 102–16.

Blomfield, Reginald. *A History of French Architecture from the Reign of Charles VIII till the Death of Mazarin, 1494–1661*. 1921; rpt. New York: Hacker, 1973.

Boase, Thomas S. R. *Boniface VIII*. London: Constable, 1933.

Boccaccio, Giovanni. *The Decameron of Giovanni Boccaccio*. Trans. Frances Winwar. The Modern Library. New York: Random House, 1930.

Boëthius, Axel. *The Golden House of Nero: Some Aspects of Roman Architecture*. Ann Arbor: University of Michigan Press, 1960.

Borghesi, S., and L. Banchi. *Nuovi documenti per la storia dell'arte senese*. Siena: Enrico Torrini, 1898.

Borsi, Franco. "I cinque ordini architettonici e L. B. Alberti." *Studi e Documenti di Architettura*, 1 (1972), 59–130.

———. *Leon Battista Alberti*. Milan: Electa Editrice, 1975.

Boulting, William. *Aeneas Sylvius, Orator, Man of Letters, Statesman and Pope*. London: Archibald Constable, 1908.

Bowsky, W. M. "City and Contado: Military Relationships and Communal Bonds in Fourteenth-Century Siena." In *Renaissance Studies in Honour of Hans Baron*. Ed. A. Molho and J. A. Tedeschi. DeKalb: Northern Illinois University Press, 1971, pp. 75–98.

Brandi, Cesare, Rosario Assunto, and Alessandro Tagliolini. *Introduzione ai giardini del senese*. S. Quirico d'Orcia: Archivio Italiano dell'Arte dei Giardino, 1976.

Braunfels, Wolfgang. *Mittelalterliche Statdtbaukunst in der Toskana*. Berlin: Gebrüder Mann, 1953.

Brown, Charlotte M. "Luca Fancelli in Mantua." *Mitteilungen des Kunsthistorischen Institutes in Florenz*, 16 (1972), 153–66.

Bruni, Leonardo. *Panegirico della città di Firenze*. Trans. Lazaro da Padova and ed. G. De Toffol. Florence: La Nuova Italia, 1974.

Bruschi, A. "Osservazioni sulla teoria architettonica rinascimentale nella formulazione albertiana." *Quaderni dell' Istituto di Storia dell'Architettura*, 31–48 (1961), 124.

Bucci, Mario. *Palazzi di Firenze*. Florence: Vallecchi, 1971.

Buchowiecki, Walther. *Handbuch der Kirchen Roms: Der Sakralbau in Geschichte und Kunst von altchristlicher Zeit bis zur Gegenwart*. Vienna: Hollinek, 1967–74.

Bulst, W. A. "Die ursprüngliche innere Aufteilung des Palazzo Medici in Florenz." *Mitteilungen des Kunsthistorischen Institutes in Florenz*, 14 (1970), 369–92.

Bürck, G. *Selbstdarstellung und Personenbildnis bei Enea Silvio Piccolomini (Pius II)*. Basel: Baseler Beiträge zur Geschichtswissenshaft, 1956.

Burckhardt, Jacob. *The Architecture of the Italian Renaissance*. Trans. James Palmes and ed. Peter Murray. Chicago: University of Chicago Press, 1985.

____. *Die Geschichte der Renaissance in Italien*. Stuttgart: Ebner and Seubert, 1868.

Burns, Howard. "Un disegno architettonico di Alberti e la questione del rapporto fra Brunelleschi ed Alberti." In Giulio Carlo Argan et al., *Filippo Brunelleschi: La sua opera e il suo tempo*. Florence: Centro Di, 1980, 1:105–23.

____. "A Drawing by L. B. Alberti." *Architectural Design (Profile 21)*, 49, 5–6 (1979), 45–56.

Burroughs, Charles. "A Planned Myth and a Myth of Planning: Nicholas V and Rome." In *Rome in the Renaissance: The City and the Myth*. Ed. P. A. Ramsey. Medieval and Renaissance Texts and Studies 18. Binghamton: State University of New York, 1982, pp. 197–207.

Calamari, Giuseppe. "Il cardinale di Pavia, Jacopo Ammannati-Piccolomini." *Bollettino di Ricerche e di Studi per la Storia di Pescia e di Valdinievole*, 3 (1929), 3ff.

____. *Il confidente di Pio II cardinale Jacopo Ammannati Piccolomini*. 2 vols. Rome: Augustea, 1932.

Calisse, Carlo. *Pio Secondo*. Siena, 1898.

Campano, G. Antonio. *Vita Pii Secundi Pontifici Maximi*. Published in *Rerum italicarum scriptores*. Ed. Ludovico Antonio Muratori. Milan: Società Palatina, 1734, 3, 2, 969–92.

Canestrelli, A. "Campanili medievali nel territorio senese." *Rassegna d'Arte Senese*, 3–4 (1915), 25–42.

Caniggia, Gianfranco. *Strutture dello spazio antropico: Studi e note*. Biblioteca di Architettura 8, Saggi e Documenti 3. Florence: Uniedit, 1976.

Caratelli, Paolo. "Pienza: La chiesa di S. Francesco." *Arte e Storia*, 17, 14, Ser. 3, 1 (1898), 110–17, and 15 (1898), 120–21.

____. *Pienza: I suoi monumenti, arredi sacri ed oggetti d'arte e d'intorni*. Rome: F. Kleinbub, 1901.

Cardellini, Ida. *Desiderio Settignano*. Milan: Edizioni di Comunità, 1962.

Cardini, Franco, and Sergio Rareggi *Palazzi pubblici di Toscana: I centri minori*. Florence: Sansoni, 1983.

Carli, Enzo. *Pienza, la città di Pio II*. Rome: Editalia, 1966.

____. *Pienza: Die Umgestaltung Corsignanos durch den Bauherrn Pius II*. Vorträge der Aeneas-Silvius Stiftung an der Universität Basel 3. Basel: Helbing and Lichtenhahn, 1965.

Carocci, G. "Pienza risorge." *Arte e Storia* (Supplement "Pienza e Pio II pubblicato in occasione del V centenario della nascita di Enea Silvio Piccolomini"), 24, Ser. 3, 8 (1905), 1–2.

Carpeggiani, Paolo. "La fortuna di un mito: Artisti e modelli fiorentini nell'architettura Mantovana dell'umanismo (e nuovi documenti per la Tribuna dell'Annunziata)." In Giulio Carlo Argan et al., *Filippo Brunelleschi: La sua opera e il suo tempo*. Florence: Centro Di, 1980, 2:817–37.

Carunchio, Tancredi. *Origini della villa rinascimentale: La ricerca di una tipologia*. Studi di Storia dell'Arte 4. Rome: Butzoni, 1974.

Casanova, E. "Un anno della vita privata di Pio II." *Bullettino Senese di Storia Patria*, 38, n.s. 2 (1931), 11–34.

Casella, N. "Recenti studi su Enea Silvio Piccolomini." *Rivista di Storia della Chiesa in Italia*, 26 (1972), 473–88.

Cataldi, Giancarlo. "Pienza e la sua piazza nuova ipotesi tipologica di lettura." *Studi e Documenti di Architettura*, 7 (1978), 73–116.

Cataldi, Giancarlo, et al. *Rilievi di Pienza*. Florence: Uniedit, 1977.

Cerasoli, F. "Il viaggio di Pio II da Roma a Mantova, 22 gennajo–27 maggio 1459: Ricerche, rettifiche, dettagli." *Buonarroti*, 4, Ser. 3, 6 (1891), 213–18.

Chambers, D. S. "The Housing Problems of Cardinal Francesco Gonzaga." *Journal of the Warburg and Courtauld Institutes*, 39 (1976), 21–58.

Chastel, André. "Un épisode de la symbolique urbaine au XV siecle: Florence et Rome, cités de Dieu." *Urbanisme et architecture: Etudes écrites et publiées en l'honneur de Pierre Lavedan*. Paris: H. Laurens, 1954.

Chierici, Gino. "Paganico." *Rassegna d'Arte Senese*, 15 (1922), 22–33.

——. *Il palazzo italiano dal secolo XI al secolo XIX.* 2d ed. rev. Milan: Antonio Vallardi, 1964.

Ciampi, Sebastiano. *Memorie di Niccolò Forteguerri istitutore del liceo e del Collegio Forteguerri di Pistoia nel secolo XV.* Pisa: Ranieri Prosperi, 1813.

La Città ideale nel Rinascimento: Scritti di Alberti, Filarete, Francesco di Giorgio Martini, Cataneo, Palladio, Vasari il Giovane, Scamozzo. Ed. Gianni Carlo Sciolla. Intro. Luigi Firpo. Turin: UTET, 1975.

Codice topografico della città di Roma. Ed. R. Valentini and G. Zucchetti. Vol. 4. Rome: Tipografia del Senato, 1940–53.

Coffin, David. Review of *Alfonso II and the Artistic Renewal of Naples, 1485–1495,* by George Hersey. *Journal of the Society of Architectural Historians,* 31 (1972), 64–67.

——. *The Villa in the Life of Renaissance Rome.* Princeton: Princeton University Press, 1979.

Contaldi, Elena. *Benozzo Gozzoli.* Milan: Hoepli, 1928.

"Convegno storico piccolominiano." In *Atti e Memorie della Deputazione di Storia Patria per le Marche,* 4, 2, Ser. 8 (1966), 1–233.

Coratelli, D. Paolo. *Pienza: I suoi monumenti, arredi sacri ed oggetti d'arte e d'intorni.* Rome: F. Kleinbub, 1901.

Costa-Messelière, Marie Geneviève de la. "Deux cités pontificales." *L'Oeil,* 73 (1961), 45–53.

Creighton, Mandell. *A History of the Papacy from the Great Schism to the Sack of Rome.* London: Longmans, Green, 1911.

"Cronaca d'arte di storia: Pienza, lavori alla cattedrale." *Arte e Storia,* 28, 1, Ser. 4, 1 (1909), 26.

Cronache e statuti della città di Viterbo. Ed. Ignazio Ciampi. Documenti di storia italiana 5. Florence: Cellini, 1872.

Cugnoni, G. *Aeneae Sylvii Piccolomini, sen qui postea fuit Pius II. Pont. Max. opera inedita descripsit ex codicibus Chisianis vulgavit notisque illustravit I. C.* Ser. 3, Memoria della classe di scienze morali, storiche e filologiche, 8. Rome: Atti della R. Accademia dei Lincei, 1883, 496–549.

Cultrera, Giuseppe. "Il Palazzo Vitelleschi in Corneto Tarquinia." *Ausonia,* 9 (1920), 260–97.

Curran, Raymond J. *Architecture and the Urban Experience.* New York: Van Nostrand Reinhold, 1983.

Dall'Acqua, Marzio. "Storia di un progetto Albertiano non realizzato: La ricostruzione della Rotonda di San Lorenzo in Mantova." In *Il Sant'Andrea di Mantova e Leon Battista Alberti: Atti del convegno di studi organizzato della città di Mantova con la collaborazione dell'Accademia Virgiliana nel quinto centenario della basilica di Sant'Andrea e della morte dell'Alberti, 1472–1972.* Mantua: Edizione della Biblioteca Comunale di Mantova, 1974, pp. 229–36.

De Carlo, Giancarlo. *Urbino: La storia di una città e il piano della sua evoluzione urbanistica.* Padua: Marsilio Editori, 1966.

De Fusco, Renato. *L'Architettura del quattrocento.* Turin: UTET, 1984.

De la Croix, Horst. *Military Considerations in City Planning: Fortifications.* New York: Braziller, 1972.

Della Giovanpaola, Arnaldo, et al. "Pienza e il suo territorio." *Bollettino Ingegneri,* 27, 3 (1980), 21–30.

Del Lungo, Isidoro. "Un creato di papa Pio II." In *Miscellanea di studi in onore Attilio Hortis.* Trieste: G. Caprin, 1910, 1:225–28.

De Lorenzo, Giuseppe. "Pienza: Impressioni e ricordi." *Arte e Storia,* 37, 1 (1918), 11–20.

Detti, Edoardo, Gian Franco Di Pietro, and Giovanni Fanelli. *Città murate e sviluppo contemporaneo: 42 centri della Toscana.* Lucca: Edizioni Centro Internazionale per lo Studio delle Cerchia Urbana, 1968.

De Wolfe, Ivor. *The Italian Townscape.* London: Architectural Press, 1963.

Di Bernardo, Flavio. *Un vescovo umanista alla corte pontificia Gianantonio Campano (1429–1477).* Miscellanea Historiae Pontificiae 39. Rome: Università Gregoriana Editrice, 1975.

Di Cristina, Lero. *Analisi geografica e storica di Pienza e del suo territorio: Proposita di risana-*

mento. Florence: Università di Firenze, 1971–72.

A Documentary History of Art, I: The Middle Ages and the Renaissance. Ed. Elizabeth G. Holt, Garden City, N.Y.: Doubleday Anchor, 1957.

Donin, Richard Kurt. *Österreichische Baugedanken am Dom von Pienza*. Forschungen zur österreichischen Kunstgeschichte 5. Vienna: Erwin Müller, 1946.

Dörner, Ludwig. *Wiener Neustadt: Ein praktisches Taschenbuch für Wiener Neustadt und Umgebung*. Bad Fischau, N.-O.: Wienerwald Verlag, 1962.

Durm, Josef. *Die Baukunst der Renaissance in Italien*. 2d ed. Stuttgart: Arnold Bergstrasser, 1914.

Edgerton, Samuel Y., Jr. *The Renaissance Rediscovery of Linear Perspective*. 2d ed. New York: Harper and Row Icon Editions, 1976.

Edler, Florence. *Glossary of Medieval Terms of Business: Italian Series, 1200–1600*. Cambridge, Mass.: Medieval Academy of America, 1934.

Elling, Christian. *Function and Form of the Roman Belvedere*. Copenhagen: I Kommission Has Ejnar Munkgaard, 1950.

Enea Silvio Piccolomini, Papa Pio II: Atti del convegno per il quinto centenario della morte e altri scritti, ed. Domenico Maffei. Siena: Accademia Senese degli Intronati, 1968.

Falconi, C. *Storia dei papi e del papato*. Rome: CEI, Vol. 4, 1972.

Faldi Guglielmi, Carla. *Duomo di Pienza*. Bologna: Officine Grafiche Poligrafici il Resto del Carlino, 1967.

Fallico, Rossella Sfogliano. "L'Alberti e l'antico nel *De re aedificatoria*." In *Il Sant'Andrea di Mantova e Leon Battista Alberti: Atti del convegno di studi organizzato dalla città di Mantova con la collaborazione dell'Accademia Virgiliana nel quinto centenario della basilica di Sant'Andrea e della morte dell'Alberti, 1472–1972*. Mantua: Edizione della Biblioteca Comunale di Mantova, 1974, pp. 157–70.

Ferrara, Miranda. "Santa Maria delle Grazie a Pistoia: Alcuni aspetti del rapporto Michelozzo-Brunelleschi." In Giulio Carlo Argan et al., *Filippo Brunelleschi: La sua opera e il suo tempo*. Florence: Centro Di, 1980, 2:571–75.

Fierville, Charles. *Le Cardinal Jean Jouffroy et son temps (1412–1473): Etude historique*. Coutances: Salettes, 1874.

Finelli, Luciana. *L'umanesimo giovane: Bernardo Rossellino a Roma e a Pienza*. Rome: Veutro Editore, 1985.

Finelli, Luciana, and Sara Rossi. *Pienza, tra ideologia e realtà*. Bari: Dedalo Libri, 1979.

———. "San Pietro come team-work." *L'Architettura, Cronache e Storia*, 22 (1977), 721–27.

Fontana, Vincenzo. *Artisti e committenti nella Roma del quattrocento: Leon Battista Alberti e la sua opera mediatrice*. Quaderni di Studi Romani I, 37. Rome: Istituto di Studi Romani, 1973.

Formichi, Fausto. "Le dodici 'case nuove' di Pienza." *Studi e Documenti di Architettura*, 7 (1978), 117–28.

Forster, Kurt W. "Discussion: The Palazzo Rucellai and Questions of Typology in the Development of Renaissance Buildings." *Art Bulletin*, 58 (1976), 109–13.

Francastel, P. "L'architettura civile del quattrocento." *Eventail de l'histoire vivante: Homage à Lucien Febvre offert à l'occasion de son 75° anniversaire*. Paris: A. Colin, 1953.

Fraser Jenkins, A. D. "Cosimo de'Medici's Patronage of Architecture and the Theory of Magnificence." *Journal of the Warburg and Courtauld Institutes*, 33 (1970), 162–70.

Frati, L. "Enea Silvio Piccolomini imitatore di Dante." *La Nuova Antologia*, 55, 1168 (1920).

Friedman, David. "Le terre nuove fiorentine." *Archeologia Medievale*, 1 (1974), 231–47.

Fritelli, U. *Giannantonio de' Pandoni detto il Porcellio*. Florence, 1900.

Frommel, Christoph Luitpold. "Francesco del Borgo, Architekt Pius' II. und Pauls II.; I. Der Petersplatz und weitere römische

Bauten Pius' II. Piccolomini." *Römisches Jahrbuch für Kunstgeschichte*, 20 (1983), 107–54.

———. "Francesco del Borgo, Architekt Pius' II. und Pauls II.; II. Palazzo Venezia, Palazzetto Venezia und San Marco." *Römisches Jahrbuch für Kunstgeschichte*, 21 (1984), 71–164.

———. *Der Palazzo Venezia in Rom.* Gerda Henkel Vorlesung. Opladen: Westdeutscher Verlag, 1982.

Gabotto, F. "Ricerche intorno allo storigrafo quattrocentista Lodrisio Crivelli." *Archivio Storico Italiano*, 7, Ser. 5 (1891), 266–98.

Gadol, Joan. *Leon Battista Alberti: Universal Man of the Renaissance.* Chicago: University of Chicago Press, 1969.

Gai, L. "Niccolò Forteguerri nei suoi rapporti con l'ambiente culturale pistoiese del quattrocento." *Studi Storici Pistoiesi* (1976), 62.

Gallimberti, Nino. "L'urbanistica della rinascita." *Atti del 1° congresso nazionale di storia dell'architettura (Firenze, 1936).* Florence: Sansoni, 1938, pp. 255–69.

Gaye, Johann (Giovanni) Wilhelm. *Carteggio inedito d'artisti dei secoli XIX, XV, XVI.* Florence: Molini, 1839–40.

Gilbert, Creighton. *Change in Piero della Francesca.* Locust Valley, N.J.: J. J. Augustin, 1968.

Gilbert, Felix. "Bernardo Rucellai and the Orti Oricellari." *Journal of the Warburg and Courtauld Institutes*, 12 (1949), 101–31.

Giovannoni, Gustavo. "L'urbanistica del Rinascimento." In G. Giovannoni et al., *L'urbanistica dall'antichità ad oggi.* Florence: Sansoni, 1943, pp. 93–115.

Goldthwaite, Richard A. *The Building of Renaissance Florence: An Economic and Social History.* Baltimore: Johns Hopkins University Press, 1980.

———. "The Florentine Palace Considered as Domestic Architecture." *American Historical Review*, 77 (1972), 977–1012.

Golzio, Vicenzo, and Giuseppe Zander. *L'arte in Roma nel secolo XV.* Bologna: Licinio Cappelli, 1968.

Gosebruch, Martin. "Florentinische Kapitelle von Brunelleschi bis zum Tempio Malatestiano und der Eigenstil der Frührenaissance." *Römisches Jahrbuch für Kunstgeschichte*, 8 (1958), 63–193.

Gottlob, Adolf. *Aus der Camera Apostolica des 15. Jahrhunderts: Ein Beitrag zur Geschichte des päpstlichen Finanzwesens und des endenden Mittelalters.* Innsbruck: Verlag der Wagner'schen Universitäts-Buchhandlung, 1889.

Grayson, Cecil. *An Autograph Letter from Leon Battista Alberti to Matteo de' Pasti, November 18, 1454.* New York: Pierpont Morgan Library, 1957.

Guidoni, Enrico. *Arte e urbanistica in Toscana, 1000–1315.* Rome: M. Bulzoni, 1970.

———. "Trasformazioni urbanistiche e teoria della città nell'età brunelleschiana." In Giulio Carlo Argan et al., *Filippo Brunelleschi: La sua opera e il suo tempo.* Florence: Centro Di, 1980, 1:65–77.

Gurrieri, Ottorino. *La basilica di San Pietro in Perugia.* Perugia: Donnini, 1954.

———. *La cattedrale di S. Lorenzo in Perugia.* Perugia: Azienda Autonoma di Turismo, 1961.

Hagenbach, Karl Rudolph. *Erinnerungen an Aeneas Sylvius Piccolomini (Papst Pius II.).* Basel, 1840.

Hale, John Rigby. "The Development of the Bastion, 1440–1534." In *Europe in the Late Middle Ages.* Ed. J. R. Hale. London: Highfield and Smalley/Evanston, Ill.: Northwestern University Press, 1965.

Haller, Johannes. "Pius II., ein Papst der Renaissance." In J. Haller, *Reden und Aufsätze zur Geschichte und Politik.* Berlin: Cotta, 1934, pp. 67–100.

Hanfstaengel, Eberhard. *Hans Stetheimer: Eine Studie zur spätgotischen Architektur Altbayerns.* Leipzig: Hermann, 1911.

Hartt, Frederick. *History of Italian Renaissance Art: Painting, Sculpture, Architecture.* Englewood Cliffs, N.J.: Prentice Hall and Harry N. Abrams, 1973.

Hartt, Frederick, Gino Corti, and Clarence Kennedy. *The Chapel of the Cardinal of Portugal, 1434–1459, at San Miniato in Flor-*

ence. Philadelphia: University of Pennsylvania Press, 1964.

Hatfield, Rab. "Some Unknown Descriptions of the Medici Palace in 1459." *Art Bulletin,* 52 (1970), 232–49.

Haupt, Albrecht. *Architettura dei palazzi dell'Italia settentrionale e della Toscana.* Milan: Bestetti e Tumminelli, 1930.

Hausmann, Frank R. "Die Benefizien des Kardinals Jacopo Ammannati-Piccolomini: Ein Beitrag zur ökonomischen Situation des Kardinals im Quattrocento." *Römische Historische Mitteilungen,* 13 (1971), 27–80.

Heckscher, William S. *Die Romruinen, die geistigen Voraussetzungen ihrer Wertung im Mittelalter und in der Renaissance.* Würzburg: R. Mayr, 1936.

———. *Sixtus IIII Aeneas insignes statuos romano populo restituendas censuit.* The Hague: M. Nijhoff, 1955.

Hermann, Frederico. *Il Palazzo di Venezia.* Rome: Libreria dello Stato, 1948.

Hersey, George L. *Pythagorean Palaces: Magic and Architecture in the Italian Renaissance.* Ithaca: Cornell University Press, 1976.

Heydenreich, Ludwig H. "Federico da Montefeltro as a Building Patron: Some Remarks on the Ducal Palace of Urbino." In *Studies in Renaissance and Baroque Art Presented to Anthony Blunt on his 60th Birthday.* London: Phaidon, 1967, pp. 1–6.

———. "Pius II. als Bauherr von Pienza." *Zeitschrift für Kunstgeschichte,* 6 (1937), 105–46. Rpt. in Ludwig H. Heydenreich, *Studien zur Architektur der Renaissance: Ausgewählte Aufsätze.* Foreword by Willibald Sauerlander. Munich: Fink, 1981, pp. 56–82.

Heydenreich, Ludwig H., and Wolfgang Lotz. *Architecture in Italy, 1400–1600.* Trans. Mary Hottinger. Pelican History of Art. Harmondsworth: Penguin Books, 1974.

Higounet, Charles. "Les 'terre nuove' Florentines du XVe Siècle." *Studi in onore di Amintore Fanfani, III: Medioevo.* Milan: A. Giuffrè, 1962, 3–17.

Hirschland, Nancy L. "The Head-Capitals of Sardis." *Papers of the British School at Rome,* 35 (1967), 12–22.

Hofmann, Walther von. *Forschungen zur Geschichte der Kurialen Behörden vom Schisma bis zur Reformation.* Bibliothek des Kgl. Preuss. Historischen Instituts in Rom 12–13. Rome: Loescher, 1914.

Holtzinger, Heinrich. *Pienza: Aufgenommen und gezeichnet von den Architekten K. Mayreder und C. Bender.* Vienna, 1882.

Hyman, Isabelle. "Notes and Speculations on S. Lorenzo, Palazzo Medici, and an Urban Project by Brunelleschi." *Journal of the Society of Architectural Historians,* 34 (1975), 98–120.

Infessura, Stefano. *Diario della città di Roma di Stefano Infessura scribasenato.* Ed. Oreste Tommasini. Fonte per la storia d'Italia. Rome: Forzani, 1890.

Johnson, Eugene J. *S. Andrea in Mantua: The Building History.* University Park: Pennsylvania State University Press, 1975.

Klotz, Heinrich. "L. B. Albertis *De re aedificatoria* in Theorie und Praxis." *Zeitschrift für Kunstgeschichte,* 32 (1969), 93–103.

Kraus, Andreas. "Die Sekretäre Pius' II.: Ein Beitrag zur Etwicklungs-geschichte des päpstlichen Sekretariats." *Römische Quartalschrift für christliche Altertumskunde und Kirchengeschichte,* 53 (1958), 25–80.

Krönig, W. "Hallenkirchen in Mittelitalien." *Kunstgeschichtliches Jahrbuch der Bibliothek Herziana,* 2 (1938), 1–142.

Lamus, Iô. *Deliciae eruditorum.* Florence, 1742.

Lang, S. "The Ideal City from Plato to Howard." *Architectural Review,* 112 (1952), 91–101.

Laspeyres, Paul. *Die Kirchen der Renaissance in Mittel-Italien.* Berlin: W. Spemann, 1882.

Lavedan, Pierre. *Histoire de l'urbanisme.* Vol. 2. Paris: Henri Laurens, 1941.

Lavedan, Piere, and Jeannel Hugueney. *L'Urbanisme au Moyen Age.* Paris: Arts et Métiers Graphiques, 1974.

Lesca, Giuseppe. *Giovannantonio Campano, detto l'episcopus aprutinus.* Pontedera: Ristori, 1892.

"Una lettera del Cardinal Papiense (Giacomo Ammannati) a Gregorio Lolli (Anno 1467)." *Arte e Storia* (Supplement "Pienza e Pio II pubblicato in occasione del V centenario della nascita di Enea Silvio Piccolomini"), 24, Ser. 3, 8 (1905), 14–15.

Levi d'Ancona, Mirella. *The Garden of the Renaissance.* Florence: Olschki, 1977.

Lisini, Alessandro, and Alfredo Liberati. *Genealogia dei Piccolomini di Siena.* Siena: Enrico Torrini, 1900.

Lorenz, Hellmut. "Zur Architektur L. B. Albertis: Die Kirchenfassaden." *Wiener Jahrbuch für Kunstgeschichte,* 29 (1976), 65–100.

Lowic, Lawrence. "Francesco di Giorgio on the Design of Churches: The Use and Significance of Mathematics in the Trattato." *Architectura,* 12 (1982), 151–63.

Lugli, Piero Maria. *Storia e cultura della città italiana.* Bari: Laterza, 1967.

Lusini, A. "La residence de Pie II a Pienza," *Terra di Siena,* 4 (1950), 18–22.

Lyttelton, Margaret, and Frank Sear. "A Roman Villa Near Anguillara Sabazia." *Papers of the British School at Rome,* 45 (1977), 227–51.

Mack, Charles R. "Bernardo Rossellino, L. B. Alberti, and the Rome of Pope Nicholas V." *Southeastern College Art Conference Review,* 10 (1982), 60–69.

——. "Brunelleschi's Spedale degli Innocenti Rearticulated." *Architectura,* 11 (1981), 129–46.

——. "Building a Florentine Palace: The Palazzo Spinelli." *Mitteilungen des Kunsthistorischen Institutes in Florenz,* 27 (1983), 261–84.

——. "Nicholas the Fifth and the Rebuilding of Rome: Reality and Legacy." In *Light on the Eternal City: Recent Observations and Discoveries in Roman Art and Architecture,* Papers in Art History from the Pennsylvania State University 2. Ed. Hellmut Hager and Susan B. Munshower. University Park: Pennsylvania State University, 1987.

——. "Notes Concerning an Unpublished Window by Bernardo Rossellino at the Badia Fiorentina." *Southeastern College Art Conference Review,* 5 (Dec. 1970), 2–5.

——. "The Palazzo Rucellai Reconsidered." In *Actas del' XXIII congreso internacional de historia del arte (1973).* Grenada: Universitad Granada, 1977, 2:344–50.

——. "The Rucellai Palace: Some New Proposals." *Art Bulletin,* 56 (1974), 517–29.

——. "Studies in the Architectural Career of Bernardo di Matteo Ghamberelli Called Rossellino." Diss., University of North Carolina at Chapel Hill, 1972.

Magnuson, Torgil. "Studies in Roman Quattrocento Architecture." *Figura,* 9 (1958).

Mancini, Girolamo. *Vita di Leon Battista Alberti.* 2d ed. Florence: Carnesecchi, 1911.

Manetti, Antonio. *The Life of Brunelleschi.* Trans. Catherine Enggass; ed. Howard Saalman. University Park: Pennsylvania State University Press, 1970.

Manetti, Giannozzo. *Vita Nicolai V summi pontificis nunc primum prodit ex manuscripta codice Florentino.* Publ. in *Rerum italicarum scriptores.* Ed. Ludovico Antonio Muratori. Milan: Società Palatina, 1734, 3, 2, 907–60.

Mannucci, Giovanni Battista. "La cattedrale di Pio II a Pienza." *Bullettino Senese di Storia Patria,* 49 (1942), 67.

——. "La chiesa di S. Francesco in Pienza." *La Diana,* 1 (1926), 275–79.

——. *Una città del Rinascimento: Pienza.* Rome: Italia Moderna Illustrata, 1906.

——. "Il convento di San Francesco in Pienza: Documenti e notizie." *Bullettino Senese di Storia Patria,* 26 (1919), 266–74.

——. "Curiosità storiche-artistiche di Pienza: Pieve dei SS. Vito e Modesto a Corsigno; il loggiato del palazzo di Pio II a Pienza; spigolature dell' Archivio Vescovile." *Arte e Storia,* 28, Ser. 4, 1 (1909), 15–18.

——. "La diocesi pientina e i suoi vescovi." *Arte e Storia,* 29, 6 (1910), 179–82; 29, 8 (1910), 247–49; 29, 9 (1910), 282; 30, 5 (1911), 144–49; 31, 10 (1912), 319–20; 31, 11 (1912), 344–48; 32, 2 (1913), 58–60.

——. "Documenti e carte d'archivio nella

biblioteca Piccolomini a Pienza." *Bullettino Senese di Storia Patria*, 48 (1941), 294–95.

——. "La famiglia Lolli-Piccolomini." *Arte e Storia*, 29, Ser. 4, 1 (1910), 27–29.

——. "Fondazione della cattedrale di Pienza." *Arte e Storia* (Supplement "Pienza e Pio II pubblicato in occasione del V centenario della nascita di Enea Silvio Piccolomini"), 24, Ser. 3, 8 (1905), 4–5.

——. *Guide-Manuel de Pienza et de ses environs avec illustrations*. Venice: Imprimerie Artistique C. Jacobi, 1909.

——. "Un nipote di Pio II per la salvezza del duomo di Pienza." *L'Unita Cattolica*, June 5, 1928.

——. "Notizie sul castello di Corsignano." *Rassegna d'Arte Senese*, 2 (1906), 63–68.

——. "L'Opera di Pio II nell'arte e la sua città natale." *Arte e Storia* (Supplement "Pienza e Pio II pubblicato in occasione del V centenario della nascita di Enea Silvio Piccolomini"), 24, Ser. 3, 8 (1905), 7–8.

——. "Il Palazzo Piccolomini di Pienza." *Arte e Storia*, 27, 17–18, Ser. 3, 2 (1908), 133–35.

——. "Il palazzo di Pio II ed i suoi restauri." *Rassegna d'Arte Senese*, 7 (1911), 22–30.

——. *Pienza: Arte e storia*. 3d ed. Siena: Stab. San Bernardino, 1937.

——. *Pienza: La città di Pio II*. Le cento città d'Italia illustrate 126. Milan: Sonzogno (Stab. graf. Matarelli), 1926.

——. *Pienza, i suoi monumenti, la sua diocesi*. Montepulciano: Tip. Madonna delle Querce, 1915.

——. "Pio II e Pienza." *Bullettino Senese di Storia Patria*, 21 (1914), 531–42, and 22 (1915), 157–65.

——. "I quattro cardinale fedeli a Pio II nelle costruzioni pientine." *Bullettino Senese di Storia Patria*, 62–63 (1955–56), 95–99.

——. *A ricordo dei restauri della cattedrale di Pienza, 1911–1935*. Siena: Poligrafica Meini, 1935.

——. "La rinascita del Duomo di Pienza." *Arte Cristiana*, 24 (1936), 75–80.

——. "Il Rossellino architetto di Pienza?" *Rassegna d'Arte Senese*, 3 (1907), 15–18.

——. "Spigolando negli Archivi di Pienza: Archivio Capitolare (1462–1464)." *Arte e Storia*, 27, 21–22, Ser. 3, 2 (1908), 170.

——. "Il viaggio di Pio II da Roma a Mantova (22 gennaio–27 maggio 1459)." *Bullettino Senese di Storia patria*, 48, n.s. 1 (1941), 62–65.

Marchini, Giuseppe, and Niccolo Rodolico. *I palazzi del popolo nei comune Toscani del Medio Evo*. Milan: Electra Editrice, 1962.

Marconi, Paolo, et al. *I castelli, architettura e difesa del territorio fra Medioevo e Rinascimento*. Novara: Istituto Geografico De Agostini, 1978.

Marcucci, Laura. "Considerazioni storico-critiche sui rilevamenti architettonici di Pienza." *Studi e Documenti di Architettura*, 7 (1978), 129–40.

Marini, Gaetano Luigi. *Degli archiatri pontifici*. Rome: Stamperia Pagliarini, 1784.

Mariotti, Giovanni. "La città di Pio II." *Terra di Siena*, 19, 3 (1965), 21–26.

Masson, Georgina. *Italian Gardens*. New York: Harry N. Abrams, 1961.

Meiss, Millard. "Light as Form and Symbol in Some Fifteenth-Century Paintings." *Art Bulletin*, 27 (1945), 43–68. Rpt. in Millard Meiss, *The Painter's Choice: Problems in the Interpretation of Renaissance Art*. New York: Harper and Row, 1976, pp. 3–18.

Melot, J. "Pienza, la ville de Pie II." *Revue générale*, 88 (1908).

Mercklin, Eugen von. *Antike Figuralkapitelle*. Berlin: De Gruyter, 1962.

Mesnil, Domenique, et al. *Builders and Humanists: The Renaissance Popes as Patrons of the Arts*. Houston: University of St. Thomas Art Department, 1966.

Michel, Alain. "Architecture et rhetorique chez Alberti: La Tradition humaniste a Pienza." In *Presence de l'architecture e de l'urbanisme romains: actes du colloque des 12, 13 decembre 1981*. Ed. R. Chevallier. Paris, 1983.

Miglio, Massimo. "Una vocazione in progresso: Michele Canesi biografo papale." *Studi Medievali*, 12, Ser. 3 (1971), 463–524.

Mitchell, R. J. *The Laurels and the Tiara: Pope*

Pius II, 1458–1464. London: Harvill Press, 1962.

Mohler, Ludwig. *Kardinal Bessarion als Theologe, Humanist, und Staatsmann.* 3 vols. Paderborn: Ferdinand Schöningh, 1923–42.

Montanari, Mario. *Mille anni della chiesa di S. Pietro in Perugia e del suo patrimonio.* Foligno: Poligrafica F. Salvati, 1966.

Moos, Stanislaus von. *Turm und Bollwerk: Beiträge zu einer politischen Ikonographie der Italienischen Renaissance-Architektur.* Zurich: Atlantis Verlag, 1974.

Moretti, Italo. *Le "terre nuove" del contado fiorentino.* Collana di Studi Storico-Territoriali 4. Florence: Salimbeni, 1979.

Moretti, Italo, and Renato Stopani. *Chiese gotiche nel contado fiorentino.* Florence: UPI, 1969.

——. "Il palazzo fortezza dei Franzesi a Staggia." *Antichità Viva,* 10, 5 (1971), 49–59.

Moretti, Mario. *L'architettura romanica religiosa nel territorio dell' antica repubblica Senese.* Parma: Scuola tipografica benedettina, 1962.

Morini, Mario. *Atlante di storia dell'urbanistica.* Milan: Hoepli, 1963.

Moschella, P. "Le case a sporti in Firenze." *Palladio,* 6 (1942), 107ff.

Müntz, Eugene. *Les Arts à la cours des papes pendant le XVe et le XVIe siècle, I (Martin V–Pie III).* 1878; rpt. Hildesheim: George Olms, 1983.

Muratori, Saverio. *Architettura e civiltà in crisi.* Rome: Centro Studi Urbanistica, 1963.

Murray, Peter. *The Architecture of the Italian Renaissance.* New York: Schocken, 1963.

Nardi-Dei, Mons. Silvio. "Una bolla santamente severa." *Arte e Storia* (Supplement "Pienza e Pio II pubblicato in occasione del V centenario della nascita di Enea Silvio Piccolomini"), 24, Ser. 3, 8 (1905), 7.

Naredi-Rainer, Paul von. "Musikalische Proportionen, Zahlenästhetik und Zahlensymbolik im architektonischen Werk L. B. Albertis." *Jahrbuch des Kunsthistorischen Institutes der Universität Graz,* 12 (1977), 81–213.

Olivato, Loredana. "La concezione urbanistica dell'Alberti e il Sant' Andrea di Mantova." In *Il Sant'Andrea di Mantova e Leon Battista Alberti: Atti del convegno di studi organizzato dalla città di Mantova con la collaborazione dell'Accademia Virgiliana nel quinto centenario della basilica di Sant'Andrea e della morte dell'Alberti, 1472–1972.* Mantua: Edizione della Biblioteca Comunale di Mantova, 1974, pp. 157–70.

Onians, John. "Alberti and ΦΙΛΑΡΕΤΗ: A Study in Their Sources." *Journal of the Warburg and Courtauld Institutes,* 34 (1971), 96–114.

——. "Brunelleschi: Humanist or Nationalist?" *Art History,* 3 (1982), 259–72.

Origo, Iris. *The World of San Bernardino.* New York: Harcourt, Brace and World, 1962.

Ortona, Erminia Gentile. "Santo Stefano Rotondo e il restauro del Rossellino." *Bollettino d'Arte,* 67 (1982), 99–106.

Paatz, Walter. "Ein antikischer Stadthaustypus im mittelalterlichen Italien." *Römisches Jahrbuch für Kunstgeschichte,* 3 (1939), 127ff.

Paatz, Walter, and Elizabeth Paatz. *Die Kirchen von Florenz.* 6 vols. Frankfurt: Klostermann, 1940–54.

Palmieri, Mattia. *De temporibus suis ab anno MCCCXLIX.* In *Rerum italicarum scriptores.* Ed. Giuseppe Maria Tartini. Florence: P. C. Viviani, 1748–70.

Palmieri, Matteo. "Libro del poema chiamato 'Città di Vita' composto da Matteo Palmieri Fiorentino, M. S. Laurentiana XL 53." Ed. M. Rooke. In *Smith College Studies in Modern Languages.* Northhampton, Mass.: Smith College, 1928.

Paparelli, Gioacchino. *Enea Silvio Piccolomini (Pio II).* Biblioteca di cultura moderna. Bari: Giuseppe Laterza e Figli, 1950.

——. *Enea Silvio Piccolomini: L'umanisimo sul soglio di Pietro.* Ravenna: Longo (Pleiadi), 1978.

Papini, Roberto. *Francesco di Giorgio architetto.* Florence: Electra Editrice, 1946.

Pastor, Ludwig von. *The History of the Popes.* 4th English ed. Vol. 3. London: Kegan Paul, Trench, Trubner, 1923.

Patzak, Bernhard. *Paläste und Villen in Toskana*. Vols. 1 and 2. Leipzig: Klinkhardt and Biermann, 1912–13.

Pauli, Sebastiano. *Disquisizione istoria della patria e compendio della vita di Giacomo Ammannati Piccolomini, cardinale di S. Chiesa, detta il papiense vescovo di Lucca e Pavia.* Lucca: Pellegrino Frediani, 1712.

Pedretti, Carlo. *Leonardo, Architect.* Trans. Sue Brill. New York: Rizzoli, 1985.

Pellecchia, Linda. Review of *La chiesa di Santa Maria delle Carceri in Prato,* by Piero Morselli and Gino Corti. *Journal of the Society of Architectural Historians,* 44 (1985), 184–86.

"Perspectives pour un pape: Pienza," *Connaissance des arts,* 178 (1966), 84–89.

Petri, Ivo. *Attualità dei Commentari di Pio II (Enea Silvio Piccolomini): Introduzione e saggi di lettura.* Siena: Cantagalli, 1984.

———. *Pienza: Storia breve di una simbolica città.* Genoa: Edigraphica, 1972.

Pica, Agnoldomenico, "Il Brunellescho e le origini del rinascimento lombardo." In *Atti del 1° congresso nazionale di storia dell' architettura, Firenze, 1936.* Florence: Sansoni, 1938, pp. 165–71.

Piccinato, Luigi. "Urbanistica medioevale." In G. Giovannoni et al., *L'urbanistica dall'antichità ad oggi.* Florence: Sansoni, 1943, pp. 63–89.

Piccolomini, Aeneas Silvius (Pius II). *I Commentari.* 5 vols. Trans. Giuseppe Bernetti. I Classici cristiani 219. Siena: Cantagalli, 1972.

———. *The Commentaries of Pius II.* Trans. Florence Alden Gragg. Ed. Leona C. Gabel. Smith College Studies in History, Northampton, Mass.: Smith College, 1936–37, 1940, 1947, 1951.

———. *Commentarii.* 1584; rpt. Frankfurt/Main: Minerva, 1974.

———. *I Commentarii rerum memorabilium, quae temporibus suis contigerii d'Enea Silvio Piccolomini (Pio II).* Ed. Giuseppe Lesca. Pisa: Nistri, 1894.

———. *Commentari rerum memorabilium, quae temporibus suis contigerunt.* Ed. Adriano van Heck, 2 vols. Studi e testi 312–13. Vatican City: Tipographia Poliglotta Vaticana, 1984.

———. *De gestis concilli Basiliensis commentariiorum.* Ed. and trans. Denys Hay and W. K. Smith. Oxford: Clarendon Press, 1967.

———. *Memoirs of a Renaissance Pope: The Commentaries of Pius II (An Abridgment).* Trans. Florence Alden Gragg. Ed. Leona C. Gabel. New York: Capricorn Books, 1959.

———. *Selected Letters of Aeneas Silvius Piccolomini.* Trans. and ed. Albert R. Baca. San Fernando Valley State College Renaissance Editions 2. Northridge, Calif.: San Fernando Valley State College, 1969.

"Pienza." In *Le cento città d'Italia 126,* Supplement 12044. Milan: Sonsogno, 31 Oct. 1899.

Pietrangeli, Carlo. *Le prime fasi architettoniche del Palazzo Senatoria.* Rome: Edizioni di Capitolium, 1965.

Pio II, MCDLXIV–MCMLXIV: A ricordo del V. centenario della morte del pontefice Pio II (Enea Silvio Piccolomini). Siena: Grafiche Meini for L'Ente Provinciale per il Turismo di Siena, 1964.

Pittaluga, Mary. *L'architettura italiana del quattrocento.* Florence: Novissima Enciclopedia Monografica Illustrata, 1943.

Planiscig, Leo. *Bernardo und Antonio Rossellino.* Vienna: Anton Schroll, 1942.

Platina, Bartolommeo. *Liber de vita Christi ad omnium Pontificum.* Publ. in *Rerum italicarum scriptores.* Ed. Ludovico Antonio Muratori. Milan: Società Palatina, 1734, 3, 2, 907–60.

———. *Le vite dei' pontifici di Bartolommeo Platina dal Salvator fino Benedetto XIII da Onofrio Panrenio.* Venice: Savioni, 1730.

Plesner, Johan. "Medieval Florentine Town-Plans." In *Résumés des communications présentés au Congrès international d'histoire de l'art.* Stockholm, 1933, p. 114.

Pressauye, Leon. "St. Bernard to St. Francis: Monastic Ideals and Iconographic Programs in the Cloister." *Gesta,* 12 (1973), 71–92.

Preyer, Brenda. "The 'Chasa overo Palagio' of Alberto di Zanobi: A Florentine Palace

of About 1400 and Its Later Remodeling."
Art Bulletin, 65 (1983), 387–401.

——. "The Rucellai Palace." In F. W. Kent et
al., *Giovanni Rucellai ed il suo Zibaldone II:
A Florentine Patrician and His Palace.* London: Warburg Institute of the University of
London, 1981, pp. 155–225.

Procacci, Ugo. "Cosimo de' Medici e la costruzione della Badia Fiesolana." *Commentari,* 19 (1968), 80–97.

Pulin, Carol. "The Palaces of an Early Renaissance Humanist, Cardinal Branda Castiglione." *Arte Lombarda,* 14 (1982), 25–32.

Quintavalle, Arturo Carlo. *Prospettiva e ideologia: Alberti e la cultura del secolo XV.*
Parma: Ediluce Studium Parmense, 1967.

Raschdorff, S. C. *Palastarchitektur von
Oberitalien und Toskana vom XV. bis XVII.
Jahrhundert.* 2 vols. Berlin: Ernst Wasmuth,
1888.

Rauty, Natale. "Le finestre a crociera del
Palazzo Panciatichi a Pistoia." In *Atti del 2°
convegno internazionale di studi: Il gotico a
Pistoia nei suoi rapporti con l'arte gotica Italiana.* Pistoia: Centro Italiano di Studio e
d'Arte Pistoia, 1966, pp. 93–101.

Redig de Campos, Deoclecio. *Di alcuni tracce
del palazzo di Niccolo III nuovamente tornate
alle luce.* Rome: Tipografia Poliglotta Vaticana, 1942.

——. *Il restauro della aule di Nicolo V e di Sisto
IV nel Palazzo Apostolico Vaticana.* Vatican
City, 1967.

Redtenbacher, Rudolf. *Die Architektur der italienischen Renaissance in Toscana.* Munich,
1885–96.

Repetti, E. *Dizionario geografico fisico storico
della Toscana.* Vol. 4. 1833–35; rpt. Florence: Cassa di Risparmio, 1972.

Richter, Maina. "Die 'Terra murata' im florentinischen Gebiet." *Mitteilungen des
Kunsthistorischen Institutes in Florence,* 5
(1940), 351–86.

Roccatelli, Carlo, and Enrico Verdozzi. *Brick-
work in Italy: A Brief Review from Ancient to
Modern Times.* Chicago: American Face
Brick Association, 1925.

Rocholl, Rudolf. *Bessarion: Studie zur
Geschichte der Renaissance.* Leipzig: A. Deichert'sche Verlags-G. Böhme, 1904.

Romanini, Angiola Maria. *L'architettura gotica
in Lombardia.* 2 vols. Milan: Ceschina,
1964.

Rossi, Adamo. "Spogli Vaticani." *Giornale
d'erudizione artistica,* 6 (1887), 129–228.

Rossi, Pietro. "Pio II a Pienza." *Bullettino
Senese di Storia Patria,* 8 (1901), 3–26.

——. "Pio II a Pienza: Contributo alla storia
sull'arte senese del quattrocento." *Bullettino
Senese di Storia Patria,* 8 (1901), 383–406.

Rotondi, Pasquale. *Il Palazzo Ducale di Urbino.* 2 vols. Urbino: Istituto Statale d'Arte
per Libro, 1950–51.

Rowe, T. G. "The Tragedy of E. S. Piccolomini, Pope Pius II." *Church History,* 30
(1961), 288–313.

Rubenstein, Nicolai. "The Piazza della Sig-
noria in Florence." In *Festschrift Herbert
Siebenhüner.* Ed. Erich Hubala and Gunter
Schweikhart. Würzburg: Herbert
Schöningh, 1978, pp. 19–30.

Rubinstein, Ruth Olitsky. "Pius II's Piazza S.
Pietro and St. Andrew's Head." In *Essays
in the History of Architecture Presented to
Rudolf Wittkower.* Ed. A. Fraser, Howard
Hibbard, M. J. Lewine. London: Phaidon,
1967, pp. 22–33. Also in *Enea Silvio Piccolomini, Papa Pio II: Atti del convegno per il
quinto centenario della morte e altri scritti.* Ed.
Domenico Maffei. Siena: Accademia Senese
degli Intronati, 1968, pp. 221–44.

Rucellai, Giovanni. *Il zibaldone quaresimile.*
Ed. A Perosa. London: The Warburg Institute of the University of London, 1960.

Rumohr, Carl F. von. "Bernardo Rossellino
und Francesco di Giorgio: Bauwerke Pius II
zu Pienza und Siena." In his *Italienische
Forschungen.* Berlin: Nicolai'schen
Buchhandlung, 1827, 2:177–201.

Rykwert, Joseph. "Inheritance or Tradition."
Architectural Design (Profile 21), 49, 5–6
(1979), 2–6.

Rykwert, Joseph, and Robert Tavernor.
"Church of S. Sebastiano in Mantua."
Architectural Design (Profile 21), 49, 5–6
(1979), 86–95.

Saalman, Howard. "Early Renaissance Architectural Theory and Practice in Antonio Filarete's *Trattato di architettura.*" *Art Bulletin,* 41 (1959), 89–106.

———. *Filippo Brunelleschi: The Cupola of Santa Maria del Fiore.* Studies in Architecture 20. London: A. Zwemmer, 1980.

———. "The Palazzo Comunale in Montepulciano: An Unknown Work by Michelozzo." *Zeitschrift für Kunstgeschichte,* 28 (1965), 1–65.

Salmi, Mario. "Bernardo Rossellino ad Arezzo." In *Scritti di storia dell'arte in onore di Ugo Procacci.* Ed. Maria Grazia Ciardi Dupré Dal Poggetto and Paolo Dal Poggetto. Milan: Electa Editrice, 1977, 1:254–61.

———. *Civiltà artistica della terra aretina.* Novara: Istituto Geografico de Agostini, 1971.

———. "Francesco di Giorgio e il Palazzo Ducale di Urbino." *Studi Artistici Urbinati,* 1 (1949), 11–15.

———. "Sant'Agostino di Anghiari." In *Atti del XII congresso di storia dell'architettura: L'architettura nell' Aretino.* Rome: Centro di Studi per la Storia dell'Architettura, 1969, pp. 200–206.

———. "Sant' Andrea a Camoggiano e la Cappella d'Pazzi." In *Festschrift Ulrich Middeldorf.* Ed. Antje Kosegarten and Peter Tigler. Berlin: Walter de Gruyter, 1968, pp. 136–42.

Salvatori, Marcello. "Considerazione sulle fortificazion del Brunelleschi." In Giulio Carlo Argan, et al., *Filippo Brunelleschi: La sua opera e il suo tempo.* Florence: Centro Di, 1980, 2:685–701.

Sandrini, Andrea. "Rapporto del 12 Ottobre 1604: La Cattedrale di Pienza." *Miscellanea Storica Senese,* 2 (1894), 135.

Sanpaolesi, Paolo. *Aspetti dell'architettura del '400 a Siena.* Urbino: Istituto d'Arte del Libro, 1948.

Santoli, Quinto. *Il Cardinale Forteguerri.* Pistoia, 1926.

Sassoli, M. G. "Michelozzo e l'architettura di villa nel primo Rinascimento." *Storia dell'Arte,* 23 (1975), 5–51.

Schiavo, Armando. *Monumenti di Pienza.* Milan: Alfieri and Lacroix for Ente Nazionale Industrie Turistiche, 1942.

Schlosser, Julius von. "Ein Künstlerproblem der Renaissance: L. B. Alberti." In *Akademie der Wissenschaften in Wien: Sitzungsberichte* 210. Vienna: Holder, Pichle, Tempsky, 1929.

Schulz, Anne Markham. *The Sculpture of Bernardo Rossellino and His Workshop.* Princeton: Princeton University Press, 1976.

Schürmayer, Walter. *Das Kardinalskollegium unter Pius II.* Historische Studien 122. 1914; rpt. Vaduz: Kraus Reprint, 1965.

Shepherd, John C., and George A. Jellicoe. *Italian Gardens of the Renaissance.* 3d ed. London: Alec Tiranti, 1966.

Simoncini, Giorgio. *Architetti e architettura nella cultura del Rinascimento.* Bologna: Il Mulino, 1967.

Simonelli, Prospero, and Giuseppe Fratadocchi. *Almo Collegio Capranica: Lavori di restauro anno Mariano.* Rome: Angelo Belardetti, 1935.

Sitte, Camillo. *The Art of Building Cites: City Building According to Artistic Fundamentals.* Trans. Charles T. Stewart. New York: Reinhold, 1945.

Smith, Leslie F. "Lodrisio Crivelli of Milan and Aeneas Silvius, 1457–1464." *Studies in the Renaissance,* 9 (1962), 31–63.

Socini, A. "Un'antica questione relativa alle fondazione del duomo di Pienza." *Rivista d'Arte,* 6 (1909), 85–94.

Spallanzani, Marco. "L'abside dell'Alberti a San Miniato a Gangalandi." *Mitteilungen des Kunsthistorischen Institutes in Florenz,* 19 (1975), 241–50.

Stefani, Carlo de. *La frana del duomo di Pienza.* Catania, 1909.

Stegmann, Carl von, and Heinrich von Geymüller. *The Architecture of the Renaissance in Tuscany Illustrating the Most Important Palaces, Villas, and Monuments.* New York: Architectural Book Publishing, 1924.

———. *Die Architektur der Renaissance in Toskana dargestellt in den hervorragensten*

Kirchen, Palästen, Villen, und Monumenten. 12 vols. Munich: Brückmann, 1885–1907.

Strnad, Alfred A. "Francesco Todeschini-Piccolomini: Politik und Mäzenatentum im Quattrocento." *Römische Historische Mitteilungen*, 8–9 (1964–65), 101–425.

———. "Pio II e suo nipote Francesco Todeschini-Piccolomini." *Atti e Memorie della Deputazione di Storia Patria per le Marche*, 5, Ser. 8 (1967), 35–84.

Suger, Abbot. *Abbot Suger on the Abbey Church of St. Denis and Its Art Treasures*. Trans. Erwin Panofsky. Princeton: Princeton University Press, 1957.

Tabarelli, Gian Maria. *Palazzi pubblici d'Italia*. Busto Arsizio: Bramante, 1978.

Tadolini, S. "Il piano per i Borghi di Nicolò V e L. B. Alberti." In *Strenna dei romanisti*. Rome: Staderni, 1971, pp. 357–64.

Tafuri, M. *L'architettura del umanesimo*. 2d ed. Bari: Laterza, 1980.

Thiem, Gunther, and Christel Thiem. *Toskanische Fassaden-Dekoration in Sgraffito und Fresko*. Munich: F. Bruckmann, 1964.

Torriti, Piero. *Pienza: Città del Rinascimento*. Genoa: Edigraphica, 1965.

———. *Pienza: La città del Rinascimento italiano*. Genoa: Sagep Editrice, 1980.

———. *Pienza e i suoi dintorni*. Genoa: Stringa, 1956.

Totaro, Luigi. *Pio II nei suoi Commentari*. Bologna: Pàtron, 1978.

Tyskiewicz, Maryla. *Bernardo Rossellino*. Florence: Stamperia Polacca, 1929.

———. *Bernardo Rossellino*. Trans. Rosa Rosmaryn. Ed. Anne Markham (Schulz). Florence: T. S. Kunsthistorisches Institut.

Ugurgieri della Berardenga, C. *Pio II Piccolomini con notizie su Pio III e altri membri della famiglia*. Biblioteca dell'Archivio Storico Italiano 18. Florence: Leo S. Olschki, 1973.

Urban, Günter. "Die Kirchenbaukunst des Quattrocento in Rom: Eine bau- und stilgeschichtliche Untersuchung." *Römisches Jahrbuch für Kunstgeschichte*, 9–10 (1961–62), 75–187.

Valentiner, W. R. "The Florentine Master of the Tomb of Pope Pius II." *Art Quarterly*, 21 (1958), 117–49.

Valtieri, Simonetta. "Rinascimento a Viterbo: Bernardo Rossellino." *Architettura, Cronache e Storia*, 17 (1972), 686–94.

Vasari, Giorgio. *The Lives of the Painters, Sculptors, and Architects*. Ed. William Gaunt. 4 vols. Everyman's Library. London: J. M. Dent, 1963.

Vast, Henri. *Le Cardinal Bessarion (1403–1472): Etude sur la Chrétienté et la Renaissance vers le milieu du XVe siècle*. 1878; rpt. Geneva: Slatkine-Megariotis Reprints, 1977.

Vecchi, V. de. "L'architettura gotica civile senese." *Bullettino Senese di Storia Patria*, 56 (1949), 3–52.

Venturi, Adolfo. *Storia dell'arte italiana: L'architettura del quattrocento*. 1923; rpt. Vaduz: Nendeln, 1967.

Verdiani-Bandi, Arnoldo. "I castelli di Val d'Orcia e la repubblica di Siena." *Bullettino Senese di Storia Patria*, 8 (1901), 410.

Verdone, M. "Enea Silvio Piccolomini ai bagni di Petriolo." *Terra di Siena*, 19, 3 (1965).

Virgil, Publius Maro. *Opera*. Ed. Frederick A. Hirtzel. Oxford: Clarendon, 1900.

Vitruvius Pollio, Marcus. *The Ten Books on Architecture*. Trans. Morris Hicky Morgan. Cambridge: Harvard University Press, 1914.

Voigt, Georg. *Enea Silvio de' Piccolomini als Papst Pius der Zweite und sein Zeitalter*. 3 vols. 1856–63; rpt. Berlin: Walter de Gruyter, 1967.

Wakayama, Eiko M. L. "Teoria prospettica albertiana e pittura del quattrocento" In *Il Sant'Andrea di Mantova e Leon Battista Alberti: Atti del convegno di studi organizzato dalla città di Mantova con la collaborazione dell'Accademia Virgiliana nel quinto centenario della basilica di Sant'Andrea e della morte dell'Alberti, 1472–1972*. Mantua: Edizione della Biblioteca Comunale di Mantova, 1974, pp. 175–88.

Weiss, Anton. *Aeneas Sylvius Piccolomini als Papst Pius II: Sein Leben und Einfluss auf die literarische Cultur Deutschlands*. Graz: U. Moser, 1897.

West, Robert (Anne Cornwallis-West). "Pienza." *Monatshefte für Kunstwissenschaft*, 8 (1915), 150–65.

Westfall, Carroll William. "Alberti and the Vatican Palace Type." *Journal of the Society of Architectural Historians*, 33 (1974), 101–21.

_____. *In This Most Perfect Paradise: Alberti, Nicholas V, and the Invention of Conscious Urban Planning in Rome, 1447–55*. University Park: Pennsylvania State University Press, 1974.

_____. "Society, Beauty, and the Humanist Architect in Alberti's *De re aedificatoria*." *Studies in the Renaissance*, 16 (1969), 61–79.

Whitfield, T. H. "Aeneas Sylvius Piccolomini." *Life of Spirit*, 15 (1961), 459–71.

Widmer, Berthe. *Enea Silvio Piccolomini in der sittlichen und politischen Entscheidung*. Baseler Beiträge zur Geschichtswissenschaft 88. Basel: Helbing and Lichtenhahn, 1963.

_____. *Enea Silvio Piccolomini, Papst Pius II, Biographie und ausgewählte Texte aus seinen Schriften*. Basel: Benno Schwabe, 1960.

Willich, Hans, and Paul Zucker. *Die Baukunst der Renaissance in Italien*. 2 vols. Wildpark-Potsdam: Akademische Verlagsgesellschaft Athenaion, 1929.

Wittkower, Rudolf. *Architectural Principles in the Age of Humanism*. Columbia University Studies in Art History and Archaeology 1. New York: Random House, 1965.

Wolkan, Rudolf. *Der Briefwechsel des Eneas Sylvius Piccolomini*. Fontes Rerum Austriacarum. Vienna: A. Hölder, 1909–18.

Zabughin, Vladimiro. *Giulio Pomponio Leto: Saggi critico*. 2 vols. Rome: La Vita Letteraria, 1909–12.

Zimolo, Giulio C. "La 'Vita Pii II P.M.,' del Platina nel cod. Vat. Ottob. lat. 2056." In *Studi in onore di mons. C. Castiglioni prefetto dell' Ambrosiana*. Milan: Guiffrè, 1957, pp. 875–904.

_____. *Le vite di Pio II di Giovanni Antonio Campano e Bartolomeo Platina*. Bologna: Zanchelli, 1964.

Zippel, Lazio G. "L'allume di Tolfa e il suo commercio." *Archivio di Società Romana di Storia Patria*, 30 (1907), 1–5, 387–462.

Zucker, Paul. *Entwicklung des Stadtbildes: Die Stadt als Form*. Munich: Drei Masken Verlag, 1929.

_____. *Raumdarstellung und Bildarchitekturen im Florentiner Quattrocento*. Leipzig: Klinkhardt and Biermann, 1913.

_____. *Town and Square from the Agora to the Village Green*. New York: Columbia University Press, 1959.

Zurko, E. R. de. "Alberti's Theory of Form and Function," *Art Bulletin*, 39 (1957), 142–45.

INDEX

Borgia, Cardinal Rodrigo (Pope Alexander VI), 108, 137, 175, 199n1

Borgo, Francesco del, 31

Boulting, William, 10, 31

Bramante, Donato, 65, 158

Brandenburg, Barbara von, 119, 137–138, 152

Bruna River project, 155

Brunelleschi, Filippo, 33, 48, 82, 87, 91, 97, 158–159, 161

Bruni, Leonardo, 9, 118, 156

Buggiano. *See* Cavalcanti, Andrea

Buonarroti, Michelangelo, 45, 60, 159

Buonconti da Pisa, Giliforte dei, 41, 104, 106, 132–133, 176

Buonconvento, 158, 161

Burckhardt, Jacob, 10

Calandrini, Cardinal Filippo, 145

Calixtus III, Pope, 30

Campano, Giannantonio, 10, 155, 165, 192n4; *Pii II vita,* 224n1; poems, 165–166, 177

Canensi, Michele, 195n21

Capranica, Cardinal Domenico, 27–28, 118

Carafa, Cardinal Oliviero, 145

Cardona, Cardinal Jaime, 137

Careggi, Villa Medicea at, 56

Carissimi, Niccolò de', 59

Carli, Enzo, 10, 127

Cascina, 158

Cassia, Via, 18, 161

Castelfranco di Sopra, 158

Castelnuovo Beradenga, 158

Cataldi, Giancarlo, 133, 135, 139–140, 142

Cavalcanti, Andrea, 87

Chambers, D. S., 137

Checho di Meo, 117

Churches: cathedral of Como, 83; cathedral of Ferrara, 92; cathedral of Graz, 208n97; cathedral of Modena, 97; cathedral of Orvieto, 208n100; cathedral of York, 83; Gumpoldskirchen, 82; Klosterneuburg, 208n97; Landshut, 83; San Agostino in Montepulciano, 91; San Andrea in Mantua, 92, 117; Santa Anna in Comprena, 137, 147; San Biagio in Montepulciano, 99; Santa Caterina in Pisa, 209n124; Saint Denis in

Churches (*cont.*)
Paris, 79; San Fortunato in Todi, 83; San Francesco (Tempio Malatestiano) in Rimini, 85, 92, 117, 125; Sankt Georgkirche in Wiener Neustadt, 208n97; Sankt Johann im Mauertale, 97; San Lorenzo in Perugia, 83; Santa Maria delle Grazie in Pistoia, 91; Sankt Nicholas in Neuötting, 95; San Pietro in Perugia, 97; San Salvatore at Monte Amiata, 22, 155; San Sebastiano in Mantua, 91; Sankt Stephan in Vienna, 97; Straubing, 82; Wasserburg, 82. *See also* Assisi; Florence; Pienza; Rome; Siena

Cicero, Marcus Tullius, 9

Cinughi, Bishop Giovanni, 77, 108

City design, 157–158, 161–162

Closed order, in medieval town planning, 157

Colonna, Fra Francesco, 203n49

Commentarii of Pius II, 9, 18, 31, 35–36, 40–41, 43, 45, 49, 51–52, 58, 60, 62, 65, 69, 72, 75, 76–77, 79, 82–83, 85, 87, 89, 92–93, 95, 99, 101–102, 104, 106–107, 108, 112, 113, 117–119, 130, 135, 136, 137, 142, 155, 165, 191n2, 201n27, 203n47, 207n92, 208n100

Corsignano. *See* Pienza

Cortona, 221n113, 222n120

Crivelli, Lodrisio, 10, 135, 145, 155, 165, 220n103, 224n2; poem, 171–177

Cugnoni, G., 10

Cuna, 192n1

Curran, Raymond, 157, 163, 224n28

Dati, Leonardo, 201n25

Della Tuccia, Niccola, 198n64, 199n74, 211n3, 213n20, 221n113

De re aedificatoria of L. B. Alberti, 30, 34, 40, 47, 65, 74–76, 92, 156, 159, 161, 210n130, 213n20

De Wolfe, Ivor, 161–162

Di Cristina, Lero, 12

Diedi, Niccolò, 138

Diether von Mainz, 82

Domenico di Antonio (Riccio), 147–148

Donatello, 85

Donin, Richard Kurt, 82

Doric order, use of at Pienza, 45, 58, 65, 85, 130

Library of Congress Cataloging-in-Publication Data

Mack, Charles R., 1940–
    Pienza : the creation of a Renaissance city.

    Bibliography: p.
    Includes index.
    1. Architecture, Renaissance—Italy—Pienza. 2. Architecture—Italy—
Pienza. 3. Cities and towns, Renaissance—Italy—Pienza. 4. Architecture and
state—Italy—Pienza. I. Title.
NA1121.P5M33   1987   720'.945'58   86-24269
ISBN 0-8014-1699-X (alk. paper)